High Performance MySQL

*Optimization, Backups, Replication,
and Load Balancing*

Other resources from O'Reilly

Related titles

Managing and Using MySQL

MySQL Cookbook

MySQL Pocket Reference

MySQL Reference Manual

Practical PostgreSQL

Web Database Applications
with PHP and MySQL

PHP 5 Essentials

Learning PHP

Programming PHP

PHP Cookbook

SQL Tuning

oreilly.com

oreilly.com is more than a complete catalog of O'Reilly books. You'll also find links to news, events, articles, weblogs, sample chapters, and code examples.

oreillynet.com is the essential portal for developers interested in open and emerging technologies, including new platforms, programming languages, and operating systems.

Conferences

O'Reilly & Associates brings diverse innovators together to nurture the ideas that spark revolutionary industries. We specialize in documenting the latest tools and systems, translating the innovator's knowledge into useful skills for those in the trenches. Visit *conferences.oreilly.com* for our upcoming events.

Safari Bookshelf (*safari.oreilly.com*) is the premier online reference library for programmers and IT professionals. Conduct searches across more than 1,000 books. Subscribers can zero in on answers to time-critical questions in a matter of seconds. Read the books on your Bookshelf from cover to cover or simply flip to the page you need. Try it today with a free trial.

High Performance MySQL

Optimization, Backups, Replication, and Load Balancing

Jeremy D. Zawodny and Derek J. Balling

O'REILLY®

Beijing · Cambridge · Farnham · Köln · Paris · Sebastopol · Talpel · Tokyo

High Performance MySQL: Optimization, Backups, Replication, and Load Balancing
by Jeremy D. Zawodny and Derek J. Balling

Published by O'Reilly Media, Inc., 1005 Gravenstein Highway North, Sebastopol, CA 95472.

O'Reilly Media, Inc. books may be purchased for educational, business, or sales promotional use. Online editions are also available for most titles (*safari.oreilly.com*). For more information, contact our corporate/institutional sales department: (800) 998-9938 or *corporate@oreilly.com*.

Editor:	Andy Oram
Production Editor:	Mary Anne Weeks Mayo
Cover Designer:	Ellie Volckhausen
Interior Designer:	David Futato

Printing History:

April 2004:	First Edition.

RepKover. This book uses RepKover™, a durable and flexible lay-flat binding.

ISBN: 0-596-00306-4
[M]   [5/04]

Table of Contents

Preface

We had several goals in mind for this book. Many of them are derived from thinking about that mythical perfect MySQL book neither of us had read but kept looking for on bookstore shelves. Others come from a lot of experience helping other users put MySQL to work in their environments.

We wanted a book that wasn't just a SQL primer. We wanted a book with a title that didn't start or end in some arbitrary time frame ("...in Thirty Days," "Seven Days To a Better...") and didn't imply that the reader was a moron of some sort because he was reading our book.

Most of all we wanted a book that would help the reader take her MySQL skills to the next level. Every book we read focused almost exclusively on SQL command syntax or covered MySQL only at a very basic level. None really helped us to understand the deeper issues. We wanted a book that went deeper and focused on real-world problems. How can you set up a cluster of MySQL servers capable of handling millions upon millions of queries and ensure that things keep running even if a couple of the servers die?

We decided to write a book that focused not just on the needs of the MySQL application developer but also on the rigorous demands of the MySQL administrator, who needs to keep the system up and running no matter what his programmers or users may throw at the server.

Having said that, we assume that you are already relatively experienced with MySQL and, ideally, have read an introductory book on MySQL. In several chapters, we'll refer to common Unix tools for monitoring system performance, such as *top*, *vmstat*, and *sar*. If you're not already familiar with them (or their equivalent on your operating system), please take a bit of time to learn the basics. It will serve you well when we look at system performance and bottlenecks.

The Basic Layout of This Book

We fit a lot of complicated topics in this book. Here we'll explain how we put them together in an order that hopefully makes them easy for you to learn.

Back to Basics

The first two chapters are dedicated to the basics—things you'll need to be familiar with before you get to additional configuration details.

Chapter 1, *Back To Basics*, reviews some rudimentary configuration basics. This book assumes a pretty good command of foundational MySQL administration, but we'll go over the fundamentals briefly before digging deeper into the world of MySQL.

After that, Chapter 2, *Storage Engines (Table Types)*, covers the various storage engines, or table types, that are part of MySQL. This is important because storage engine selection is one of the few things that can be nontrivial to change after you create a table. We review the various benefits (and potential pitfalls) of the various storage engines, and try to provide enough information to help you decide which engine is best for your particular application and environment.

Things to Reference as You Read the Rest of the Book

The next two chapters cover things you'll find yourself referencing time and again throughout the course of the book.

Chapter 3, *Benchmarking*, discusses the basics of benchmarking—determining what sort of workloads your server can handle, how fast it can perform certain tasks, and so on. You'll want to benchmark your application both before and after a major change, so you can judge how effective your changes are. What seems to be a positive change may turn out to be a negative one under real-world stress.[*]

In Chapter 4, *Indexes*, we cover the various nuances of indexes. Many of the things we discuss in later chapters hinge on how well your application puts MySQL's indexes to work. A firm understanding of indexes and how to optimize their use is something you'll find yourself returning to repeatedly throughout the process.

Places to Tune Your Application

The next two chapters discuss areas in which the MySQL administrator, application designer, or MySQL programmer can make changes to improve performance of a MySQL application.

---

[*] Management folks also tend to like metrics they can point at and say, "See, this is how much our system improved after we spent $39.95 on that O'Reilly book! Wasn't that a great investment?"

In Chapter 5, *Query Performance*, we discuss how the MySQL programmer might improve the performance of the MySQL queries themselves. This includes basics, such as how the query parser will parse the queries provided, as well as how to optimize queries for ideal performance.

Once the queries are optimized, the next step is to make sure the server's configuration is optimized to return those queries in the fastest possible manner. In Chapter 6, *Server Performance Tuning*, we discuss some ways to get the most out of your hardware, and to suggest hardware configurations that may provide better performance for larger-scale applications.

Scaling Upward After Making Changes

Once you've got a server up and running as best it can, you may find that one server simply isn't enough. In Chapter 7, *Replication*, we discuss replication—that is, getting your data copied automatically to multiple servers. When combined with the load-balancing lessons in Chapter 8, *Load Balancing and High Availability*, this will provide you with the groundwork for scaling your applications in a significant way.

Make Sure All That Work Isn't for Naught

Once you have configured your application, gotten it up and running, and replicated your database across multiple servers, your next task as a MySQL administrator is to keep it all going.

In Chapter 9, *Backup and Recovery*, we discuss various backup and recovery strategies for your MySQL databases. These strategies help minimize your downtime in the event of inevitable hardware failure and ensures that your data survives such catastrophes.

Finally, Chapter 10, *Security*, provides you with a firm grasp of some of the security issues involved in running a MySQL server. More importantly, we offer many suggestions to allow you to prevent outside parties from harming the servers you have spent all this time trying to configure and optimize.

The Miscellany

There's a couple things we delve into that either don't "fit" in a particular chapter or are referenced often enough by multiple chapters that they deserve a bit of special attention all to themselves.

In Appendix A, *The SHOW STATUS and SHOW INNODB STATUS Commands*, we cover the output of the SHOW STATUS and SHOW INNODB STATUS commands. We attempt to decipher for the average administrator what all those variables mean and offer some ways to find potential problems based on their values relative to each other.

Appendix B, *mytop*, covers a program called *mytop*, which Jeremy wrote as an easy-to-use interface to what your MySQL server is presently doing. It functions much like the Unix *top* command and can be invaluable at all phases of the tuning process to find which MySQL threads are using the most resources.

Finally, in Appendix C, *phpMyAdmin*, we discuss *phpMyAdmin*, a web-based tool for administration of a MySQL server. *phpMyAdmin* can simplify many of the administrator's routine jobs and allow users to issue queries against the database without having to build a client or have shell access to the server.

Software Versions and Availability

Writing a MySQL book has proven to be quite a challenge. One reason is that MySQL is a moving target. In the two-plus years since Jeremy first wrote the outline for this book, numerous releases of MySQL have appeared. MySQL 4.0 went from testing to stable, and as we go to press, MySQL 4.1 and 5.0 are both available as alpha versions. We had to revise the older text occasionally to remove references to limitations that were fixed after the fact.[*]

We didn't use a single version of MySQL for this book. Instead, we used a handful of MySQL 4.0 and 4.1 releases, while occasionally looking back at how things used to be in the 3.23 days. MySQL 5.0 is still in so much flux that we simply could not attempt to cover it in the first edition. The same is true for the (currently) new MySQL Administrator GUI tool.

Throughout this book, we assume a baseline version of MySQL 4.0.14 and have made an effort to note features or functionality that may not exist in older releases or that may exist only in the 4.1 series. However, the definitive reference for mapping features to specific versions is the MySQL documentation itself. We expect that you'll find yourself visiting the annotated online documentation (*http://www.mysql.com/doc/*) from time to time as you read this book.

Another great aspect of MySQL is that it runs on all of today's popular platforms: Mac OS X, Windows, Linux, Solaris, FreeBSD: you name it! However, our experience is heavily skewed toward Linux and FreeBSD. When possible, we've tried to note differences Windows users are likely to encounter, which tend to come in two flavors. First, file paths are completely different. Chapter 1 contains numerous references to *C:\mysql* and the location of configuration files on Windows.

Perl is the other rough spot when dealing with MySQL on Windows. MySQL comes with several useful utilities that are written in Perl and certain chapters in this book present example Perl scripts that form the basis of more complex tools you'll build. However, Windows doesn't come with Perl. In order to use these scripts, you'll need

---

[*] Note to budding authors: write as fast as you can. The longer you drag it out, the more work you have to do.

to download a Windows version of Perl from ActiveState and install the necessary add-on modules (DBI and DBD::mysql) for MySQL access.

Conventions Used in This Book

The following typographical conventions are used in this book:

Plain text

> Indicates menu titles, menu options, menu buttons, and keyboard accelerators (such as Alt and Ctrl).

Italic

> Indicates new terms, URLs, email addresses, usernames, hostnames, filenames, file extensions, pathnames, directories, and utilities.

Constant width

> Indicates elements of code, configuration options, variables, functions, modules, the contents of files, or the output from commands.

Constant width bold

> Shows commands or other text that should be typed literally by the user.

Constant width italic

> Shows text that should be replaced with user-supplied values.

Using Code Examples

This book is here to help you get your job done. In general, you may use the code in this book in your programs and documentation. You don't need to contact us for permission unless you're reproducing a significant portion of the code. For example, writing a program that uses several chunks of code from this book doesn't require permission. Selling or distributing a CD-ROM of examples from O'Reilly books *does* require permission. Answering a question by citing this book and quoting example code doesn't require permission. Incorporating a significant amount of example code from this book into your product's documentation *does* require permission.

We appreciate, but don't require, attribution. An attribution usually includes the title, author, publisher, and ISBN. For example: *"High Performance MySQL: Optimization, Backups, Replication, and Load Balancing*, by Jeremy D. Zawodny and Derek J. Balling. Copyright 2004 O'Reilly Media, Inc., 0-596-00306-4."

If you feel your use of code examples falls outside fair use or the permission given above, feel free to contact us at *permissions@oreilly.com.*

How to Contact Us

Please address comments and questions concerning this book to the publisher:

O'Reilly Media, Inc.
1005 Gravenstein Highway North
Sebastopol, CA 95472
(800) 998-9938 (in the United States or Canada)
(707) 829-0515 (international or local)
(707) 829-0104 (fax)

We have a web page for this book, where we list errata, examples, and any additional information. You can access this page at:

http://www.oreilly.com/catalog/hpmysql/

To comment or ask technical questions about this book, send email to:

bookquestions@oreilly.com

For more information about our books, conferences, Resource Centers, and the O'Reilly Network, see our web site at:

http://www.oreilly.com

The authors maintain a site called:

http://highperformancemysql.com

There you will find new information on MySQL releases, updates to the tools shown in the book, and possibly other goodies such as question-and-answer forums. Visit regularly!

Acknowledgments

A book like this doesn't come into being without help from literally dozens of people. Without their assistance, the book you hold in your hands would probably still be a bunch of sticky notes on the side of our monitors. This is the part of the book where we get to say whatever we like about the folks who helped us out, and we don't have to worry about music playing in the background telling us to shut up and go away, as you might see on TV during an awards show.

We couldn't have completed this project without the constant prodding, begging, pleading, and support from our editor, Andy Oram.* If there is one person most responsible for the book in your hands, it's Andy. We really do appreciate the weekly nag sessions.

---

* Then again, if there's a second edition on the horizon, one might argue that this project is *not* complete.

Andy isn't alone, though. At O'Reilly there are a bunch of other folks who had some part in getting those sticky notes converted to a cohesive book that you'd be willing to read, so we also have to thank the production, illustration, and marketing folks for helping to pull this book together. And, of course, thanks to Tim O'Reilly for his continued commitment to producing some of the industry's finest documentation for popular open source software.

Finally, we'd both like to give a big thanks to the folks who agreed to look over the various drafts of the book and tell us all the things we were doing wrong: our reviewers. They spent part of their 2003 holiday break looking over roughly formatted versions of this text, full of typos, misleading statements, and outright mathematical errors. In no particular order, thanks to Brian "Krow" Aker, Mark "JDBC" Matthews, Jeremy "the other Jeremy" Cole, Mike "VBMySQL.com" Hillyer, Raymond "Rainman" De Roo, Jeffrey "Regex Master" Friedl, Jason DeHaan, Dan Nelson, Steve "Unix Wiz" Friedl, and last but not least, Kasia "Unix Girl" Trapszo.

From Jeremy

I would again like to thank Andy for agreeing to take on this project and for continually beating on us for more chapter material. Derek's help was essential for getting the last 20–30% of the book completed so that we wouldn't miss yet another target date. Thanks for agreeing to come on board late in the process and deal with my sporadic bursts of productivity, and for handling XML grunt work, Chapter 10 Appendix C, and all the other stuff I threw your way.

I also need to thank my parents for getting me that first Commodore 64 computer so many years ago. They not only tolerated the first 10 years of what seems to be a lifelong obsession with electronics and computer technology, but quickly became supporters of my never-ending quest to learn and do more.

Next I'd like to thank a group of people I've had the distinct pleasure of working with while spreading MySQL religion at Yahoo during the last few years. Jeffrey Friedl and Ray Goldberger provided encouragement and feedback from the earliest stages of this undertaking. Along with them, Steve Morris, James Harvey, and Sergey Kolychev put up with my seemingly constant experimentation on the Yahoo! Finance MySQL servers, even when it interrupted their important work. Thanks also to the countless other Yahoos who have helped me find interesting MySQL problems and solutions. And, most importantly, thanks for having the trust and faith in me needed to put MySQL into some of the most important and visible parts of Yahoo's business.

Adam Goodman, the publisher and owner of *Linux Magazine*, helped me ease into the world of writing for a technical audience by publishing my first feature-length MySQL articles back in 2001. Since then, he's taught me more than he realizes about editing and publishing and has encouraged me to continue on this road with my own monthly column in the magazine. Thanks, Adam.

Thanks to Monty and David for sharing MySQL with the world. Speaking of MySQL AB, thanks to all the other great folks there who have encouraged me in writing this: Kerry, Larry, Joe, Marten, Brian, Paul, Jeremy, Mark, Harrison, Matt, and the rest of the team there. You guys rock.

Finally, thanks to all my weblog readers for encouraging me to write informally about MySQL and other technical topics on a daily basis. And, last but not least, thanks to the Goon Squad.

From Derek

Like Jeremy, I've got to thank my family, for much the same reasons. I want to thank my parents for their constant goading that I should write a book, even if this isn't anywhere near what they had in mind. My grandparents helped me learn two valuable lessons, the meaning of the dollar and how much I would fall in love with computers, as they loaned me the money to buy my first Commodore VIC-20.

I can't thank Jeremy enough for inviting me to join him on the whirlwind book-writing roller coaster. It's been a great experience and I look forward to working with him again in the future.

A special thanks goes out to Raymond De Roo, Brian Wohlgemuth, David Calafrancesco, Tera Doty, Jay Rubin, Bill Catlan, Anthony Howe, Mark O'Neal, George Montgomery, George Barber, and the myriad other people who patiently listened to me gripe about things, let me bounce ideas off them to see whether an outsider could understand what I was trying to say, or just managed to bring a smile to my face when I needed it most. Without you, this book might still have been written, but I almost certainly would have gone crazy in the process.

## CHAPTER 1

Back To Basics

Many MySQL users and administrators slide into using MySQL. They hear its benefits, find that it's easy to install on their systems (or better yet, comes pre-installed), and read a quick book on how to attach simple SQL operations to web sites or other applications.

It may take several months for the dragons to raise their heads. Perhaps one particular web page seems to take forever, or a system failure corrupts a database and makes recovery difficult.

Real-life use of MySQL requires forethought and care—and a little benchmarking and testing. This book is for the MySQL administrator who has the basics down but realizes the need to go further. It's a good book to read after you've installed and learned how to use MySQL but before your site starts to get a lot of traffic, and the dragons are breathing down your neck. (When problems occur during a critical service, your fellow workers and friendly manager start to take on decidedly dragon-like appearances.)

The techniques we teach are valuable in many different situations, and sometimes to solve different problems. Replication, for instance, may be a matter of reliability for you—an essential guarantee that your site will still be up if one or two systems fail. But replication can also improve performance; we show you architectures and techniques that solve multiple problems.

We also take optimization far beyond the simple use of indexes and diagnostic (EXPLAIN) statements: this book tells you what the factors in good performance are, where bottlenecks occur, how to benchmark MySQL, and other advanced performance topics.

We ask for a little more patience and time commitment than the average introductory computer book. Our approach involves a learning cycle, and experience convinces us that it's ultimately the fastest and most efficient way to get where you want.

After describing the problems we're trying to solve in a given chapter, we start with some background explanation. In other words, we give you a mental model for understanding what MySQL is doing. Then we describe the options you have to solve the problem, and only after all that do we describe particular tools and techniques.

This book is clearly not the end of the line in terms of information. Knowing that, we've started a web site, *http://www.highperformancemysql.com*, where we put useful scripts and new topics. See the Preface for more information.

Before we dig into how to tune your MySQL system to optimum performance, it's best if we go over a couple of ground rules and make sure everyone is on the same page.

Binary Versus Compiled-From-Source Installations

There are two ways you can install MySQL. As a novice administrator, you may have simply installed a binary package that had precompiled executables, libraries, and configuration files, and placed those files wherever the maker of the binary package decided they should go.

 It's exceedingly rare for a Windows user to compile his own copy of MySQL. If you're running MySQL on Windows, feel free to download your copy from the MySQL web site and skip this discussion.

Alternatively, for any number of reasons, you might have decided to compile the MySQL binaries on your own, by downloading a source tarball and configuring the installation to best meet your needs. However, don't do so lightly. Compiling from source has led to countless hours of pain for some users, mostly due to subtle bugs in their compilers or thread libraries. For this very reason, the standard binaries provided by MySQL AB are statically linked. That means they are immune to any bugs in your locally installed libraries.

There aren't too many places where the issue of "binary versus compiled-from-source" will come into play in the average MySQL tuning regimen, but they do happen. For example, in Chapter 10, our advice on chrooting your installation can be used only if every file MySQL needs is brought into a single directory tree, which might not be the case in a binary installation.

For a novice administrator on a simple installation, we recommend using a binary package (such as an RPM) to set up your system. However, once you progress to the point of really needing to tinker with the "guts" of MySQL, you will probably want to quickly go back, change a `configure` flag, and recompile.

MySQL.com Binary Versus Distribution Binary

One thing to keep in mind is that there are a number of sources for binary packages, and nearly all of them set up the system differently.

For example, you can download the binary installation from the MySQL.com web site. You can also nstall the binary distribution included by your Linux distribution vendor, or the one you grabbed from the FreeBSD ports collection. Finally, you can downloaded a binary for a platform that isn't officially supported, but on which someone is keeping a MySQL version current, such as the Amiga architecture.* In any of these cases, you will end up with different directory layouts, compilation options, etc.

If you use the binary distributions from anyone other than MySQL AB, your support options may be significantly decreased, simply by virtue of having limited yourself to seeking help from those who use that particular distribution. Even a question as simple as, "Where is the *my.cnf* file located on the FreeBSD port of MySQL?" is going to limit those who can respond to two groups: those who have run MySQL using the FreeBSD port, and those on the mailing list or newsgroup, etc. who have encountered that question before. On the plus side, if your distribution has automated security announcements and updates, you probably never need to worry about patching MySQL if a security flaw is discovered.

Many binary distributors of MySQL mold it to fit "their" layout. For example, the Debian distribution places the config files in */etc/mysql/*, some language-specific files in */usr/share/mysql/*, the executables directly into */usr/bin/*, etc. It's not "the Debian way" to segregate an application's binaries; it incorporates them into the system as a whole. Likewise, in those places it does incorporate them, it does so in what may seem like an odd manner. For instance, you might expect config files to go directly into */etc/*, but instead they get put in */etc/mysql/*. It can be confusing if you're trying to find everything you need to modify, or if you're trying to later convert from one type of installation to the other.

The MySQL.com-supplied tarball binary packages, however, behave more like the source-compilation process. All the files—configuration files, libraries, executables, and the database files themselves—end up in a single directory tree, created specifically for the MySQL install. This is typically */usr/local/mysql*, but it can be altered as needed at installation time. Because this behavior is much the same as a source-compiled installation, the available support from the MySQL community is much greater. It also makes things easier if you decide later to instead use a MySQL installation you compile from source.

---

* At the time that sentence was written, it was entirely theoretical: the thinking was "I'm not aware of anything, but surely someone *will* do that!" In researching it, we found that MySQL for Amiga was, indeed, happening. For those who read German, there's an article from *Amiga Magazine* at *http://www.amiga-magazin. de/magazin/a08-01/mysql/* that describes how to do it, and a mailing list at *http://groups.yahoo.com/group/ Amiga_MySql/* for people working on it as well.

On the other hand, the MySQL-supplied binary packages that are distributed using package-management formats such as RPM are laid out similarly to the format of the system they are designed for. For example, the RPM installation you get from MySQL.com will have its files laid out similarly to the Red Hat-supplied RPM. This is so because it's not uncommon for a Linux distribution to ship an RPM that hasn't been thoroughly tested and is broken in fairly serious ways. The RPM files MySQL.com distributes are intended as upgrade paths for users with such a problem so they can have "just what they have now, but it works."

Because of that, if you're going to install a binary you download from MySQL.com, we highly recommend using the tarball formatted files. They will yield the familiar directory structure the average MySQL administrator is used to seeing.

Configuration Files

Configuring a MySQL server is often just a matter of editing the configuration file to make any changes you need and then restarting the server. While that sounds rather simple, adjusting the server's configuration is something you're not likely to do on a daily basis. More likely, you've installed MySQL, configured it minimally or with the defaults, and then let it run. Most users never go back and adjust the server configuration until a problem arises. As a result, it's easy to forget how to configure MySQL.

Another possibility is that you didn't even know there was a configuration file for MySQL. For the majority of projects, MySQL's default configuration is more than sufficient on modern hardware. It may not be as fast as it can be (because you haven't optimized it), but it will certainly meet your basic needs.

File Locations

When MySQL starts, it reads its configuration files in a particular order, unless told otherwise. On Unix, the order is:

1. */etc/my.cnf*
2. *datadir/my.cnf*
3. *~/.my.cnf*

On Windows, the order:

1. *%SystemRoot%/my.ini*
2. *C:\my.cnf*

Three command-line arguments affect how MySQL reads its configuration files:

--no-defaults
    Tells MySQL not to read any configuration files.

--defaults-file=/path/to/file
>   Tells MySQL to read this file only, and any other files explicitly declared with `--defaults-extra-file`.

--defaults-extra-file=/path/to/file
>   Tells MySQL to read this file after reading the */etc/my.cnf* global configuration file .

Files read later in the process override those set in previously read files. If both */etc/my.cnf* and *datadir/my.cnf* specify a value for the TCP port that MySQL should listen to, the latter takes precedence.

This behavior can be quite helpful when you need to run multiple servers either on the same host or on several different hosts. You can give all servers an identical copy of */etc/my.cnf* that specifies all the values that aren't specific to a single host. With that out of the way, the few host-specific settings can be maintained in a small supplemental file such as *datadir/my.cnf*.

A similar strategy works if you'd like to run multiple servers on a single host. By putting all the common settings in */etc/my.cnf* and the server-specific settings in each *datadir/my.cnf*, it's easy to keep several servers running with a minimum of effort.

For example, perhaps you want to run a couple different instances of the MySQL server, one for each character set you plan to use (to make your life easier). You might put all your "common" settings in */etc/my.cnf* and the following in */etc/my.english.cnf*:

```
default-character-set=latin1
port=3306
socket=/var/lib/mysql/english.sock
```

Your */etc/my.german.cnf* file has:

```
default-character-set=latin1_de
port=3307
socket=/var/lib/mysql/german.sock
```

You might even have */etc/my.korean.cnf* with:

```
default-character-set=euc_kr
port=3308
socket=/var/lib/mysql/korean.sock
```

Now, when you start up the three servers, you want each to load all the settings from the shared */etc/my.cnf* file, and then get settings from one of each of the previous language-based configuration files. You can use a command like the following:

```
$ mysqld_safe --defaults-extra-file=/etc/my.german.cnf
$ mysqld_safe --defaults-extra-file=/etc/my.english.cnf
$ mysqld_safe --defaults-extra-file=/etc/my.korean.cnf
```

This command yields three different *mysqld* instances, running on ports 3306 through 3308, each using the language-specific configuration options mentioned in the file indicated by the defaults-extra-file switch.

MySQL is usually installed as a service on Windows. As a result, Windows users must call *c:\mysql\bin\mysqld* directly to pass command-line arguments.

File Format

The configuration file format consists of one or more sections, each of which may contain one or more lines. Sections begin with a name in square brackets, such as [*mysqld*]; this identifies the program to which the options should be applied. Each line contains a comment, a key/value pair, a set-variable directive, or a Boolean directive. Blank lines are ignored.

Two special section names can occur in each configuration file: [server] and [client]. Items listed in the [server] block apply to the MySQL server process. Those in the [client] section apply to all client programs that use the MySQL C client library, including *mysql*, *mysqlhotcopy*, and *mysqldump*.

Comments begin with # or ; and continue to the end of the line:

```
# this is a comment
; so is this
```

There is no multiline comment format. You can't place a comment at the end of an otherwise non-empty line:

```
key_buffer=128M # a comment can't go here
```

The key/value pairs are settings such as:

```
user = mysql
port = 3306
```

The set-variable statements look like key/value pairs in which the value is a key/value pair itself:

```
set-variable = key_buffer=384M
set-variable = tmp_table_size=32M
```

Spaces aren't important in set-variable lines. You can also write the two previous lines as follows:

```
set-variable = key_buffer = 384M
set-variable=tmp_table_size=32M
```

Either way, MySQL will understand you. However, consider using some space to enhance readability.

As of Version 4.1, the `set-variable=` portion of the variable definition is no longer needed and is deprecated. In current versions:

```
set-variable = key_buffer=384M
```

and:

```
key_buffer=384M
```

are both interpreted in an identical manner by the server at startup time. If you are running a version that supports leaving out the `set-variable` clause, it probably is best to do so because it won't be supported forever. We've chosen to use the older format here because it's what you're likely to have already, and the sample configuration files in the standard MySQL distribution continue to use it.

The few boolean directives are just stated plainly:

```
skip-bdb
```

Individual lines in the configuration file are limited to 2 KB in length. While it's rare that you'll ever need to use a line that long, it can occasionally be a problem.

Sample Files

The *support-files* directory of the MySQL distribution* contains four sample configuration files:

- *my-small.cnf*
- *my-medium.cnf*
- *my-large.cnf*
- *my-huge.cnf*

The names of the files are meant to signify the size of the machine on which the MySQL server will run. Each contains comments describing where the size comes from. For example, *my-medium.cnf* says:

```
# This is for a system with little memory (32M - 64M) where MySQL plays
# a important part and systems up to 128M very MySQL is used together with
# other programs (like a web server)
```

To use a sample file, simply copy it to */etc/my.cnf* (or *systemdir\win.ini* on Windows) and making changes as necessary. While none is likely to be ideal for any particular setup, each file is a good starting point for setting up a new system. Failure to make adjustments to the sample configuration can lead to worse performance in some cases.

Let's look at the sample *my-medium.cnf* file from a newly installed system. Some of the information may not make sense right away (depending on how much experience

---

* These files aren't included in the Windows distribution of older MySQL releases.

you have), but the more examples you see, the more you'll begin to understand them.

The file starts with some helpful comments about the type of system this configuration is appropriate for and information needed to install it:

```
# Example mysql config file for medium systems.
#
# This is for a system with little memory (32M - 64M) where MySQL plays
# a important part and systems up to 128M very MySQL is used together with
# other programs (like a web server)
#
# You can copy this file to
# /etc/mf.cnf to set global options,
# mysql-data-dir/my.cnf to set server-specific options (in this
# installation this directory is /usr/local/mysq/var) or
# ~/.my.cnf to set user-specific options.
#
# One can in this file use all long options that the program supports.
# If you want to know which options a program support, run the program
# with --help option.
```

Next are the options that apply to all the client tools you might run on this host:

```
# The following options will be passed to all MySQL clients
[client]
#password       = your_password
port            = 3306
socket          = /tmp/mysql.sock
```

What follows next are the parameters specific to the server. The port and socket options, of course, should agree with what the clients were just told. The remaining settings allow MySQL to allocate more RAM for various caches and buffers as well as enable some basic replication options:

```
# Here follows entries for some specific programs

# The MySQL server
[mysqld]
port            = 3306
socket          = /tmp/mysql.sock
skip-locking
set-variable    = key_buffer=16M
set-variable    = max_allowed_packet=1M
set-variable    = table_cache=64
set-variable    = sort_buffer=512K
set-variable    = net_buffer_length=8K
set-variable    = myisam_sort_buffer_size=8M
log-bin
server-id       = 1
```

Next are a few options you probably don't need to change if you have sufficient disk space:

```
# Point the following paths to different dedicated disks
#tmpdir          = /tmp/
#log-update      = /path-to-dedicated-directory/hostname
```

The BDB options refer to the BDB storage engine, which provide MySQL's first transaction-safe storage. You'll learn more about storage engines in Chapter 2.

```
# Uncomment the following if you are using BDB tables
#set-variable    = bdb_cache_size=4M
#set-variable    = bdb_max_lock=10000
```

InnoDB, another of MySQL's storage engines, has numerous options that must be configured before you can use them. Because it provides transaction-safe tables with its own memory management and storage system, you need to specify where the data files will live, as well as how much RAM should be used. (InnoDB was briefly known as Innobase, so you may see that name in configuration files.)

```
# Uncomment the following if you are using Innobase tables
#innodb_data_file_path = ibdata1:400M
#innodb_data_home_dir = /usr/local/mysql/var/
#innodb_log_group_home_dir = /usr/local/mysql/var/
#innodb_log_arch_dir = /usr/local/mysql/var/
#set-variable = innodb_mirrored_log_groups=1
#set-variable = innodb_log_files_in_group=3
#set-variable = innodb_log_file_size=5M
#set-variable = innodb_log_buffer_size=8M
#innodb_flush_log_at_trx_commit=1
#innodb_log_archive=0
#set-variable = innodb_buffer_pool_size=16M
#set-variable = innodb_additional_mem_pool_size=2M
#set-variable = innodb_file_io_threads=4
#set-variable = innodb_lock_wait_timeout=50
```

The final option groups are for specific MySQL command-line utilities, including the *mysql* shell:

```
[mysqldump]
quick
set-variable      = max_allowed_packet=16M

[mysql]
no-auto-rehash
# Remove the next comment character if you are not familiar with SQL
#safe-updates

[isamchk]
set-variable      = key_buffer=20M
set-variable      = sort_buffer=20M
set-variable      = read_buffer=2M
set-variable      = write_buffer=2M
```

```
[myisamchk]
set-variable     = key_buffer=20M
set-variable     = sort_buffer=20M
set-variable     = read_buffer=2M
set-variable     = write_buffer=2M

[mysqlhotcopy]
interactive-timeout
```

That file would be considerably larger and certainly more confusing if all the possible settings were listed. For 90% (or more) of MySQL users, there is simply never a need to adjust more than a few of the settings listed in the sample files.

Reconfiguration

When an administrator adjusts the server parameters, it's common to go through an iterative process that involves making changes, restarting the server, performing some tests, and repeating the process. In fact, we'll look at doing just that in Chapter 3. In the meantime, it's worth mentioning that you should strongly consider putting your MySQL configuration files into some sort of revision control system (RCS, CVS, Subversion, etc.). Doing so gives you an easy way to track changes and back out of a bad configuration change.

As of MySQL 4.0, it's possible to change server variables on the fly at runtime. For example, if you wanted to increase the size of the key buffer from what it was set to at startup, you might do the following:

```
mysql> SET GLOBAL key_buffer=50M;
```

This sets the global value for key_buffer to 50 MB.

Some variables, such as sort_buffer_size, can be set globally so that they affect all new threads on the server, or they can be defined so that they apply only to the current MySQL client session. For example, if you wish to make a series of queries that might better use a large sort buffer, you can type:

```
mysql> SET SESSION sort_buffer_size=50M;
```

Variables set using the SESSION syntax are thread-specific and don't alter the values other threads use.

It's important to note that any change you make here, using either GLOBAL or SESSION syntax, will not survive a restart of the MySQL server; it's completely transient in that regard. Runtime changes like this are excellent for testing scenarios such as, "If I increase my key_buffer value, will it improve my query performance?" Once you've found a value that works for you, though, remember to go back to your */etc/my.cnf* file and put that value into your configuration file, or you may find yourself wondering weeks or months later why performance was so horrible after that reboot, completely forgetting the variable change you made on the fly months prior.

It's also possible to use arguments on the *mysqld_safe* command line to override values defined in the configuration files. For example, you might do something like the following:

```
$ mysqld_safe -O key_buffer=50M
```

Like the earlier set-variable syntax, the -O syntax is deprecated as of Version 4.0. Here is a better way to issue that command:

```
$ mysqld_safe --key_buffer=50M
```

Command-line argument changes made in the *mysql.server* startup script will, obviously, survive from server restart to server restart, as long as that startup script is used to disable and reenable the server. It's important to point out, though, that it's usually better to have all your configuration declarations in a single place, so that maintenance doesn't become a game of hide-and-seek with the configuration options, trying to remember where you set which values.

The SHOW Commands

MySQL users often wonder how to find out what their server is actually doing at any point in time—usually when things start to slow down or behave strangely. You can look at operating system statistics to figure out how busy the server is, but that really doesn't reveal much. Knowing that the CPU is at 100% utilization or that there's a lot of disk I/O occurring provides a high-level picture of what is going on, but MySQL can tell far more.

Several SHOW commands provide a window into what's going on inside MySQL. They provide access to MySQL's configuration variables, ongoing statistics, and counters, as well as a description of what each client is doing.

SHOW VARIABLES

The easiest way to verify that configuration changes have taken effect is to ask MySQL for its current variable settings. The SHOW VARIABLES command does just that. Executing it produces quite a bit of output, which looks something like this:

```
mysql> SHOW VARIABLES;
```

```
+---------------------------------+--------------------------------------------+
| Variable_name                   | Value                                      |
+---------------------------------+--------------------------------------------+
| back_log                        | 20                                         |
| basedir                         | mysql                                      |
| binlog_cache_size               | 32768                                      |
| character_set                   | latin1                                     |
| concurrent_insert               | ON                                         |
| connect_timeout                 | 5                                          |
| datadir                         | /home/mysql/data/                          |
```

The output continues from there, covering over 120 variables in total. The variables are listed in alphabetical order, which is convenient for reading, but sometimes related variables aren't anywhere near each other in the output. The reason for this is because as MySQL evolves, new variables are added with more descriptive names, but the older variable names aren't changed; it would break compatibility for any program that expects them.*

Many of the variables in the list may be adjusted by a set-variable entry in any of MySQL's configuration files. Some of them are compiled-in values that can not be changed. They're really constants (not variables), but they still show up in the output of SHOW VARIABLES. Still others are boolean flags.

Notice that the output of SHOW VARIABLES (and all of the SHOW commands, for that matter) looks just like the output of any SQL query. It's tabular data. MySQL returns the output in a structured format, making it easy to write tools that can summarize and act on the output of these commands. We'll put that to good use in later chapters.

SHOW PROCESSLIST

The other SHOW command we'll look at is SHOW PROCESSLIST. It outputs a list of what each thread is doing at the time you execute the command.† It's roughly equivalent to the ps or top commands in Unix or the Task Manager in Windows.

Executing it produces a process list in tabular form:

```
mysql> SHOW PROCESSLIST;

+----+---------+-----------+------+---------+------+-------+------------------+
| Id | User    | Host      | db   | Command | Time | State | Info             |
+----+---------+-----------+------+---------+------+-------+------------------+
| 17 | jzawodn | localhost | NULL | Query   | 0    | NULL  | show processlist |
+----+---------+-----------+------+---------+------+-------+------------------+
```

It's common for the State and Info columns to contain more information that produces lines long enough to wrap onscreen. So it's a good idea to use the \G escape in the *mysql* command interpreter to produce vertical output rather than horizontal output:

```
mysql> SHOW PROCESSLIST \G
*************************** 1. row ***************************
     Id: 17
   User: jzawodn
   Host: localhost
     db: NULL
Command: Query
```

---

* In the rare event they do change, MySQL retains the old names as aliases for the new ones.

† Not all threads appear in the SHOW PROCESSLIST output. The thread that handles incoming network connections, for example, is never listed.

```
    Time: 0
   State: NULL
    Info: show processlist
```

No matter which way you look at it, the same fields are included:

Id The number that uniquely identifies this process. Since MySQL is a multi-threaded server, it really identifies the thread (or connection) and is unrelated to process IDs the operating system may use. As the operating system does with processes, MySQL starts numbering the threads at 1 and gives each new thread an ID one higher than the previous thread.

User
The name of the MySQL user connected to this thread.

Host
The name of the host or IP address from which the user is connected.

db The database currently selected. This may be NULL if the user didn't specify a database.

Command
This shows the command state (from MySQL's internal point of view) that the thread is currently in. Table 1-1 lists each command with a description of when you are likely to see it. The commands roughly correspond to various function calls in MySQL's C API. Many commands represent very short-lived actions. Two of those that don't, Sleep and Query, appear frequently in day-to- day usage.

Table 1-1. Commands in SHOW PROCESSLIST output

Command	Meaning
Binlog Dump	The slave thread is reading queries from the master's binary log.
Change user	The client is logging in as a different user.
Connect	A new client is connecting.
Connect Out	The slave thread is connecting to the master to read queries from its binary log.
Create DB	A new database is being created.
Debug	The thread is producing debugging output. This is very uncommon.
Delayed_insert	The thread is processing delayed inserts.
Drop DB	A database is being dropped.
Field List	The client has requested a list of fields in a table.
Init DB	The thread is changing to a different database, typically as the result of a USE command.
Kill	The thread is executing a KILL command.
Ping	The client is pinging the server to see if it's still connected.
Processlist	The client is running SHOW PROCESSLIST.
Query	The thread is currently executing a typical SQL query: SELECT, INSERT, UPDATE, DELETE. This is the most common state other than Sleep.
Quit	The thread is being terminated as part of the server shutdown process.

Table 1-1. Commands in SHOW PROCESSLIST output (continued)

Command	Meaning
Refresh	The thread is issuing the FLUSH PRIVILEGES command.
Register Slave	A slave has connected and is registering itself with the master.
Shutdown	The server is being shut down.
Sleep	The thread is idle. No query is being run.
Statistics	Table and index statistics are being gathered for the query optimizer.

Time

The number of seconds that the process has been running the current command. A process with a Time of 90 and Command of Sleep has been idle for a minute and a half.

State

Additional human-readable information about the state of this thread. Here's an example:

```
Slave connection: waiting for binlog update
```

This appears on the master server when a slave is actively replicating from it.

Info

This is the actual SQL currently being executed, if any. Only the first 100 characters are displayed in the output of SHOW PROCESSLIST. To get the full SQL, use SHOW FULL PROCESSLIST.

SHOW STATUS

In addition to all the variable information we can query, MySQL also keeps track of many useful counters and statistics. These numbers track how often various events occur. The SHOW STATUS command produces a tabular listing of all the statistics and their names.

To confuse matters a bit, MySQL refers to these counters as variables too. In a sense, they are variables, but they're not variables you can set. They change as the server runs and handles traffic; you simply read them and reset them using the FLUSH STATUS command.

The SHOW STATUS command, though, offers a lot of insight into your server's performance. It's covered in much greater depth in Appendix A.

SHOW INNODB STATUS

The SHOW INNODB STATUS status command provides a number of InnoDB-specific statistics. As we said earlier, InnoDB is one of MySQL's storage engines; look for more on storage engines in Chapter 2.

The output of SHOW INNODB STATUS is different from that of SHOW STATUS in that it reads more as a textual report, with section headings and such. There are different sections of the report that provide information on semaphores, transaction statistics, buffer information, transaction logs, and so forth.

SHOW INNODB STATUS is covered in greater detail along with SHOW STATUS in Appendix A. Also, note that in a future version of MySQL, this command will be replaced with a more generic SHOW ENGINE STATUS command.

CHAPTER 2

Storage Engines (Table Types)

One powerful aspect of MySQL that sets it apart from nearly every other database server is that it offers users many choices and options depending upon the user's environment. From the server point of view, its default configuration can be changed to run well on a wide range of hardware. At the application development level, you have a variety of data types to choose from when creating tables to store records. But what's even more unusual is that you can choose the type of table in which the records will be stored. You can even mix and match tables of different types in the same database!

 Storage engines used to be called table types. From time to time we refer to them as table types when it's less awkward to do so.

In this chapter, we'll show the major differences between the storage engines and why those differences are important. We'll begin with a look at locking and concurrency as well as transactions—two concepts that are critical to understanding some of the major differences between the various engines. Then we'll discuss the process of selecting the right one for your applications. Finally, we'll look deeper into each of the storage engines and get a feel for their features, storage formats, strengths and weaknesses, limitations, and so on.

Before drilling down into the details, there are a few general concepts we need to cover because they apply across all the storage engines. Some aren't even specific to MySQL at all; they're classic computer science problems that just happen to occur frequently in the world of multiuser database servers.

MySQL Architecture

It will greatly aid your thinking about storage engines and the capabilities they bring to MySQL if you have a good mental picture of where they fit. Figure 2-1 provides a logical view of MySQL. It doesn't necessarily reflect the low-level implementation, which is bound to be more complicated and less clear cut. However, it does serve as a guide that will help you understand how storage engines fit in to MySQL. (The NDB storage engine was added to MySQL just before this book was printed. Watch for it in the second edition.)

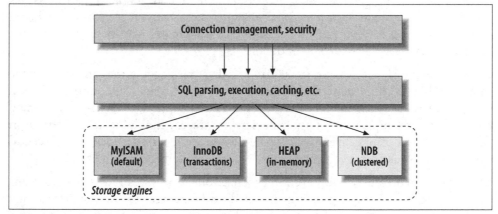

Figure 2-1. A logical view of MySQL's architecture

The topmost layer is composed of the services that aren't unique to MySQL. They're services most network-based client/server tools or servers need: connection handling, authentication, security, etc.

The second layer is where things get interesting. Much of the brains inside MySQL live here, including query parsing, analysis, optimization, caching, and all the built-in functions (dates, times, math, encryption, etc.). Any functionality provided across storage engines lives at this level. Stored procedures, which will arrive in MySQL 5.0, also reside in this layer.

The third layer is made up of storage engines. They're responsible for the storage and retrieval of all data stored "in" MySQL. Like the various filesystems available for Linux, each storage engine has its own benefits and drawbacks. The good news is that many of the differences are transparent at the query layer.

The interface between the second and third layers is a single API not specific to any given storage engine. This API is made up of roughly 20 low-level functions that perform operations such as "begin a transaction" or "fetch the row that has this primary key" and so on. The storage engines don't deal with SQL or communicate with each other; they simply respond to requests from the higher levels within MySQL.

Locking and Concurrency

The first of those problems is how to deal with concurrency and locking. In any data repository you have to be careful when more than one person, process, or client needs to change data at the same time. Consider, for example, a classic email box on a Unix system. The popular *mbox* file format is incredibly simple. Email messages are simply concatenated together, one after another. This simple format makes it very easy to read and parse mail messages. It also makes mail delivery easy: just append a new message to the end of the file.

But what happens when two processes try to deliver messages at the same time to the same mailbox? Clearly that can corrupt the mailbox, leaving two interleaved messages at the end of the mailbox file. To prevent corruption, all well-behaved mail delivery systems implement a form of locking to prevent simultaneous delivery from occurring. If a second delivery is attempted while the mailbox is locked, the second process must wait until it can acquire the lock before delivering the message.

This scheme works reasonably well in practice, but it provides rather poor concurrency. Since only a single program may make any changes to the mailbox at any given time, it becomes problematic with a high-volume mailbox, one that receives thousands of messages per minute. This exclusive locking makes it difficult for mail delivery not to become backlogged if someone attempts to read, respond to, and delete messages in that same mailbox. Luckily, few mailboxes are actually that busy.

Read/Write Locks

Reading from the mailbox isn't as troublesome. There's nothing wrong with multiple clients reading the same mailbox simultaneously. Since they aren't making changes, nothing is likely to go wrong. But what happens if someone tries to delete message number 25 while programs are reading the mailbox? It depends. A reader could come away with a corrupted or inconsistent view of the mailbox. So to be safe, even reading from a mailbox requires special care.

Database tables are no different. If you think of each mail message as a record and the mailbox itself as a table, it's easy to see that the problem is the same. In many ways, a mailbox is really just a simple database table. Modifying records in a database table is very similar to removing or changing the content of messages in a mailbox file.

The solution to this classic problem is rather simple. Systems that deal with concurrent read/write access typically implement a locking system that consists of two lock types. These locks are usually known as *shared locks* and *exclusive locks*, or *read locks* and *write locks*.

Without worrying about the actual locking technology, we can describe the concept as follows. Read locks on a resource are shared: many clients may read from the resource at the same time and not interfere with each other. Write locks, on the other hand, are exclusive, because it is safe to have only one client writing to the resource at given time and to prevent all reads when a client is writing. Why? Because the single writer is free to make any changes to the resource—even deleting it entirely.

In the database world, locking happens all the time. MySQL has to prevent one client from reading a piece of data while another is changing it. It performs this lock management internally in a way that is transparent much of the time.

Lock Granularity

One way to improve the concurrency of a shared resource is to be more selective about what is locked. Rather than locking the entire resource, lock only the part that contains the data you need to change. Better yet, lock only the exact piece of data you plan to change. By decreasing the amount of data that is locked at any one time, more changes can occur simultaneously—as long as they don't conflict with each other.

The downside of this is that locks aren't free. There is overhead involved in obtaining a lock, checking to see whether a lock is free, releasing a lock, and so on. All this business of lock management can really start to eat away at performance because the system is spending its time performing lock management instead of actually storing and retrieving data. (Similar things happen when too many managers get involved in a software project.)

To achieve the best performance overall, some sort of balance is needed. Most commercial database servers don't give you much choice: you get what is known as row-level locking in your tables. MySQL, on the other hand, offers a choice in the matter. Among the storage engines you can choose from in MySQL, you'll find three different granularities of locking. Let's have a look at them.

Table locks

The most basic and low-overhead locking strategy available is a *table lock*, which is analogous to the mailbox locks described earlier. The table as a whole is locked on an all-or-nothing basis. When a client wishes to write to a table (insert, delete, or update, etc.), it obtains a write lock that keeps all other read or write operations at bay for the duration of the operation. Once the write has completed, the table is unlocked to allow those waiting operations to continue. When nobody is writing, readers obtain read locks that allow other readers to do the same.

For a long time, MySQL provided only table locks, and this caused a great deal of concern among database geeks. They warned that MySQL would never scale up beyond toy projects and work in the real world. However, MySQL is so much faster than most commercial databases that table locking doesn't get in the way nearly as much as the naysayers predicted it would.

Part of the reason MySQL doesn't suffer as much as expected is because the majority of applications for which it is used consist primarily of read queries. In fact, the MyISAM engine (MySQL's default) was built assuming that 90% of all queries run against it will be reads. As it turns out, MyISAM tables perform very well as long as the ratio of reads to writes is very high or very low.

Page locks

A slightly more expensive form of locking that offers greater concurrency than table locking, a *page lock* is a lock applied to a portion of a table known as a page. All the records that reside on the same page in the table are affected by the lock. Using this scheme, the main factor influencing concurrency is the page size; if the pages in the table are large, concurrency will be worse than with smaller pages. MySQL's BDB (Berkeley DB) tables use page-level locking on 8-KB pages.

The only hot spot in page locking is the last page in the table. If records are inserted there at regular intervals, the last page will be locked frequently.

Row locks

The locking style that offers the greatest concurrency (and carries the greatest overhead) is the *row lock*. In most applications, it's relatively rare for several clients to need to update the exact same row at the same time. Row-level locking, as it's commonly known, is available in MySQL's InnoDB tables. InnoDB doesn't use a simple row locking mechanism, however. Instead it uses row-level locking in conjunction with a multiversioning scheme, so let's have a look at that.

Multi-Version Concurrency Control

There is a final technique for increasing concurrency: Multi-Version Concurrency Control (MVCC). Often referred to simply as *versioning*, MVCC is used by Oracle, by PostgreSQL, and by MySQL's InnoDB storage engine. MVCC can be thought of as a new twist on row-level locking. It has the added benefit of allowing nonlocking reads while still locking the necessary records only during write operations. Some of MVCC's other properties will be of particular interest when we look at transactions in the next section.

So how does this scheme work? Conceptually, any query against a table will actually see a snapshot of the data as it existed at the time the query began—no matter how long it takes to execute. If you've never experienced this before, it may sound a little crazy. But give it a chance.

In a versioning system, each row has two additional, hidden values associated with it. These values represent when the row was created and when it was expired (or deleted). Rather than storing the actual time at which these events occur, the database stores the version number at the time each event occurred. The *database version* (or *system version*) is a number that increments each time a query* begins. We'll call these two values the *creation id* and the *deletion id*.

Under MVCC, a final duty of the database server is to keep track of all the running queries (with their associated version numbers). Let's see how this applies to particular operations:

SELECT

When records are selected from a table, the server must examine each row to ensure that it meets several criteria:

- Its creation id must be less than or equal to the system version number. This ensures that the row was created before the current query began.

- Its deletion id, if not null, must be greater than the current system version. This ensures that the row wasn't deleted before the current query began.

- Its creation id can't be in the list of running queries. This ensures that the row wasn't added or changed by a query that is still running.

Rows that pass all of these tests may be returned as the result of the query.

INSERT

When a row is added to a table, the database server records the current version number along with the new row, using it as the row's creation id.

DELETE

To delete a row, the database server records the current version number as the row's deletion id.

UPDATE

When a row is modified, the database server writes a new copy of the row, using the version number as the new row's creation id. It also writes the version number as the old row's deletion id.

The result of all this extra record keeping is that read queries never lock tables, pages, or rows. They simply read data as fast as they can, making sure to select only rows that meet the criteria laid out earlier. The drawbacks are that the server has to store a bit more data with each row and do a bit more work when examining rows. Table 2-1 summarizes the various locking models and concurrency in MySQL.

---

* That's not quite true. As you'll see when we start talking about transactions later, the version number is incremented for each transaction rather than each query.

Table 2-1. *Locking models and concurrency in MySQL*

Locking strategy	Concurrency	Overhead	Engines
Table socks	Lowest	Lowest	MyISAM, Heap, Merge
Page locks	Modest	Modest	BDB
Multiversioning	Highest	High	InnoDB

Transactions

You can't examine the more advanced features of a database system for very long before transactions enter the mix. A transaction is a group of SQL queries that are treated *atomically*, as a single unit of work. Either the entire group of queries is applied to a database, or none of them are. Little of this section is specific to MySQL. If you're already familiar with ACID transactions, feel free to skip ahead to the section "Transactions in MySQL."

A banking application is the classic example of why transactions are necessary. Imagine a bank's database with a two tables: checking and savings. To move $200 from Jane's checking account to her savings account, you need to perform at least three steps:

1. Make sure her checking account balance is greater than $200.

2. Subtract $200 from her checking account balance.

3. Add $200 to her savings account balance.

The entire operation should be wrapped in a transaction so that if any one of the steps fails, they can all be rolled back.

A transaction is initiated (or opened) with the BEGIN statement and applied with COMMIT or *rolled back* (undone) with ROLLBACK. So the SQL for the transaction might look like this:

```
          BEGIN;
[step 1] SELECT balance FROM checking WHERE customer_id = 10233276;
[step 2] UPDATE checking SET balance = balance - 200.00 WHERE customer_id = 10233276;
[step 3] UPDATE savings  SET balance = balance + 200.00 WHERE customer_id = 10233276;
          COMMIT;
```

But transactions alone aren't the whole story. What happens if the database server crashes while performing step 3? Who knows? The customer probably just lost $200. What if another process comes along between Steps 2 and 3 and removes the entire checking account balance? The bank has given the customer a $200 credit without even knowing it.

Simply having transactions isn't sufficient unless the database server passes what is known as the *ACID test*. ACID is an acronym for Atomicity, Consistency, Isolation, and Durability—four tightly related criteria that are required in a well-behaved transaction processing system. Transactions that meet those four criteria are often referred to as *ACID transactions*.

Atomicity

Transactions must function as a single indivisible unit of work. The entire transaction is either applied or rolled back. When transactions are atomic, there is no such thing as a partially completed transaction: it's all or nothing.

Consistency

The database should always move from one consistent state to the next. Consistency ensures that a crash between Steps 2 and 3 doesn't result in $200 missing from the checking account. Because the transaction is never committed, none of the transaction's changes are ever reflected in the database.

Isolation

The results of a transaction are usually invisible to other transactions until the transaction is complete. This ensures that if a bank account summary runs after Step 2, but before Step 3, it still sees the $200 in the checking account. When we discuss isolation levels, you'll understand why we said *usually* invisible.

Durability

Once committed, the results of a transaction are permanent. This means that the changes must be recorded in such a way that system crashes won't lose the data. Of course, if the database server's disks fail, all bets are off. That's a hardware problem. We'll talk more about how you can minimize the effects of hardware failures in Chapter 6.

Benefits and Drawbacks

ACID transactions ensure that banks don't lose your money. By wrapping arbitrarily complex logic into single units of work, the database server takes some of the burden off application developers. The database server's ACID properties offer guarantees that reduce the need for code guarding against race conditions and handling crash recovery.

The downside of this extra security is that the database server has to do more work. It also means that a database server with ACID transactions will generally require more CPU power, memory, and disk space than one without them. As mentioned earlier, this is where MySQL's modularity comes into play. Because you can decide on a per-table basis if you need ACID transactions or not, you don't need to pay the performance penalty on a table that really won't benefit from transactions.

Isolation Levels

The previous description of isolation was a bit simplistic. Isolation is more complex than it might first appear because of some peculiar cases that can occur. The SQL standard defines four isolation levels with specific rules for which changes are and aren't visible inside and outside a transaction. Let's look at each isolation level and the type of problems that can occur.

Read uncommitted

In the *read uncommitted* isolation level, transactions can view the results of uncommitted transactions. At this level, many problems can occur unless you really, really know what you are doing and have a good reason for doing it. Read uncommitted is rarely used in practice. Reading uncommitted data is also known as a *dirty read*.

Read committed

The default isolation level for most database systems is *read committed.* It satisfies the simple definition of isolation used earlier. A transaction will see the results only of transactions that were already committed when it began, and its changes won't be visible to others until it's committed.

However, there are problems that can occur using that definition. To visualize the problems, refer to the sample data for the Stock and StockPrice tables as shown in Tables 2-2 and 2-3.

Table 2-2. The Stock table

id	Ticker	Name
1	MSFT	Microsoft
2	EBAY	eBay
3	YHOO	Yahoo!
4	AMZN	Amazon

Table 2-3. The StockPrice table

stock_id	date	open	high	low	close
1	2002-05-01	21.25	22.30	20.18	21.30
2	2002-05-01	10.01	10.20	10.01	10.18
3	2002-05-01	18.23	19.12	18.10	19.00
4	2002-05-01	45.55	46.99	44.87	45.71
1	2002-05-02	21.30	21.45	20.02	20.21
2	2002-05-02	10.18	10.55	10.10	10.35
3	2002-05-02	19.01	19.88	19.01	19.22
4	2002-05-02	45.69	45.69	44.03	44.30

Imagine you have a Perl script that runs nightly to fetch price data about your favorite stocks. For each stock, it fetches the data and adds a record to the StockPrice table with the day's numbers. So to update the information for Amazon.com, the transaction might look like this:

```
BEGIN;
SELECT @id := id FROM Stock WHERE ticker = 'AMZN';
INSERT INTO StockPrice VALUES (@id, '2002-05-03', 20.50, 21.10, 20.08, 21.02);
COMMIT;
```

But what if, between the select and insert, Amazon's id changes from 4 to 17 and a new stock is added with id 4? Or what if Amazon is removed entirely? You'll end up inserting a record with the wrong id in the first case. And in the second case, you've inserted a record for which there is no longer a corresponding row in the Stock table. Neither of these is what you intended.

The problem is that you have a *nonrepeatable read* in the query. That is, the data you read in the SELECT becomes invalid by the time you execute the INSERT. The repeatable read isolation level exists to solve this problem.

Repeatable read

At the *repeatable read* isolation level, any rows that are read during a transaction are locked so that they can't be changed until the transaction finishes. This provides the perfect solution to the problem mentioned in the previous section, in which Amazon's id can change or vanish entirely. However, this isolation level still leaves the door open to another tricky problem: phantom reads.

Using the same data, imagine that you have a script that performs some analysis based on the data in the StockPrice table. And let's assume it does this while the nightly update is also running.

The analysis script does something like this:

```
BEGIN;
SELECT * FROM StockPrice WHERE close BETWEEN 10 and 20;
// think for a bit
SELECT * FROM StockPrice WHERE close BETWEEN 10 and 20;
COMMIT;
```

But the nightly update script inserts between those two queries new rows that happen to match the close BETWEEN 10 and 20 condition. The second query will find more rows that the first one! These additional rows are known as *phantom rows* (or simply phantoms). They weren't locked the first time because they didn't exist when the query ran.

Having said all that, we need to point out that this is a bit more academic than you might think. Phantom rows are such a common problem that InnoDB's locking (known as *next-key locking*) prevents this from happening. Rather than locking only the rows you've touched in a query, InnoDB actually locks the slot following them in the index structure as well.

Serializable

The highest level of isolation, *serializable*, solves the phantom read problem by ordering transactions so that they can't conflict. At this level, a lot of timeouts and lock contention may occur, but the needs of your application may bring you to accept the decreased performance in favor of the data stability that results.

Table 2-2 summarizes the various isolation levels and the drawbacks associated with each one. Keep in mind that as you move down the list, you're sacrificing concurrency and performance for increased safety.

Table 2-4. ANSI SQL isolation levels

Isolation level	Dirty reads possible	Non-repeatable reads possible	Phantom reads possible
Read uncommitted	Yes	Yes	Yes
Read committed	No	Yes	Yes
Repeatable read	No	No	Yes
Serializable	No	No	No

Deadlocks

Whenever multiple transactions obtain locks, there is the danger of encountering a deadlock condition. Deadlocks occur when two transactions attempt to obtain conflicting locks in a different order.

For example, consider these two transactions running against the StockPrice table:

Transaction #1:

```
BEGIN;
UPDATE StockPrice SET close = 45.50 WHERE stock_id = 4 and date = '2002-05-01';
UPDATE StockPrice SET close = 19.80 WHERE stock_id = 3 and date = '2002-05-02';
COMMIT;
```

Transaction #2:

```
BEGIN;
UPDATE StockPrice SET high = 20.12 WHERE stock_id = 3 and date = '2002-05-02';
UPDATE StockPrice SET high = 47.20 WHERE stock_id = 4 and date = '2002-05-01';
COMMIT;
```

If you're unlucky, each transaction will execute its first query and update a row of data, locking it in the process. Each transaction will then attempt to update its second row only to find that it is already locked. Left unchecked, the two transactions will wait for each other to complete—forever.

To combat this problem, database systems implement various forms of deadlock detection and timeouts. The more sophisticated systems, such as InnoDB, will notice circular dependencies like the previous example and return an error. Others will give up after the query exceeds a timeout while waiting for a lock. InnoDB's default timeout is 50 seconds. In either case, applications that use transactions need to be able to handle deadlocks and possibly retry transactions.

Transaction Logging

Some of the overhead involved with transactions can be mitigated through the use of a transaction log. Rather than directly updating the tables on disk each time a change occurs, the system can update the in-memory copy of the data (which is very fast) and write a record of the change to a *transaction log* on disk. Then, at some later time, a process (or thread) can actually apply the changes that the transaction log recorded. The serial disk I/O required to append events to the log is much faster than the random seeks required to update data in various places on disk.

As long as events are written to the transaction log before a transaction is considered committed, having the changes in a log will not affect the durability of the system. If the database server crashes before all changes have been applied from the transaction log, the database will continue applying changes from the transaction log when it is restarted and before it accepts new connections.

Transactions in MySQL

MySQL provides two transaction-safe storage engines: Berkeley DB (BDB) and InnoDB. Their specific properties are discussed in next section. Each one offers the basic BEGIN/COMMIT/ROLLBACK functionality. They differ in their supported isolation levels, locking characteristics, deadlock detection, and other features.

AUTOCOMMIT

By default MySQL operates in AUTOCOMMIT mode. This means that unless you've explicitly begun a transaction, it automatically executes each query in a separate transaction. You can enable AUTOCOMMIT for the current connection by running:

```
SET AUTOCOMMIT = 1;
```

Disable it by executing:

```
SET AUTOCOMMIT = 0;
```

Changing the value of AUTOCOMMIT has no effect on non-transaction-safe tables such as MyISAM or HEAP.

Implicit commits

Certain commands, when issued during an open transaction, cause MySQL to commit the transaction before they execute. Typically these are commands that make significant changes, such as removing or renaming a table.

Here is the list of commands for which MySQL implicitly commits a transaction:

- `ALTER TABLE`
- `BEGIN`
- `CREATE INDEX`
- `DROP DATABASE`
- `DROP TABLE`
- `RENAME TABLE`
- `TRUNCATE`
- `LOCK TABLES`
- `UNLOCK TABLES`

As additional features are added to MySQL, it is possible that other commands will be added to the list, so be sure to check the latest available documentation.

Isolation levels

MySQL allows you to set the isolation level using the `SET TRANSACTION ISOLATION LEVEL` command. Unless otherwise specified, the isolation level is changed beginning with the next transaction.

To set the level for the whole session (connection), use:

```
SET SESSION TRANSACTION ISOLATION LEVEL READ COMMITTED
```

Here's how to set the global level:

```
SET GLOBAL TRANSACTION ISOLATION LEVEL SERIALIZABLE
```

MySQL recognizes all four ANSI standard isolation levels, and as of Version 4.0.5 of MySQL, InnoDB supports all of them:

- `READ UNCOMMITTED`
- `READ COMMITTED`
- `REPEATABLE READ`
- `SERIALIZABLE`

The default isolation level can also be set using the `--transaction-isolation` command-line option when starting the server or set via *my.cnf*.

Mixing storage engines in transactions

Transaction management in MySQL is currently handled by the underlying storage engines, not at a higher level. Thus, you can't reliably mix tables stored in transactional engines (such as InnoDB and BDB) in a single transaction. A higher-level transaction management service may someday be added to MySQL, making it safe to mix and match transaction-safe tables in a transaction. Until then, don't expect it to work.

If you mix transaction-safe and non-transaction-safe tables (such as InnoDB and MyISAM) in a transaction, the transaction will work properly if all goes well. However, if a rollback is required, the changes to the non-transaction-safe table won't be undone. This leaves the database in an inconsistent state that may be difficult to recover from (and renders the entire point of transactions moot).

Simulating transactions

At times you may need the behavior of transactions when you aren't using a transaction-safe table. You can achieve something like transactions using MySQL's LOCK TABLES and UNLOCK TABLES commands. If you lock the tables that will be involved in the transaction and keep track of any changes that you make (in case you need to simulate a rollback), you'll have something equivalent to running at the serializable isolation level. But the process is kludgy and error prone, so if you really need transactions, we recommend using a transactional storage engine.

Selecting the Right Engine

When designing MySQL-based applications, you should decide which engine to use for storing your data. If you don't think about it during the design phase, you will likely face complications later in the process. You might find that the default engine doesn't provide a feature you need, such as transactions. Or maybe the mix of read and write queries your application generates will require more granular locking than MyISAM's table locks.

Because you can make the choice on a table-by-table basis, you'll need a clear idea of how each table is used and the data it stores. Of course, it also helps to have a good understanding of the application as a whole and its potential for growth. Armed with this information, you can begin to make good choices about which table engines can do the job.

Considerations

While there are many factors that can affect your decision, it usually boils down to just a few considerations: transactions and concurrency, backups, and special features.

Transactions and concurrency

When it comes to transactions and concurrency, consider the following guidelines:

- If your application requires transactions and high read/write concurrency, InnoDB is probably your best bet.

- If your application requires transactions but only moderate read/write concurrency, either BDB or InnoDB tables should work fine.

- If your application doesn't require transactions and issues primarily SELECT or primarily INSERT/UPDATE queries, MyISAM is a good choice. Many web applications fall into this category.

Backups

The need to perform regular backups may also influence your table choices. If your server can be shut down at regular intervals for backups, the storage engines are equally easy to deal with. However, if you need to perform online backups in one form or another, the choices become less clear. Chapter 9 deals with this topic in more detail.

Another way of looking at this is simplicity. As you'll see in Chapter 9, using multiple storage engines increases the complexity of backups and server tuning. You may decide that it's just easier to use a single storage engine rather than those that are theoretically best.

Special features

Finally, you sometimes find that an application relies on particular features or optimizations that are provided by only some of MySQL's storage engines. For example, not all tables provide a quick answer to queries like the following:

```
SELECT COUNT(*) FROM mytable
```

If your application depends on accurate and fast row counts, MyISAM is the answer. InnoDB must actually count up all the rows, but the MyISAM storage engine always knows the exact row count of a table without the need to do any work.

If your application requires referential integrity with foreign keys, you're limited to just InnoDB tables. Do you need full-text search capabilities? Only MyISAM tables provide it.

Keep this in mind as you read the more detailed information about each table's features. There will come a time when you find that the feature you really, really need is available only in one table engine. When that happens, you need to either compromise or break a table into multiple tables of different types.

Practical Examples

These issues may seem rather abstract without some sort of real-world context. So let's consider some common uses for tables in various database applications. For each table, we'll look at which engine best matches with the table's needs. The details of each engine are covered in the next section.

Logging

Suppose you want to use MySQL to log a record of every telephone call from a central telephone switch in real time. Or maybe you've installed *mod_log_sql* for Apache so you can log all visits to your web site directly in a table. In such an application, speed is probably the most important goal; you don't want the database to be the bottleneck. Using MyISAM tables works very well because they have very low overhead and can handle inserting thousands of records per second.

Things will get interesting if you decide it's time to start running reports to summarize the data you've logged. Depending on the queries you use, there's a good chance you will significantly slow the process of inserting records while gathering data for the report. What can you do?

You can use MySQL's built-in replication (Chapter 7) to clone the data onto a second (slave) server. You can then run your time- and CPU-intensive queries against the data on the slave. This keeps the master free to insert records as fast as it possibly can while also giving you the freedom to run any query you want without worrying about how it could affect the real-time logging.

Another option is to use a MyISAM Merge table. Rather than always logging to the same table, adjust the application to log to a table that contains the name or number of the month in its name, such as `web_logs_2004_01` or `web_logs_2004_jan`. Then define a Merge table that contains the data you'd like to summarize and use it in your queries. If you need to summarize data daily or weekly, the same strategy works; you just need to create tables with more specific names, such as `web_logs_2004_01_01`. While you're busy running queries against tables that are no longer being written to, your application can log records to its current table uninterrupted. Merge tables are discussed in the later section "MyISAM Merge tables."

A final possibility is simply to switch to using a table that has more granular locking than MyISAM does. Either BDB or InnoDB works well in this case. Non-MyISAM tables will generally use more CPU and disk space, but that may be a reasonable tradeoff in this case. Also, in the event of a crash, MyISAM tables may take quite a long time to check and repair while InnoDB tables should recover quickly.

Read-only or read-mostly tables

Tables that contain the data used to construct a catalog or listing of some sort (jobs, auctions, real estate, etc.) are usually read from far more often than they are written to. This makes them great candidates for MyISAM.

Order processing

When you deal with any sort of order processing, transactions are a requirement. Half-completed orders aren't going to endear customers to your service. Using transaction-safe table types (InnoDB or BDB), these unfortunate "data surprises" can be avoided. Considering that BDB tables use—at best—locking at the page level, applications with high transaction volumes should consider InnoDB tables.

In the case of order processing, InnoDB has a distinct advantage because it supports referential integrity through the use of foreign keys. These keys allow a field in one table to have an enforced relationship to the key of another table (e.g., an `Order` record contains a `CustomerID` field that "points" to the primary key of the `Customer` table). Foreign keys effectively point to those other tables and indicate that data is maintained in them, and they help you keep data consistent across your tables. (Keep in mind that a foreign key in an InnoDB table must reference another InnoDB table. Currently they can't cross storage engines.)

You might want to design your tables so that customers can't be removed without also removing all their orders. Or maybe you'd like to ensure that products aren't deleted from the catalog table before the orders that reference those products are archived. With InnoDB's foreign keys, you can.

Stock quotes

If you're collecting stock quotes for your own analysis, MyISAM tables work great. However, if you're running a high-traffic web service that has a real-time quote feed and thousands of users, a query should never have to wait. At any time, there could be many clients attempting to read and write to the table, so the row-level locking provided by InnoDB tables is the way to go.

If you have sufficient memory, MySQL's in-memory Heap tables might be an option, too. However, their indexes have some interesting restrictions you need to investigate first. See the "Heap Tables" section in Chapter 4 for more details.

Bulletin boards and threaded discussion forums

Threaded discussions are an interesting problem for MySQL users. There are hundreds of freely available PHP and Perl-based systems available that provide threaded discussions. Many of them aren't written with database efficiency in mind, so they tend to perform a large number of queries for each request they serve, as well as updates to counters and usage statistics about the various discussions. Many of the systems also use a small number of monolithic tables to store all their data. As a result, a few central tables become the focus of heavy read and write activity, and the locks required to enforce concurrency become a substantial source of contention.

Despite their design shortcomings, most of the systems work well for small and medium loads. However, if a web site grows large enough and generates a significant amount of traffic, it may begin to get very slow. The obvious solution is to switch to a different table type that can handle the heavy read/write volume. Users who have attempted this are sometimes surprised to find that the system runs even more slowly than it did before!

What they don't realize is that the system is using a particular query, normally something like:

```
SELECT COUNT(*) FROM table WHERE ...
```

The problem is that not all engines can run that query quickly. MyISAM tables keep accurate row counts available, so they can. But BDB and InnoDB must actually scan the data to count all the rows. The developers of the popular web site Slashdot (*http://slashdot.org/*) ran into this problem when they moved their system from MyISAM to InnoDB tables. They spent time going through their code to eliminate all those queries.

MySQL's query cache, which we'll cover in more detail in Chapter 5, can often be a big help in situations in which an application issues the same query over and over with the same parameters.

CD-ROM applications

If you ever need to distribute a CD-ROM- or DVD-ROM-based application that uses MySQL data files, consider using MyISAM or Compressed MyISAM tables. They can be easily isolated and copied to other media. Compressed MyISAM tables take far less space than uncompressed ones, but they are read-only. Since the data is going to be on read-only media anyway, there's little reason not to use compressed tables.

Table Conversions

Several techniques are available to convert one table type to another, each with advantages and disadvantages. In the following sections, we cover three of the most common.

ALTER TABLE

The easiest way to move a table from one engine to another is by using an ALTER TABLE statement. The following command converts mytable to BDB:

```
ALTER TABLE mytable TYPE = BDB;
```

 As of MySQL Versions 4.0.18 and 4.1.2, you may use ENGINE instead of TYPE. In a later version of MySQL (probably in the 5.x series), support for TYPE will be removed entirely.

The previous syntax works for all storage engines, but there's a catch: it can take a lot of time. MySQL will perform a row-by-row copy of your old table into your new table. During that time, you'll probably be using all the server's disk I/O capacity, and the original table will be locked while the conversion runs. So take care before trying this technique on a busy table. Instead, you can use one of the following methods, which involve making a copy of the table first.

Dump and reimport

To gain more control over the process, you might choose to dump the table to a text file using the *mysqldump* utility. Once the table is dumped, simply edit the dump file to adjust the CREATE TABLE statement it contains. Be sure to change the table name as well as its type because you can't have two tables with the same name in the same database even if they are of different types.

If you import into InnoDB or BDB, be sure to use the --no-autocommit option to disable AUTOCOMMIT mode. Otherwise each individual insert will be performed in its own transaction.

The downside of using *mysqldump* is that it isn't terribly fast and uses far more disk space. Not only will the dump file contain all the data from the table, it will also contain all the SQL necessary to repopulate the table. Also, you won't be able to delete the dump file until the new table has been created.

Furthermore, if the dump file happens to be quite large, editing it can be a challenge. You can't simply load a 6-GB file into *vi* or *emacs* on most systems.* Instead, you'll need to craft a Perl or *sed* script to do the job.

CREATE and SELECT

The third technique is a compromise between the speed of the first mechanism and the safety of the second. Rather than dumping the entire table or converting it all at once, you create the new table and use MySQL's INSERT INTO ... SELECT syntax to populate it incrementally. If, for example, you have a MyISAM table called myisam_table that you'd like to convert to an InnoDB table named innodb_table, you need to run queries like this:

```
BEGIN;
INSERT INTO innodb_table SELECT * FROM myisam_table WHERE id BETWEEN x AND y;
COMMIT;
```

Assuming that id is the primary key, you run that query using larger values of x and y each time until all the data has been copied to the new table. After doing so, you are left with the original table, which you can drop after you're done with it, and the new table, which is now fully populated.

Alternatively, if you use MySQL 4.1 or newer, you can create the new table and copy the table in two steps:

```
CREATE TABLE newtable LIKE mytable;
INSERT INTO newtable SELECT * FROM mytable;
```

Whichever method you use, if you're dealing with a large volume of data, it's often more efficient to copy the data before adding indexes to the new table.

---

* Maybe you can, but it'll be pretty painful.

The Storage Engines

Now it's time to look at each of MySQL's storage engines in more detail. Table 2-3 summarizes some of the high-level characteristics of the handlers. The following sections provide some basic highlights and background about each table handler as well as any unusual characteristics and interesting features.

Before going further, it's worth noting that this isn't an exhaustive discussion of MySQL's storage engines. We assume that you've read (or at least know where to find) the information in the *MySQL Reference Manual*.

Table 2-5. Storage engine features in MySQL

Attribute	MyISAM	Heap	BDB	InnoDB
Transactions	No	No	Yes	Yes
Lock granularity	Table	Table	Page (8 KB)	Row
Storage	Split files	In-memory	Single file per table	Tablespace(s)
Isolation levels	None	None	Read committed	All
Portable format	Yes	N/A	No	Yes
Referential integrity	No	No	No	Yes
Primary key with data	No	No	Yes	Yes
MySQL caches data records	No	Yes	Yes	Yes
Availability	All versions	All versions	MySQL-Max	All Versions[a]

[a] Prior to MySQL 4.0, InnoDB was available in MySQL-Max only.

Most of MySQL's disk-based tables have some basic things in common. Each database in MySQL is simply a subdirectory of MySQL's data directory in the underlying filesystem.* Whenever you create a table, MySQL stores the table definition in a *.frm* file with the same name as the table. Thus, when you create a table named `MyTable`, MySQL stores the table definition in *MyTable.frm*.

To determine the type of a table, use the `SHOW TABLE STATUS` command. For example, to examine the user table in the `mysql` database, you execute the following:

```
mysql> SHOW TABLE STATUS LIKE 'user' \G
*************************** 1. row ***************************
           Name: user
           Type: MyISAM
     Row_format: Dynamic
           Rows: 6
 Avg_row_length: 59
    Data_length: 356
Max_data_length: 4294967295
```

---

* In MySQL 5.0, the term "database" will likely morph into "schema."

```
      Index_length: 2048
          Data_free: 0
     Auto_increment: NULL
        Create_time: 2002-01-24 18:07:17
        Update_time: 2002-01-24 21:56:29
         Check_time: NULL
      Create_options:
            Comment: Users and global privileges
1 row in set (0.06 sec)
```

Notice that it's a MyISAM table. You might also notice a lot of other information and statistics in the output. Let's briefly look at what each line means:

Name
  The table's name.

Type
  The table's type. Again, in some versions of MySQL, this may say "Engine" rather than "Type."

Row_format
  Dynamic, Fixed, or Compressed. Dynamic rows vary in length because they contain variable-length fields such as VARCHAR or BLOB. Fixed rows, which are always the same size, are made up of fields that don't vary in length, such as CHAR and INTEGER. Compressed rows exist only in compressed tables (see the later section "Compressed MyISAM").

Rows
  The number of rows in the table. For non-transactional tables, this number is always accurate. For transactional tables, it is usually an estimate.

Avg_row_length
  How many bytes the average row contains.

Data_length
  How much data (in bytes) the entire table contains.

Max_data_length
  The maximum amount of data this table can hold. In a MyISAM table with dynamic (variable length) rows, the index file for a table (*tablename.MYI*) stores row locations using 32-bit pointers into the data file (*tablename.MYD*). That means it can address only up to 4 GB of space by default. See the next section, "MyISAM Tables" for more details. For MyISAM tables with fixed-length rows, the limit is just under 4.3 billion rows.

Index_length
  How much space is consumed by index data.

Data_free
  The amount of space that has been allocated but is currently unused.

Auto_increment
  The next AUTO_INCREMENT value.

Create_time
> When the table was first created.

Update_time
> When data in the table last changed.

Check_time
> When the table was last checked using `CHECK TABLE` or `myisamchk`.

Create_options
> Any other options that were specified when the table was created.

Comment
> The comments, if any, that were set when the table was created.

MyISAM Tables

As MySQL's default storage engine, MyISAM provides a good compromise between performance and useful features. Versions of MySQL prior to 3.23 used the Index Sequential Access Method (ISAM) table format. In Version 3.23, ISAM tables were deprecated in favor of MyISAM, an enhanced ISAM format.[*] MyISAM tables don't provide transactions or a very granular locking model, but they do have full-text indexing (see Chapter 4), compression, and more.

Storage

In MyISAM storage, there are typically two files: a data file and an index file. The two files bear *.MYD* and *.MYI* extensions, respectively. The MyISAM format is platform-neutral, meaning you can copy the data and index files from an Intel-based server to a Macintosh PowerBook or Sun SPARC without any trouble.

MyISAM tables can contain either dynamic or static (fixed-length) rows. MySQL decides which format to use based on the table definition. The number of rows a MyISAM table can hold is limited primarily by the available disk space on your database server and the largest file your operating system will let you create. Some (mostly older) operating systems have been known to cut you off at 2 GB, so check your local documentation.

However, MyISAM files with variable-length rows, are set up by default to handle only 4 GB of data, mainly for efficiency. The index uses 32-bit pointers to the data records. To create a MyISAM table that can hold more than 4 GB, you must specify values for the `MAX_ROWS` and `AVG_ROW_LENGTH` options that represent ballpark figures for the amount of space you need:

```
CREATE TABLE mytable (
  a   INTEGER  NOT NULL PRIMARY KEY,
```

---

[*] ISAM tables may be used in MySQL 4.0 and 4.1. Presumably they'll vanish sometime in the 5.x release cycle. If you're still using ISAM tables, it's time to upgrade to MyISAM!

```
       b    CHAR(18) NOT NULL
) MAX_ROWS = 1000000000 AVG_ROW_LENGTH = 32;
```

In the example, we've told MySQL to be prepared to store at least 32 GB of data in the table. To find out what MySQL decided to do, simply ask for the table status:

```
mysql> SHOW TABLE STATUS LIKE 'mytable' \G
*************************** 1. row ***************************
           Name: mytable
           Type: MyISAM
     Row_format: Fixed
           Rows: 0
 Avg_row_length: 0
    Data_length: 0
Max_data_length: 98784247807
   Index_length: 1024
      Data_free: 0
 Auto_increment: NULL
    Create_time: 2002-02-24 17:36:57
    Update_time: 2002-02-24 17:36:57
     Check_time: NULL
 Create_options: max_rows=1000000000 avg_row_length=32
        Comment:
1 row in set (0.05 sec)
```

As you can see, MySQL remembers the create options exactly as specified. And it chose a representation capable of holding 91 GB of data!

Other stuff

As one of the oldest storage engines included in MySQL, MyISAM tables have a number of features that have been developed over time specifically to fill niche needs uncovered through years of use:

Locking and concurrency
> Locking in MyISAM tables is performed at the table level. Readers obtain shared (read) locks on all tables they need to read. Writers obtain exclusive (write) locks.

Automatic repair
> If MySQL is started with the --myisam-recover option, the first time it opens a MyISAM table, it examines the table to determine whether it was closed properly. If it was not (probably because of a hardware problem or power outage), MySQL scans the table for problems and repairs them. The downside, of course, is that your application must wait while a table it needs is being repaired.

Manual repair
> You can use the CHECK TABLE mytable and REPAIR TABLE mytable commands to check a table for errors and repair them. The *myisamchk* command-line tool can also be used to check and repair tables when the server is offline.

Concurrency improvements

If a MyISAM table has no deleted rows, you can insert rows into the table while select queries are running against it.

Index features

BLOB and TEXT columns in a MyISAM table can be indexed. MyISAM tables have a limit of 500 bytes on each key, however, so the index uses only the first few hundred bytes of a BLOB or TEXT field. MyISAM tables also allow you to index columns that may contain NULL values. You can find more information on MyISAM indexes in Chapter 4.

Delayed key writes

MyISAM tables marked with the DELAY_KEY_WRITE create option don't have index changes written to disk as they are made. Instead, the changes are made to the in-memory key buffer only and flushed to disk when the associated blocks are pruned from the key buffer or when the table is closed. This can yield quite a performance boost on heavily used tables that change frequently.

Compressed MyISAM Tables

For circumstances in which the data never changes, such as CD-ROM- or DVD-ROM-based applications, or in some embedded environments, MyISAM tables can be compressed (or packed) using the *myisampack* utility. Compressed tables can't be modified, but they generally take far less space and are faster as a result. Having smaller tables means fewer disk seeks are required to find records.

On relatively modern hardware, the overhead involved in decompressing the data is insignificant for most applications. The individual rows are compressed, so MySQL doesn't need to unpack an entire table (or even a page) just to fetch a single row.

RAID MyISAM Tables

While they're not really a separate table type, MyISAM RAID tables do serve a particular niche. To use them, you need to compile your own copy of MySQL from source or use the MySQL-Max package. RAID tables are just like MyISAM tables except that the data file is split into several data files. Despite the reference to RAID in the name, these data files don't have to be stored on separate disks, although it is easy to do so. Writes to the table are striped across the data files, much like RAID-0 would do across physical disks. This can be helpful in two circumstances. If you have an operating system that limits file sizes to 2 or 4 GB but you need larger tables, using RAID will get you past the limit. If you're have an I/O bound table that is read from and written to very frequently, you might achieve better performance by storing each of the RAID files on a separate physical disk.

To create a RAID table, you must supply some additional options at table-creation time:

```
CREATE TABLE mytable (
  a    INTEGER  NOT NULL PRIMARY KEY,
  b    CHAR(18) NOT NULL
) RAID_TYPE = STRIPED RAID_CHUNKS = 4 RAID_CHUNKSIZE = 16;
```

The RAID_TYPE option, while required, must be STRIPED or RAID0, which are synonymous. No other RAID algorithms are available. The RAID_CHUNKS parameter tells MySQL how many data files to break the table into. The RAID_CHUNKSIZE option specifies how many kilobytes of data MySQL will write in each file before moving to the next.

In the previous example, MySQL would create four subdirectories named *00*, *01*, *02*, and *03* in which it would store a file named *mytable.MYD*. When writing data to the table, it would write 16 KB of data to one file and then move to the next one. Once created, RAID tables are transparent. You can use them just as you would normal MyISAM tables.

With the availability of inexpensive RAID controllers and the software RAID features of some operating systems, there isn't much need for using RAID tables in MySQL. Also, it's important to realize that RAID tables split only the data file, not the indexes. If you're trying to overcome file size limits, keep an eye on the size of your index files.

MyISAM Merge Tables

Merge tables are the final variation of MyISAM tables that MySQL provides. Where a RAID table is a single table split into smaller pieces, a Merge table is the combination of several similar tables into one virtual table.

This is particularly useful when MySQL is used in logging applications. Imagine you store web server logs in MySQL. For ease of management, you might create a table for each month. However, when it comes time to generate annual statistics, it would be easier if all the records were in a single table. Using Merge tables, that's possible. You can create 12 normal MyISAM tables, log_2004_01, log_2004_02, … log_2004_12, and then a Merge table named log_2004.

Queries for a particular month can be run against the specific table that holds the data. But queries that may need to cross month boundaries can be run against the Merge table log_2004 as if it was a table that contained all the data in the underlying twelve tables.

The requirements for a Merge table are that the underlying tables must:

- Have exactly the same definition
- Be MyISAM tables

- Exist in the same database (this limitation is removed in MySQL Versions 4.1.1 and higher, however)

Interestingly, it's possible for some underlying tables to be compressed MyISAM tables. That means you can compress tables as they get old (since they're no longer being written to anyway), but still use them as part of a Merge table. Just make sure to remove the table from the Merge table before compressing it, then re-add it after it has been compressed.

Using the example table from earlier, let's create several identical tables and a Merge table that aggregates them:

```
CREATE TABLE mytable0 (
    a    INTEGER  NOT NULL PRIMARY KEY,
    b    CHAR(18) NOT NULL
);

CREATE TABLE mytable1 (
    a    INTEGER  NOT NULL PRIMARY KEY,
    b    CHAR(18) NOT NULL
);

CREATE TABLE mytable2 (
    a    INTEGER  NOT NULL PRIMARY KEY,
    b    CHAR(18) NOT NULL
);

CREATE TABLE mytable (
    a    INTEGER  NOT NULL PRIMARY KEY,
    b    CHAR(18) NOT NULL
) TYPE = MERGE UNION = (mytable0, mytable1, mytable2) INSERT_METHOD = LAST;
```

The only difference between the Merge table and the underlying tables is that it has a few extra options set at creation time. The type, of course, is MERGE. The UNION option specifies the tables that make up the Merge table. Order is important if you plan to insert into the Merge table rather than the underlying tables. The INSERT_METHOD option, which can be NO, FIRST, or LAST, tells MySQL how to handle inserts to the Merge table. If the method is NO, inserts aren't allowed. Otherwise, inserts will always go to either the first or last of the underlying tables based on the value of INSERT_METHOD.

The order of the tables is also important for unique-key lookups because as soon as the record is found, MySQL stops looking. Thus, the earlier in the list the table is, the better. In most logging applications where you'll be doing searches on the Merge table, it might make sense to put the tables in reverse chronological order. The order is also important for making ORDER BY as fast as possible because the required merge-sort will be faster when the rows are nearly in order already. If you don't specify INSERT_METHOD, the default is NO.

As with other tables, you can use SHOW TABLE STATUS to get information about a Merge table:

```
mysql> SHOW TABLE STATUS LIKE 'mytable' \G
*************************** 1. row ***************************
           Name: mytable
           Type: MRG_MyISAM
     Row_format: Fixed
           Rows: 2
 Avg_row_length: 23
    Data_length: 46
Max_data_length: NULL
   Index_length: 0
      Data_free: 0
 Auto_increment: NULL
    Create_time: NULL
    Update_time: NULL
     Check_time: NULL
 Create_options:
        Comment:
1 row in set (0.01 sec)
```

Not all of the data is available. MySQL doesn't keep track of the creation, update, and check times for merge tables. It also doesn't store the create options that you might expect. However, you can retrieve that information using SHOW CREATE TABLE:

```
mysql> SHOW CREATE TABLE mytable \G
*************************** 1. row ***************************
       Table: mytable
Create Table: CREATE TABLE `mytable` (
  `a` int(11) NOT NULL default '0',
  `b` char(18) NOT NULL default '',
  PRIMARY KEY  (`a`)
) TYPE=MRG_MyISAM INSERT_METHOD=LAST UNION=(mytable0,mytable1,mytable2)
1 row in set (0.00 sec)
```

This demonstrates that Merge tables really aren't full-fledged tables. In fact, Merge tables have some important limitations and surprising behavior:

- REPLACE queries don't work on them.
- AUTO_INCREMENT columns aren't updated on insert. They are updated if you insert directly into one of the underlying tables.
- DROP TABLE mytable will drop only the virtual table, not the underlying tables. This may or may not be what you'd expect.

InnoDB Tables

The InnoDB table handler is the newest addition to the MySQL family. Developed by Heikki Tuuri of Innobase Oy in Helsinki, Finland, InnoDB was designed with transaction processing in mind and modeled largely after Oracle.

Storage

The InnoDB table handler breaks from MySQL tradition and stores all its data in a series of one or more data files that are collectively known as a *tablespace*. A tablespace is essentially a black box that is completely managed by InnoDB. If a tablespace if composed of several underlying files, you can't choose or influence which of the underlying files will contain the data for any particular database or table.

InnoDB can also use raw disk partitions in building its tablespace, but that's not very common. Using disk partitions makes it more difficult to back up InnoDB's data, and the resulting performance boost is on the order of a few percent on most operating systems.

As of MySQL 4.1, you have the option of slightly more MyISAM-like storage for InnoDB. You can enable multiple tablespace support by adding `innodb_file_per_table` to *my.cnf*; this makes InnoDB create one tablespace file per newly created InnoDB table. The filename will be of the form *tablename.ibd*. In all other respects, they're simply dynamically sized InnoDB tablespace files. Each one just happens to contain data for only one specific table.

Locking and concurrency

InnoDB uses MVCC to achieve very high concurrency. InnoDB defaults to the repeatable read isolation level, and as of MySQL Version 4.0.5, it implements all four levels: read uncommitted, read committed, repeatable read, and serializable.

In an InnoDB transaction, You may explicitly obtain either exclusive or shared locks on rows using the MySQL statements: SELECT ... FOR UPDATE and SELECT ... LOCK IN SHARE MODE.

Special features

Besides its excellent concurrency, InnoDB's next most popular feature is *referential integrity* in the form of foreign key constraints. This means that given the following schema:

```
CREATE TABLE master (
   id        INTEGER NOT NULL PRIMARY KEY,
   stuff     TEXT    NOT NULL
) TYPE = InnoDB;

CREATE TABLE detail (
   master_id INTEGER      NOT NULL,
   detail1   VARCHAR(80) NOT NULL,
   detail2   VARCHAR(20) NOT NULL,
   INDEX     master_idx (master_id),
   FOREIGN KEY (master_id) REFERENCES master(id)
) TYPE = InnoDB;
```

InnoDB doesn't allow you to insert add records to the detail table until there is a corresponding record in the master table. Attempting to do so yields an error:

```
mysql> INSERT INTO detail VALUES (10, 'blah', 'blah');
ERROR 1216: Cannot add a child row: a foreign key constraint fails
```

InnoDB also provides lightning fast record lookups for queries that use a primary key. Its clustered index system (described in more detail in Chapter 4) explains how it works.

Heap (In-Memory) Tables

MySQL provides in-memory Heap tables for applications in which you need incredibly fast access to data that either never changes or doesn't need to persist after a restart. Using a Heap table means that a query can complete without even waiting for disk I/O. This makes sense for lookup or mapping tables, such as area code to city/state name, or for caching the results of periodically aggregated data.

Limitations

While Heap tables are very fast, they often don't work well as replacements for disk-based tables. Until MySQL Version 4.1, Heap tables used only hash-based indexes rather than B-tree indexes (which MyISAM uses). Hash indexes are suited to only a subset of queries. The section "Heap Tables" in Chapter 4 covers this in more detail.

Berkeley DB (BDB) Tables

MySQL's first transaction-safe storage engine, BDB is built on top of the Berkeley DB database library, which is now maintained and developed by Sleepycat Software. In fact, the original work to integrate the Berkeley DB technology with MySQL was performed jointly by MySQL AB and Sleepycat Software. Other than transactions, the BDB table handler's other main feature is that it uses page-level locking to achieve higher concurrency than MyISAM tables.

Though BDB tables have been available in MySQL since Version 3.23, they haven't proven very popular among users. Many users looking for transactions in MySQL were also looking for row-level locking or MVCC. Further dampening interest in BDB, by the time the BDB code had stabilized, word of InnoDB began to circulate. This prompted many users to hold out for the real thing and use MyISAM tables a bit longer.

If nothing else, the inclusion of BDB tables in MySQL served as a stepping stone in many ways. It prompted the MySQL developers to put the transaction-handling infrastructure into MySQL, while at the same time proving to the skeptics that MySQL wasn't a toy.

## CHAPTER 3

Benchmarking

We decided to cover benchmarking very early in this book because it's a critically important skill. Much of this book focuses on information and techniques you need to keep MySQL fast or make it run even faster. You need a good performance testing framework to judge the difference between one configuration and another, one query and another, or even one server and another. You also need a lot of patience and a willingness to experiment. This chapter can't give you all the answers, but we try to provide some tools that will help you find them.

If you care about database performance in your applications (and if you're reading this book, you probably do), benchmarking needs to become part of your development testing process. When you're testing an upgrade to MySQL or some MySQL configuration changes, run the benchmark tests you developed while building the application. Look at the results. Make sure they don't surprise you.

This chapter isn't long, but it contains essential material that we'll refer back to and apply in future chapters. If you're planning to skip around in the book, be sure to read this chapter first.

We begin with a look at the importance of benchmarking in database applications, then continue with a look at benchmarking strategies—things you need to think about in the planning process. Finally we get our hands dirty with a look at benchmarking tools.

We'll build on the strategies and tools presented in this chapter in those that follow. When considering performance questions, we'll consider the factors involved and present a benchmark test that can assist in the decision-making process. Take some time now to experiment with the tools and examples presented here. The skills you build now will benefit you in later chapters and in your own projects.

The Importance of Benchmarking

Benchmarking is fundamentally a "what if" game. By setting up a simple test, you can quickly answer questions such as the following:

- What if I increase the number of rows by a factor of 10? Will my queries still be fast?
- Will a RAM upgrade really help? If so, how much?
- Is the new server really twice as fast as the old one?
- What if I disable the query cache?
- Which is faster, using a subquery or two shorter queries?
- What happens when this query is run multiple times or is run with other queries?

Benchmarking is often about comparisons. When deciding to make an important change, you'll want first to test the alternative(s) and then decide what to do based on the results of the test.

Our goal is to make benchmarking MySQL easy. Anytime you catch yourself wondering if A is faster than B, or whether A or B uses more memory, just pull out your favorite benchmarking tool and find out. Sometimes you'll be surprised by the results. To achieve the goal of easy MySQL benchmarking, we've tried to document how to use the available tools.

Beyond answering what-if questions, benchmarking is especially important in database-driven applications because it can highlight problems that are otherwise difficult to pinpoint. When an application slows down, the database may not be the first suspect. After spending a lot of time testing the application code, you'll eventually need to isolate the database to see whether it is a significant bottleneck. Having a prebuilt benchmark makes that task trivial.

Benchmarking Strategies

We'll look at the mechanics of benchmarking shortly. First it's important to convey some of strategies and ideas that make up the philosophy behind benchmarking.

To start with, it's important to make a distinction between performance testing and stress testing. Both processes use the tools we'll look at in this chapter, but the goals are very different. When doing performance testing, you're usually comparing two alternatives—most often in isolation from everything else. For instance, would it be faster to use a UNION or run two separate queries? Stress testing, on the other hand, is about finding limits: what's the maximum number of requests I can handle with this configuration?

If the two types of benchmarking still sound similar, look at it this way: in performance testing, the numbers you get aren't as important as the difference between them. You may see that alternative #1 usually runs in 0.01 seconds (or 100 queries/second), while alternative #2 runs in 0.20 seconds (or 5 queries/second). That tells you the first alternative is 20 times faster than the second one. However, knowing that you can handle 100 queries per second doesn't tell you how your application *as a whole* will perform unless, of course, your application always runs the same query. In contrast, stress testing can help in situations such as: "We expect the promotion we just offered to bring in 30% more hits than we have now. What will the effects on our server be?"

To make benchmarking as realistic and hassle-free as possible, here are several suggestions to consider:

Change one thing at a time

> In science this is called isolating the variable. No matter how well you think you understand the effects your changes will have, don't make more than one change between test runs. Otherwise you'll never know which one was responsible for the doubling (or halving) of performance. You might be surprised to find that an adjustment you made once before to improve performance actually makes it worse in your current tests.

Test iteratively

> Try not to make dramatic changes. When adjusting MySQL's buffers and caches, you'll often be trying to find the smallest value that comfortably handles your load. Rather than increasing a value by 500%, start with a 50% or 100% increase and continue using that percentage increase on subsequent tests. You'll probably find the optimal value faster this way. Similarly, if you're working from larger values to smaller, the time-tested "divide and conquer" technique is your best bet. Cut the current value in half, retest, and repeat the process until you've zeroed in close to the correct value.

Always repeat tests

> No matter how carefully you control the environment, something can creep in and really mess up your numbers. Maybe you forgot to disable *cron*, or you have some disk-intensive script running in the background. Because the disk is already being hit, you may not notice the new process, but it sure can slow down MySQL.

> By running each test several times (we recommend no fewer than four) and throwing out the first result, you minimize the chance of an outside influence getting in the way. It will be pretty clear that something was wrong with the first result when the second and third set of tests run twice as fast as the first. Also, consider restarting MySQL and even rebooting your server between test runs to factor out caching artifacts.

Use real data

It sounds like common sense, doesn't it? If you're not testing with real data, it's difficult to draw conclusions based on the numbers you get. As you'll see in Chapter 4, MySQL will often behave differently when presented with different sets of data. The query optimizer makes decisions based on what it knows about the data you've stored. If you're testing with fake data, there's a chance that the optimizer's decisions aren't the same as they'll be when you switch to using your real data.

In a similar vein, try to use a realistic amount of data. If you plan to have 45 million rows in a table but test with only 45 thousand, you'll find that performance drops off quite a bit after the table is filled up—and it has nothing to do with limits in MySQL. The simple fact is that your server probably has enough memory to keep 45 thousand rows cached, but 45 million rows aren't nearly as likely to be entirely cached.

Don't use too many clients

Try not to go crazy with benchmarking. It's fun to see how hard you can push your server, but unless you're doing stress testing, there's little need to run more than 40 or 50 concurrent clients in day-to-day benchmarking.* What you'll likely find is that performance (measured in queries/second) reaches a plateau when you try to increase the simulated clients beyond a certain number.

When you attempt to use too many clients, your server will refuse to accept any more connections than specified by the max_clients setting. Be careful not to increase this value too much; if you do, the server may start to swap wildly and grind to a halt simply because it doesn't have the resources (typically memory) to handle huge numbers of clients. We'll come back to this in Chapter 6 when we look at service performance. But the test doesn't help you evaluate your server realistically.

You can find the optimal number of clients by using a simple iterative testing method. Start with a small number such as 20, and run the benchmark. Double the number, and run it again. Continue doubling it until the performance does not increase, meaning that the total queries per second stays the same or decreases. Another option is to use data from your logs to find out roughly how many concurrent users you handle during peak times.

Separate the clients from the server

Even if your real application runs on the same host as MySQL, it's best to run the benchmarking client on a separate machine. In this way, you need not worry about the resources required by the client interfering with MySQL's performance during the test.

---

* There will always be exceptions. If your site must routinely handle 450 connections, you'll obviously need to test with numbers close to 450.

Benchmarking Tools

In this chapter we'll introduce three useful benchmarking tools:

- The MySQL Benchmark Suite, which is useful for making comparisons between different database engines or different installations of one database engine. It isn't meant to benchmark your site-specific data or needs.
- MySQL super-smack, a stress-testing tool.
- MyBench, a tool developed in Perl by one of the authors. It is another stress-testing tool that is easier to customize and extend than super-smack.

> The benchmark tools presented in this chapter may not run under Windows due to the lack of a Perl interpreter or binaries compiled for Windows. Because versions of Perl for Windows are readily (and freely) available from ActiveState, there's a good chance MyBench may work. However, neither of the authors use Windows, and we have not tried to confirm this.
>
> However, these tools do run on Linux and most Unix-like platforms and can be used to test remote servers. So you might run them on Linux or Solaris to remotely benchmark a Windows 2000 server running MySQL.

The MySQL Benchmark Suite

The MySQL distribution comes with a rather comprehensive set of generic tests that have been bundled together so you can run them as a group and examine the results. The tests will do little to help you figure out whether a configuration change will speed up your application. But they're very helpful when used as a high-level benchmark, meaning they provide a good overall indication of how well one server performs relative to another.

You can also run the tests individually if you'd like compare a subset of the results from several servers. If you're mainly interested in UPDATE speed, run one of the UPDATE-intensive tests a few times on each server.

The benchmark suite can be used to test non-MySQL servers as well. According to the *README*, PostgreSQL, Solid, and mSQL have been tested. This may be helpful if you're trying to choose between MySQL and PostgreSQL. All the benchmark code is relatively generic Perl using the DBI and Benchmark modules. If needed, you can add support for nearly any database server that has a DBI driver (Oracle, Sybase, Informix, DB2, etc.). If you do so, be sure to look at the *bench-init.pl* for any global options you may need to add or change.

By running the benchmarks against several different servers, you'll get an idea of how much faster one server is than another. The tests are largely CPU-bound, but there are portions of the test that demand a lot of disk I/O (for short times). You'll likely find that the 2.4-GHz CPU doesn't necessarily make MySQL run twice as fast as the 1.2-GHz CPU.

The benchmark suite will not help you test the benefits of multi-CPU machines because the benchmark process is completely serialized. It executes one query after another, so MySQL will not benefit from the addition of a second CPU. To test that, you'll need to use MySQL super-smack or a home-grown solution. Both are covered in the following sections.

To run the tests, use the *run-all-tests* script located in the *sql-bench* directory. Be sure to read the *README* in that directory. It provides a complete list of the command-line options you can use.

```
$ cd sql-bench
sql-bench$ ./run-all-tests --server=mysql --user=root --log --fast
Test finished. You can find the result in:
output/RUN-mysql_fast-Linux_2.4.18_686_smp_i686
```

The benchmarks may take quite a while to run, depending on your hardware and configuration. On a dual 933-MHz Pentium 3, it took over an hour to execute the tests using MySQL 4.0.13. While it's running, however, you can watch the progress. The --log flag causes results from each test to be logged in a subdirectory named *output*. Each file contains a series of timings for the various operations in each benchmark test. Here's a small sampling, slightly reformatted for printing:

```
sql-bench/output$ tail -5 select-mysql_fast-Linux_2.4.18_686_smp_i686
Time for count_distinct_group_on_key (1000:6000):
  34 wallclock secs ( 0.20 usr  0.08 sys +  0.00 cusr  0.00 csys =  0.28 CPU)
Time for count_distinct_group_on_key_parts (1000:100000):
  34 wallclock secs ( 0.57 usr  0.27 sys +  0.00 cusr  0.00 csys =  0.84 CPU)
Time for count_distinct_group (1000:100000):
  34 wallclock secs ( 0.59 usr  0.20 sys +  0.00 cusr  0.00 csys =  0.79 CPU)
Time for count_distinct_big (100:1000000):
   8 wallclock secs ( 4.22 usr  2.20 sys +  0.00 cusr  0.00 csys =  6.42 CPU)
Total time:
  868 wallclock secs (33.24 usr  9.55 sys +  0.00 cusr  0.00 csys = 42.79 CPU)
```

As you can see, the count_distinct_group_on_key (1000:6000) test took 34 "wallclock" seconds to execute. That's the total amount of time the client took to run the test. The other values (usr, sys, cursr, csys) that added up to 0.28 seconds constitute the overhead for this test. That's how much of the time was spent running the benchmark client code rather than waiting for the MySQL server's response. This means that the figure we care about—how much time was tied up by things outside the client's control—totalled 33.72 seconds.

It's also worth noting that you can run the tests individually if you need to. Rather than rerun the entire suite, you may decide to focus on the *insert test*. By doing so, you see a bit more detail than was in the summarized files left in the output directory:

```
sql-bench$ ./test-insert
Testing server 'MySQL 4.0.13 log' at 2003-05-18 11:02:39
```

```
Testing the speed of inserting data into 1 table and do some selects on it.
The tests are done with a table that has 100000 rows.

Generating random keys
Creating tables
Inserting 100000 rows in order
Inserting 100000 rows in reverse order
Inserting 100000 rows in random order
Time for insert (300000):
   42 wallclock secs ( 7.91 usr  5.03 sys +  0.00 cusr  0.00 csys = 12.94 CPU)
Testing insert of duplicates
Time for insert_duplicates (100000):
   16 wallclock secs ( 2.28 usr  1.89 sys +  0.00 cusr  0.00 csys =  4.17 CPU)
```

MySQL super-smack

Developed by Sasha Pachev, a former MySQL AB employee, super-smack is a stress-testing tool that can talk to both MySQL and PostgreSQL. The super-smack tool really deserves wider recognition, because it's very powerful. Using a simple configuration file syntax, you can define a series of tests (a *query barrel*) to run against your server along with the data and tables needed to support the tests. When running the tests, you control how many concurrent clients will be simulated (one per thread) and how many iterations of each test the clients will execute using command-line arguments.

Because the tool simulates many simultaneous users, it works very well for testing multi-CPU servers. And even on single CPU machines, it allows you to generate more realistic test scenarios as well as perform stress tests.

A typical test with super-smack involves creating one or more large tables and populating them with various data, chosen from an input file or generated on the fly. It then proceeds to beat on the created tables using a series of queries that are defined by the user via a configuration file. The values used in the queries are selected from an external file in either random or sequential order.

As you'll see, using MySQL super-smack requires more work than using the supplied benchmarks. While it will take some time to get super-smack set up and running the first time, you'll benefit from having much greater control over the tests. With a little practice, you can create custom tailored benchmarks in very little time.

You'll first need to download and build super-smack before you can begin testing; it doesn't come with MySQL. As of this writing, the current release is available from *http://jeremy.zawodny.com/mysql/super-smack/*. It uses GNU *autoconf*, so the installation process is relatively simple as long as your build tools are reasonably current.

```
/tmp$ tar -zxf super-smack-1.1.tar.gz
/tmp$ cd super-smack-1.1
/tmp/super-smack-1.1$ ./configure --with-mysql
... lots of configure output ...
/tmp/super-smack-1.1$ make
```

```
... lots of compilation output ...
/tmp/super-smack-1.1$ sudo make install
```

Be sure to read the *MANUAL* and *TUTORIAL* files included in the distribution. They cover topics that we may not—especially if you're using a newer version.

To get started with super-smack, let's look at the example benchmarks it includes. In */usr/share/smacks*, you'll find a small collection of *smack* files:

```
/usr/share/smacks$ ls -l
total 8
-rw-r--r--   1 jzawodn  jzawodn     3211 Feb  2  2004 select-key.smack
-rw-r--r--   1 jzawodn  jzawodn     3547 Feb  2  2004 update-select.smack
```

These files contain the commands necessary to populate a table and execute a bunch of queries against it. Before diving into the configuration file, let's give it a quick run. We'll ask it to simulate 30 concurrent users, each running 10,000 iterations of the test queries.

```
/usr/share/smacks$ super-smack update-select.smack 30 10000
Error running query select count(*) from http_auth:Table 'test.http_auth' doesn't
exist
Creating table 'http_auth'
Loading data from file '/var/smack-data/words.dat' into table 'http_auth'
Table http_auth is now ready for the test
Query Barrel Report for client smacker
connect: max=49ms  min=0ms avg= 14ms from 30 clients
Query_type       num_queries    max_time       min_time       q_per_s
select_index     300000         10             0              2726.41
update_index     300000         5              0              2726.41
```

The test requires a table named http_auth to operate. Since the table didn't exist, the test used the data in */var/smack-data/words.dat* to populate the table. Then super-smack ran the tests and produced results.

After the "Query Barrel Report" line, you can see the performance stats from this benchmark run. (A query barrel, as you'll see later, is a set of queries run by super-smack in each iteration.) The first line provides connection stats, which list the maximum, minimum, and average connection times for each of the 30 clients—that is, how long the client waited for the server when establishing a connection.[*]

The remaining lines provide statistics for each type of test defined in the *smack* file. For each, you see the number of times the query was executed (this should always match what you specified on the command line), the maximum time the query took, the minimum time the query took, and the number of queries executed per second.

Running with different values (fewer clients), you'll see the performance was actually higher: 3,306 queries/sec versus 2,726 queries/sec.

---

[*] The super-smack tool uses persistent connections. Each client connects once and remains connected for the duration of the test run. You can't use super-smack to simulate nonpersistent connections.

```
/usr/share/smacks$ super-smack update-select.smack 5 10000
Query Barrel Report for client smacker
connect: max=2ms  min=1ms avg= 1ms from 5 clients
Query_type      num_queries     max_time        min_time        q_per_s
select_index    50000           1               0               3306.66
update_index    50000           1               0               3306.66
```

That's likely because we ran the super-smack client on the same machine as MySQL, so the two were competing for CPU time. In real-world testing, you'd probably have the client and server separated, and you'd want to run the same benchmark several times to rule out any anomalies.

Preparing test data

Using the *words.dat* data as input works in the http_auth benchmark, but when testing your applications, you'll need to supply your own data. There is no one-size-fits-all answer for how to generate your test data. You have to determine what data to create or extract for use in the tests. Once you've done that and loaded the data into MySQL, you need to extract the relevant values into a file that super-smack can read during testing.

For example, if you're testing an online product catalog in which items will be selected based on their product ID, you'll need a list of product IDs to use during testing. For a comprehensive test, use all the product IDs. If you have millions of products, it may be sufficient to test a subset of them.

In either case, first get a list of the product IDs into a text file that you can then drop into */var/smack-data/* to use during the testing. The easiest way to do that to use MySQL's SELECT ... INTO OUTFILE construct:

```
SELECT id INTO OUTFILE "/tmp/product.dat" FROM product
```

That produces a file containing one product ID per line—perfect for use with super-smack. If your test requires multiple columns of data, you can produce a file of quoted comma-separated values:

```
SELECT id, type INTO OUTFILE "/tmp/product.dat"
FIELDS TERMINATED BY ','
OPTIONALLY ENCLOSED BY '"'
LINES TERMINATED BY "\n"
FROM product
```

super-smack allows you to specify a field delimiter to be used for input files, as you'll see. Also be sure to copy your file to */var/smack-data/*.

Configuration

Having installed and tested super-smack, let's spend some time dissecting one of the standard *smack* files. Along the way, we'll consider how you might adapt the file to your own testing needs.

The file presented here is a bit different from the one contained in the super-smack distribution. The functionality is the same, but the comments and formatting have been adjusted.

The *smack* file looks like a stripped-down scripting language that's loosely based on C or Perl. Each *smack* file defines several objects that are used in the `main` block of the file: clients, tables, dictionaries, and queries.

```
client "admin"
{
  user "root";
  host "localhost";
  db "test";
  pass "";
  socket "/var/lib/mysql/mysql.sock";
}
```

The first section defines an `admin` client using the root account on *localhost*'s server and assumes there's no password on the account.* If you plan to run super-smack on a remote client, be sure to update the settings appropriately. The socket should be left empty (or removed) in that case. If you're running MySQL on a nonstandard port, specify that in the `client` section(s):

```
port "3307";
```

Next, define the table and data used for the tests:

```
table "http_auth"
{
  client "admin";

  create "create table http_auth
    (username char(25) not null primary key,
     pass char(25),
     uid integer not null,
     gid integer not null
    )";

  min_rows "90000";
  data_file "words.dat";
  gen_data_file "gen-data -n 90000 -f %12-12s%n,%25-25s,%n,%d";
}
```

There's a lot going on here. First, we specify that the table will be created and populated using the `admin` user options specified previously. Then we provide a CREATE TABLE specification. If the table doesn't already exist, super-smack creates it. We also specify a minimum number of rows. If the table exists but doesn't have sufficient

---

* If you don't specify a password, super-smack does not prompt you for one. We point this out only because many other MySQL tools prompt you.

rows, super-smack will drop and recreate the table. Then, if needed, it will load the data from the *words.dat* file, which is expected to live in */var/smack-data*. Finally, if that file doesn't exist, super-smack uses gen-data (which comes with super-smack) to create 90,000 rows of random data.

The gen-data command isn't documented, but as you can see, it requires a number of rows (-n) and a printf-style format string (-f). Sample output for our command looks like:

```
$ gen-data -n 5 -f %12-12s%n,%25-25s,%n,%d
pajgyycklwiv1,qbnvqtcewpwvxpobgpcgwppkw,1,763719779
epqjynjbrpew2,mhvcdpmifuefqdmjblodvlset,2,344858293
fbntssvvmwck3,cfydxkranoqfiuvyhqvtprmpx,3,2125632375
fcwtayvakrxr4,ldaprgacrwsbujrnlxxsxqwse,4,1513050921
jnaixvfvktpf5,htihaukugfiurnnmxnysypsnr,5,1872952907
```

super-smack loads the output into the table using the LOAD DATA command.

In real-life testing, you probably won't be using super-smack to populate your tables. Instead, you can simply use a copy of your real data.

Next we have a dictionary definition:

```
dictionary "word"
{
  type "rand";
  source_type "file";
  source "words.dat";
  delim ",";
  file_size_equiv "45000";
}
```

A dictionary is simply a source for words that will later be used when constructing queries. It's a simple mechanism that gives you control over which values are used in queries and how they are used.

The dictionary type can be one of the following:

rand
> Values are selected randomly from the list.

seq
> Values are used sequentially.

unique
> Generate unique values using the same method as gen-data.

The source_type may be one of the following:

file
> A file read from disk.

list
> A user-supplied list of words, comma-separated.

template

The format to use when type is unique. For example, `"jzawodn_%07d"` generates values composed of `jzawodn_` and a seven-digit number.

The source is either a filename (assumed to be in the */var/smack-data* directory) or a comma-separated list of quoted values (`"one"`,`"two"`,`"three"`) when using a `source_type` of `list`.

If you use a delimited file, the `delim` option tells super-smack which character separates the input fields in your source file. The `file_size_equiv` option is helpful when you have a very large dictionary. Rather than use every word, super-smack divides the file size by this number. The result is then used to skip records in the input.

For example, if your file is 100 KB in size and you specify a `file_size_equiv` of 10,240, super-smack divides the two and knows to use only one tenth of the input. It will test using every tenth value in the source file.

Next are two query definitions, one for a series of SELECT queries followed by an UPDATE query generator:

```
query "select_by_username"
{
  query "select * from http_auth where username = '$word'";
  type "select_index";
  has_result_set "y";
  parsed "y";
}
query "update_by_username"
{
  query "update http_auth set pass='$word' where username = '$word'";
  type "update_index";
  has_result_set "n";
  parsed "y";
}
```

The queries are relatively simple. If you'd like to substitute a word from the dictionary in the query, simply use the `$word` placeholder and be sure to set `parsed` to `y`; otherwise super-smack uses your query as is.

The type is simply a tag or name for this set of queries. It is reported by name in the final statistics. The `has_result_set` option tells super-smack whether the query returns data.

Next, one more `client` is defined:

```
client "smacker"
{
  user "test";
  pass "";
  host "localhost";
  db "test";
```

```
        socket "/var/lib/mysql/mysql.sock";
        query_barrel "1 select_by_username 1 update_by_username";
    }
```

Unlike the previous client, this one has a query_barrel associated with it. The query barrel defines the order and number of queries the client will run during each iteration. In this case, we've instructed it to execute one select_by_username query followed by one update_by_username query. You can adjust the numbers to suit your particular testing needs, of course.

Finally, we get to the main section of the *smack* file. It controls the actual flow.

```
    main
    {
      smacker.init();
      smacker.set_num_rounds($2);
      smacker.create_threads($1);
      smacker.connect();
      smacker.unload_query_barrel();
      smacker.collect_threads();
      smacker.disconnect();
    }
```

One of the first things to notice is that command-line arguments are available in shell-style numbered variables ($1, $2, etc.). So if you'd like to reverse the order of arguments on the command line, you can do so.

The code's flow is straightforward. It begins by initializing the smacker client. Then we set the number of rounds and create the necessary threads. Each thread then connects to the server and unloads its barrel of queries, keeping statistics along the way. The collect_threads function causes the main thread to wait for the others to complete. The clients then disconnect, and the statistics are reported.

When you look at the setup piece by piece, it's easy to digest. The same framework works for a wide variety of testing. The main section rarely changes. And, for very simple tests (such as a single query), there's no need to define multiple users. If you are creating a benchmark to simulate a relatively complex application that requires various username and password combinations to access all the necessary data, you'll need to also define them in your *smack* file.

MyBench: A Home-Grown Solution

MySQL super-smack is a great tool, but it's not terribly extensible unless you want to dive into the C++ code. When you need custom logic that's not easy to express in super-smack's configuration, it's probably time to turn to your favorite scripting language.

When Jeremy encountered this problem in back in 2001, he developed a very simple Perl-based system called MyBench. It handles the details of spawning clients, gathering and computing statistics, and so on. The downside is that it's quite a bit heavier on the client side. You really shouldn't run the benchmark client on the same machine as MySQL.

You can download the code from *http://jeremy.zawodny.com/mysql/mybench/*. To use it you'll need DBI, DBD::mysql, and Time::HiRes installed. The MyBench.pm module contains the common logic. Creating a simple benchmark is a matter of adding your logic to the supplied *bench_example* script.

As we did with super-smack, let's look through the *bench_example* script to understand how it works. The first few lines simply import the required modules and set up some simple command-line option handling. It requires two command-line arguments. The -n argument specifies the number of clients to simulate (children to fork), and -r sets the number of iterations each client will run. The optional -h argument can specify a hostname.

```perl
#!/usr/bin/perl -w

use strict;
use MyBench;
use Getopt::Std;
use Time::HiRes qw(gettimeofday tv_interval);
use DBI;

my %opt;
Getopt::Std::getopt('n:r:h:', \%opt);

my $num_kids  = $opt{n} || 10;
my $num_runs  = $opt{r} || 100;
my $db        = "test";
my $user      = "test";
my $pass      = "";
my $port      = 3306;
my $host      = $opt{h} || "192.168.0.1";
my $dsn       = "DBI:mysql:$db:$host;port=$port";
```

Of course, you can hardcode the values if you'd like, or you can make the script more generic by parameterizing the connection information (db, user, pass, port, host).

With the setup out of the way, the script sets up a callback function. It will be called by the code to set up an initial connection and run the tests.

```perl
my $callback = sub
{
    my $id  = shift;
    my $dbh = DBI->connect($dsn, $user, $pass, { RaiseError => 1 });
    my $sth = $dbh->prepare("SELECT * FROM mytable WHERE ID = ?");

    my $cnt = 0;
    my @times = ( );
```

```
## wait for the parent to HUP me
local $SIG{HUP} = sub { };
sleep 600;

while ($cnt < $num_runs)
{
    my $v = int(rand(100_000));
    ## time the query
    my $t0 = [gettimeofday];
    $sth->execute($v);
    my $t1 = tv_interval($t0, [gettimeofday]);
    push @times, $t1;
    $sth->finish( );
    $cnt++;
}

## cleanup
$dbh->disconnect( );
my @r = ($id, scalar(@times), min(@times), max(@times), avg(@times),
                    tot(@times));
return @r;
};
```

The callback first establishes a connection to the server and prepares the query that will be executed. Next, it sets a few variables and then sets a dummy signal handler. It then sleeps, waiting for a SIGHUP. After the parent has started all the children, it signals them to start using SIGHUP.

After the signal has been handled, the main loop starts. In each iteration, it selects a random value to test, starts a timer, executes the query, and stops the timer. The resulting time is pushed to the @times list for later use. We finish the statement to dispose of any returned data and increment the loop counter.

After the loop completes, we disconnect from the server and return the time information back to the caller:

```
my @results = MyBench::fork_and_work($num_kids, $callback);
MyBench::compute_results('test', @results);

exit;

__END__
```

The fork_and_work( ) subroutine from the MyBench package is what gets everything rolling. The results are then passed to compute_results( ) and printed. The first argument passed is simply a name that will appear in the output to identify the results.

Here's a simple run, using a SELECT 1 query with 10 clients for 100,000 iterations:

```
$ ./bench_select_1 -n 10 -r 100000
forking: ++++++++++
sleeping for 2 seconds while kids get ready
waiting: ----------
test: 1000000 7.5e-05 0.65045 0.000561082981999975 561.082981999975 17822.6756483597
```

```
clients  : 10
queries  : 1000000
fastest  : 7.5e-05
slowest  : 0.65045
average  : 0.000561082981999975
serial   : 561.082981999975
q/sec    : 17822.6756483597
```

The first three lines are merely status updates so you can tell that the test is doing something while it runs. The test: line produces all the statistics on a single line, suitable for processing in another script or pasting into a spreadsheet. They're followed by human readable output.

There you can see how many clients were used, the total number of queries executed, and the response times (in seconds) of fastest and slowest queries as well as the average. The serial value explains approximately how many seconds the queries would have taken if executed serially. Finally, the q/sec number tells us how many queries per second (on average) the server handled during the test.

Because the code times only the query and not the work done by the Perl script, you can add arbitrarily complex logic to the main loop. Rather than generate a random number, maybe you need to read a value from a file or from another database table. Perhaps you need to run a few special queries every 785th iteration, to simulate the behavior of your real application. Doing so with MyBench would be easy; using super-smack would be more of a challenge.

## CHAPTER 4

Indexes

Indexes allow MySQL to quickly find and retrieve a set of records from the millions or even billions that a table may contain. If you've been using MySQL for any length of time, you've probably created indexes in the hopes of getting lighting-quick answers to your queries. And you've probably been surprised to find that MySQL didn't always use the index you thought it would.

For many users, indexes are something of a black art. Sometimes they work wonders, and other times they seem just to slow down inserts and get in the way. And then there are the times when they work fine for a while, then begin to slowly degrade.

In this chapter, we'll begin by looking at some of the concepts behind indexing and the various types of indexes MySQL provides. From there, we'll cover some of the specifics in MySQL's implementation of indexes. The chapter concludes with recommendations for selecting columns to index and the longer term care and feeding of your indexes.

Indexing Basics

To understand how MySQL uses indexes, it's best first to understand the basic workings and features of indexes. Once you have a basic understanding of their characteristics, you can start to make more intelligent choices about the right way to use them.

Index Concepts

To understand what indexes allow MySQL to do, it's best to think about how MySQL works to answer a query. Imagine that phone_book is a table containing an aggregate phone book for the state of California, with roughly 35 million entries.

And keep in mind that records within tables aren't inherently sorted. Consider a query like this one:

```
SELECT * FROM phone_book WHERE last_name = 'Zawodny'
```

Without any sort of index to consult, MySQL must read all the records in the phone_book table and compare the last_name field with the string "Zawodny" to see whether they match. Clearly that's not efficient. As the number of records increases, so does the effort necessary to find a given record. In computer science, we call that an $O(n)$ problem.

But given a real phone book, we all know how to quickly locate anyone named Zawodny: flip to the Zs at the back of book and start there. Since the second letter is "a," we know that any matches will be at or near the front of the list of all names starting with Z. The method used is based on knowledge of the data and how it is sorted.

That's cheating, isn't it? Not at all. The reason you can find the Zawodnys so quickly is that they're sorted alphabetically by last name. So it's easy to find them, provided you know your ABCs, of course.

Most technical books (like this one) provide an index at the back. It allows you to find the location of important terms and concepts quickly because they're listed in sorted order along with the corresponding page numbers. Need to know where *mysqlhotcopy* is discussed? Just look up the page number in the index.

Database indexes are similar. Just as the book author or publisher may choose to create an index of the important concepts and terms in the book, you can choose to create an index on a particular column of a database table. Using the previous example, you might create an index on the last name to make looking up phone numbers faster:

```
ALTER TABLE phone_book ADD INDEX (last_name)
```

In doing so, you're asking MySQL to create an ordered list of all the last names in the phone_book table. Along with each name, it notes the positions of the matching records—just as the index at the back of this book lists page numbers for each entry.*

From the database server's point of view, indexes exist so that the database can quickly eliminate possible rows from the result set when executing a query. Without any indexes, MySQL (like any database server) must examine every row in a table. Not only is that time consuming, it uses a lot of disk I/O and can effectively pollute the disk cache.

In the real world, it's rare to find dynamic data that just happens to be sorted (and stays sorted). Books are a special case; they tend to remain static.

---

* That's a bit of a lie. MySQL doesn't always store the position of the matching records. We'll see why soon enough.

Because MySQL needs to maintain a separate list of indexes' values and keep them updated as your data changes, you really don't want to index every column in a table. Indexes are a trade-off between space and time. You're sacrificing some extra disk space and a bit of CPU overhead on each INSERT, UPDATE, and DELETE query to make most (if not all) your queries much faster.

Much of the MySQL documentation uses the terms *index* and *key* interchangeably. Saying that last_name is a key in the phone_book table is the same as saying that the last_name field of the phone_book table is indexed.

Partial indexes

Indexes trade space for performance. But sometimes you'd rather not trade too much space for the performance you're after. Luckily, MySQL gives you a lot of control over how much space is used by the indexes. Maybe you have a phone_book table with 2 billion rows in it. Adding an index on last_name will require a lot of space. If the average last_name is 8 bytes long, you're looking at roughly 16 GB of space for the data portion of the index; the row pointers are there no matter what you do, and they add another 4–8 bytes per record.*

Instead of indexing the entire last name, you might index only the first 4 bytes:

```
ALTER TABLE phone_book ADD INDEX (last_name(4))
```

In doing so, you've reduced the space requirements for the data portion of the index by roughly half. The trade-off is that MySQL can't eliminate quite as many rows using this index. A query such as:

```
SELECT * FROM phone_book WHERE last_name = 'Smith'
```

retrieves all fields beginning with Smit, including all people with name Smith, Smitty, and so on. The query must then discard Smitty and all other irrelevant rows.

Multicolumn indexes

Like many relational database engines, MySQL allows you to create indexes that are composed of multiple columns:

```
ALTER TABLE phone_book ADD INDEX (last_name, first_name)
```

Such indexes can improve the query speed if you often query all columns together in the WHERE clause or if a single column doesn't have sufficient variety. Of course, you can use partial indexes to reduce the space required:

```
ALTER TABLE phone_book ADD INDEX (last_name(4), first_name(4))
```

---

* That's a bit of an oversimplification, too. MySQL has some strategies for reducing the size of the index, but they also come at a price.

In either case, a query to find Josh Woodward executes quickly:

```
SELECT * FROM phone_book
  WHERE last_name = 'Woodward'
    AND first_name = 'Josh'
```

Having the last name and first name indexed together means that MySQL can eliminate rows based on both fields, thereby greatly reducing the number of rows it must consider. After all, there are a lot more people in the phone book whose last name starts with "Wood" than there are folks whose last name starts with "Wood" and whose first name also starts with "Josh."

When discussing multicolumn indexes, you may see the individual indexed columns referred to as *key parts* or "parts of the key." Multicolumn indexes are also referred to as composite indexes or compound indexes.

So why not just create two indexes, one on `last_name` and one on `first_name`? You could do that, but MySQL won't use them both at the same time. In fact, MySQL will only ever use one index per table per query—except for UNIONs.* This fact is important enough to say again: *MySQL will only ever use one index per table per query.*

With separate indexes on `first_name` and `last_name`, MySQL will choose one or the other. It does so by making an educated guess about which index allows it to match fewer rows. We call it an educated guess because MySQL keeps track of some index statistics that allow it to infer what the data looks like. The statistics, of course, are generalizations. While they often let MySQL make smart decisions, if you have very clumpy data, MySQL may make suboptimal choices about index use. We call data *clumpy* if the key being indexed is sparse in some areas (such as names beginning with X) and highly concentrated in others (such as the name `Smith` in English-speaking countries). This is an important topic that we'll revisit later in this book.

Index order

How does MySQL order values in the index? If you've used another RDBMS, you might expect MySQL to have syntax for specifying that an index be sorted in ascending, descending, or some other order. MySQL gives you no control over its internal sorting of index values. It has little reason to. As of Version 4.0, it does a good job of optimizing cases that cause slower performance for other database systems.

For example, some database products may execute this query quickly:

```
SELECT * FROM phone_book WHERE last_name = 'Zawodny'
  ORDER BY first_name DESC
```

And this query slowly:

```
SELECT * FROM phone_book WHERE last_name = 'Zawodny'
  ORDER BY first_name ASC
```

* In a UNION, each logical query is run separately, and the results are merged.

Why? Because some databases store the indexes in descending order and are optimized for reading them in that order. In the first case, the database uses the multicolumn index to locate all the matching records. Since the records are already stored in descending order, there's no need to sort them. But in the second case, the server finds all matching records and then performs a second pass over those rows to sort them.

MySQL is smart enough to "traverse the index backwards" when necessary. It will execute both queries very quickly. In neither case does it need to sort the records.

Indexes as constraints

Indexes aren't always used to locate matching rows for a query. A *unique index* specifies that a particular value may only appear once in a given column.* In the phone book example, you might create a unique index on phone_number to ensure that each phone number appears only once: †

```
ALTER TABLE phone_book ADD UNIQUE (phone_number)
```

The unique index serves a dual purpose. It functions just like any other index when you perform a query based on a phone number:

```
SELECT * FROM phone_book WHERE phone_number = '555-7271'
```

However, it also checks every value when attempting to insert or update a record to ensure that the value doesn't already exist. In this way, the unique index acts as a constraint.

Unique indexes use as much space as nonunique indexes do. The value of every column as well as the record's location is stored. This can be a waste if you use the unique index as a constraint and never as an index. Put another way, you may rely on the unique index to enforce uniqueness but never write a query that uses the unique value. In this case, there's no need for MySQL to store the locations of every record in the index: you'll never use them.

Unfortunately, there's no way to signal your intentions to MySQL. In the future, we'll likely find a feature introduced for this specific case. The MyISAM storage engine already has support for unique columns without an index (it uses a hash-based system), but the mechanism isn't exposed at the SQL level yet.

Clustered and secondary indexes

With MyISAM tables, the indexes are kept in a completely separate file that contains a list of primary (and possibly secondary) keys and a value that represents the byte

---

* Except for NULL, of course. NULL is always a special case.

† In the real world, however, this would be a very bad practice, as anyone who has shared a phone with several housemates can tell you.

offset for the record. These ensure MySQL can find and then quickly skip to that point within the database to locate the record. MySQL has to store the indexes this way because the records are stored in essentially random order.

With *clustered indexes*, the primary key and the record itself are "clustered" together, and the records are all stored in primary-key order. InnoDB uses clustered indexes. In the Oracle world, clustered indexes are known as "index-organized tables," which may help you remember the relationship between the primary key and row ordering.

When your data is almost always searched on via its primary key, clustered indexes can make lookups incredibly fast. With a standard MyISAM index, there are two lookups, one to the index, and a second to the table itself via the location specified in the index. With clustered indexes, there's a single lookup that points directly to the record in question.

Some operations render clustered indexes less effective. For instance, consider when a secondary index is in use. Going back to our phone book example, suppose you have last_name set as the primary index and phone_number set as a secondary index, and you perform the following query:

```
SELECT * FROM phone_book WHERE phone_number = '555-7271'
```

MySQL scans the phone_number index to find the entry for 555-7271, which contains the primary key entry Zawodny because phone_book's primary index is the last name. MySQL then skips to the relevant entry in the database itself.

In other words, lookups based on your primary key happen exceedingly fast, and lookups based on secondary indexes happen at essentially the same speed as MyISAM index lookups would.

But under the right (or rather, the wrong) circumstances, the clustered index can actually degrade performance. When you use one together with a secondary index, you have to consider the combined impact on storage. Secondary indexes point to the primary key rather than the row. Therefore, if you index on a very large value and have several secondary indexes, you will end up with many duplicate copies of that primary index, first as the clustered index stored alongside the records themselves, but then again for as many times as you have secondary indexes pointing to those clustered indexes. With a small value as the primary key, this may not be so bad, but if you are using something potentially long, such as a URL, this repeated storage of the primary key on disk may cause storage issues.

Another less common but equally problematic condition happens when the data is altered such that the primary key is changed on a record. This is the most costly function of clustered indexes. A number of things can happen to make this operation a more severe performance hit:

- Alter the record in question according to the query that was issued.
- Determine the new primary key for that record, based on the altered data record.

- Relocate the stored records so that the record in question is moved to the proper location in the tablespace.
- Update any secondary indexes that point to that primary key.

As you might imagine, if you're altering the primary key for a number of records, that UPDATE command might take quite some time to do its job, especially on larger tables. Choose your primary keys wisely. Use values that are unlikely to change, such as a Social Security account number instead of a last name, serial number instead of a product name, and so on.

Unique indexes versus primary keys

If you're coming from other relational databases, you might wonder what the difference between a primary key and a unique index is in MySQL. As usual, it depends. In MyISAM tables, there's almost no difference. The only thing special about a primary key is that it can't contain NULL values. The primary key is simply a NOT NULL UNIQUE INDEX named PRIMARY. MyISAM tables don't require that you declare a primary key.

InnoDB and BDB tables require primary keys for every table. There's no requirement that you specify one, however. If you don't, the storage engine automatically adds a hidden primary key for you. In both cases, the primary keys are simply incrementing numeric values, similar to an AUTO-INCREMENT column. If you decide to add your own primary key at a later time, simply use ALTER TABLE to add one. Both storage engines will discard their internally generated keys in favor of yours. Heap tables don't require a primary key but will create one for you. In fact, you can create Heap tables with no indexes at all.

Indexing NULLs

It is often difficult to remember that SQL uses tristate logic when performing logical operations. Unless a column is declared NOT NULL, there are three possible outcomes in a logical comparison. The comparison may be true because the values are equivalent; it may be false because the values aren't equivalent; or it may not match because one of the values is NULL. Whenever one of the values is NULL, the outcome is also NULL.

Programmers often think of NULL as undefined or unknown. It's a way of telling the database server "an unknown value goes here." So how do NULL values affect indexes?

NULL values may be used in normal (nonunique) indexes. This is true of all database servers. However, unlike many database servers, MySQL allows you to use

NULL values in unique indexes.* You can store as many NULL values as you'd like in such an index. This may seem a bit counterintuitive, but that's the nature of NULL. Because NULL represents an undefined value, MySQL needs to assert that all NULL values are the same if it allowed only a single value in a unique index.

To make things just a bit more interesting, a NULL value may appear only once as a primary key. Why? The SQL standard dictates this behavior. It is one of the few ways in which primary keys are different from unique indexes in MySQL. And, in case you're wondering, allowing NULL values in the index really doesn't impact performance.

Index Structures

Having covered some of the basic ideas behind indexing, let's turn to the various types (or structures) of indexes in MySQL. None of the index types are specific to MySQL. You'll find similar indexes in PostgreSQL, DB2, Oracle, etc.

Rather than focus too much on the implementation details,† we'll look at the types of data or applications each type was designed to handle and find answers to questions like these: Which index types are the fastest? Most flexible? Use the most or least space?

If this were a general-purpose textbook for a computer science class, we might delve deeper into the specific data structures and algorithms that are employed under the hood. Instead, we'll try to limit our scope to the practical. If you're especially curious about the under-the-hood magic, there are plenty of excellent computer science books available on the topic.

B-Tree Indexes

The B-tree, or balanced tree, is the most common types of index. Virtually all database servers and embedded database libraries offer B-tree indexes, often as the default index type. They are usually the default because of their unique combination of flexibility, size, and overall good performance.

As the name implies, a B-tree is a tree structure. The nodes are arranged in sorted order based on the key values. A B-tree is said to be balanced because it will never become lopsided as new nodes are added and removed. The main benefit of this balance is that the worst-case performance of a B-tree is always quite good. B-trees offer $O(\log n)$ performance for single-record lookups. Unlike binary trees, in which each node has at most two children, B-trees have many keys per node and don't grow "tall" or "deep" as quickly as a binary tree.

---

* MySQL Version 3.23 and older don't allow this, Versions 4.0 and newer do.

† As with many products, the specific implementation details are subject to change over time. By trying to take advantage of what's under the hood, you're inviting future problems when it does change.

B-tree indexes offer a lot of flexibility when you need to resolve queries. Range-base queries such as the following can be resolved very quickly:

```
SELECT * FROM phone_book WHERE last_name
BETWEEN 'Marten' and 'Mason'
```

The server simply finds the first "Marten" record and the last "Mason" record. It then knows that everything in between are also matches. The same is true of virtually any query that involves understanding the range of values, including MIN( ) and MAX( ) and even an open-ended range query such as the following:

```
SELECT COUNT(*) FROM phone_book WHERE last_name > 'Zawodny'
```

MySQL will simply find the last Zawodny and count all the records beyond it in the index tree.

Hash Indexes

The second most popular indexes are hash-based. These *hash indexes* resemble a hash table rather than a tree. The structure is very flat compared to a tree. Rather than ordering index records based on a comparison of the key value with similar key values, hash indexes are based on the result of running each key through a *hash function*. The hash function's job is to generate a semiunique hash value (usually numeric) for any given key. That value is then used to determine which bucket to put the key in.

Consider a common hashing function such as MD5( ). Given similar strings as input, it produces wildly different results:

```
mysql> SELECT MD5('Smith');
+----------------------------------+
| MD5('Smith')                     |
+----------------------------------+
| e95f770ac4fb91ac2e4873e4b2dfc0e6 |
+----------------------------------+
1 row in set (0.46 sec)

mysql> SELECT MD5('Smitty');
+----------------------------------+
| MD5('Smitty')                    |
+----------------------------------+
| 6d6f09a116b2eded33b9c871e6797a47 |
+----------------------------------+
1 row in set (0.00 sec)
```

However, the MD5 algorithm produces 128-bit values (represented as base-64 by default), which means there are just over 3.4×10^{38} possible values. Because most computers don't have nearly enough disk space (let alone memory) to contain that many slots, hash tables are always governed by the available storage space.

A common technique that reduces the possible key space of the hash table is to allocate a fixed number of buckets, often a relatively large prime number such as 35,149. You then divide the result of the hash function by the prime number and use the remainder to determine which bucket the value falls into.

That's the theory. The implementation details, again, can be quite a bit more complex, and knowing them tends not to help much. The end result is that the hash index provides very fast lookups, generally O(1) unless you're dealing with a hash function that doesn't produce a good spread of values for your particular data.

While hash-based indexes generally provide some of the fastest key lookups, they are also less flexible and less predictable than other indexes. They're less flexible because range-based queries can't use the index. Good hash functions generate very different values for similar values, so the server can't make any assumptions about the ordering of the data within the index structure. Records that are near each other in the hash table are rarely similar. Hash indexes are less predictable because the wrong combination of data and hash function can result in a hash table in which most of the records are clumped into just a few buckets. When that happens, performance suffers quite a bit. Rather than sifting through a relatively small list of keys that share the same hash value, the computer must examine a large list.

Hash indexes work relatively well for most text and numeric data types. Because hash functions effectively reduce arbitrarily sized keys to a small hash value, they tend not to use as much space as many tree-based indexes.

R-Tree Indexes

R-tree indexes are used for spatial or N-dimensional data. They are quite popular in mapping and geoscience applications but work equally well in other situations in which records are often queried based on two axes or dimensions: length and width, height and weight, etc.

Having been added for Version 4.1, R-tree indexes are relatively new to MySQL. MySQL's implementation is based on the OpenGIS specifications, available online at *http://www.opengis.org/*. The spatial data support in other popular database servers is often based on the OpenGIS specifications, so the syntax should be familiar if you've similar products.

Spatial indexes may be unfamiliar to many long-time MySQL users, so let's look at a simple example. We'll create a table to contain spatial data, add several points using X, Y coordinates, and ask MySQL which points fall within the bounds of some polygons.

First, create the table with a small BLOB field to contain the spatial data:

```
mysql> create table map_test
    -> (
    ->    name varchar(100) not null primary key,
    ->    loc  geometry,
```

```
   ->    spatial index(loc)
   -> );
Query OK, 0 rows affected (0.00 sec)
```

Then add some points:

```
mysql> insert into map_test values ('One Two', point(1,2));
Query OK, 1 row affected (0.00 sec)

mysql> insert into map_test values ('Two Two', point(2,2));
Query OK, 1 row affected (0.00 sec)

mysql> insert into map_test values ('Two One', point(2,1));
Query OK, 1 row affected (0.00 sec)
```

Now, ensure that it looks right in the table:

```
mysql> select name, AsText(loc) from map_test;
+---------+-------------+
| name    | AsText(loc) |
+---------+-------------+
| One Two | POINT(1 2)  |
| Two Two | POINT(2 2)  |
| Two One | POINT(2 1)  |
+---------+-------------+
3 rows in set (0.00 sec)
```

Finally, ask MySQL which points fall within a polygon:

```
mysql> SELECT name FROM map_test WHERE
    -> Contains(GeomFromText('POLYGON((0 0, 0 3, 3 3, 3 0, 0 0))'), loc);
+---------+
| name    |
+---------+
| One Two |
| Two Two |
| Two One |
+---------+
3 rows in set (0.00 sec)
```

Figure 4-1 shows the points and polygon on a graph.

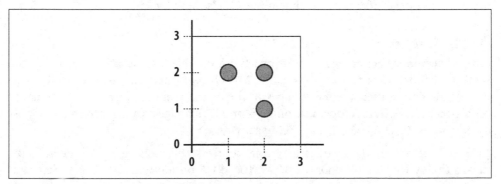

Figure 4-1. 2-D points and a polygon that contains them

MySQL indexes the various shapes that can be represented (points, lines, polygons) using the shape's minimum bounding rectangle (MBR). To do so, it computes the smallest rectangle you can draw that completely contains the shape. MySQL stores the coordinates of that rectangle and uses them when trying to find shapes in a given area.

Indexes and Table Types

Now that we have discussed the common index types, terminology, and uses in relatively generic terms so far, let's look at the indexes implemented in each of MySQL's storage engines. Each engine implements a subset of the three index types we've looked at. They also provide different optimizations that you should be aware of.

MyISAM Tables

MySQL's default table type provides B-tree indexes, and as of Version 4.1.0, it provides R-tree indexes for spatial data. In addition to the standard benefits that come with a good B-tree implementation, MyISAM adds two other important but relatively unknown features prefix compression and packed keys.

Prefix compression is used to factor out common prefixes in string keys. In a table that stores URLs, it would be a waste of space for MySQL to store the "http://" in every node of the B-tree. Because it is common to large number of the keys, it will compress the common prefix so that it takes significantly less space.

Packed keys are best thought of as prefix compression for integer keys. Because integer keys are stored with their high bytes first, it's common for a large group of keys to share a common prefix because the highest bits of the number change far less often. To enable packed keys, simply append:

```
PACKED_KEY = 1
```

to the CREATE TABLE statement.

MySQL stores the indexes for a table in the table's *.MYI* file.

Delayed key writes

One performance-enhancing feature of MyISAM tables is the ability to delay the writing of index data to disk. Normally, MySQL will flush modified key blocks to disk immediately after making changes to them, but you can override this behavior on a per-table basis or globally. Doing so provides a significant performance boost during heavy INSERT, UPDATE, and DELETE activity.

MySQL's delay_key_write tristate setting controls this behavior. The default, ON, means that MySQL will honor the DELAY_KEY_WRITE option in CREATE TABLE. Setting it to OFF means that MySQL will never delay key writes. And setting it to ALL tells

MySQL to delay key writes on all MyISAM tables regardless of the `DELAY_KEY_WRITE` used when the table was created.

The downside of delayed key writes is that the indexes may be out of sync with the data if MySQL crashes and has unwritten data in its key buffer. A `REPAIR TABLE`, which rebuilds all indexes and may consume a lot of time, is necessary to correct the problem.

Heap Tables

MySQL's only in-memory table type was originally built with support just for hash indexes. As of Version 4.1.0, however, you may choose between B-tree and hash indexes in Heap tables. The default is still to use a hash index, but specifying B-tree is simple:

```
mysql> create table heap_test (
    -> name varchar(50) not null,
    -> index using btree (name)
    -> ) type = HEAP;
Query OK, 0 rows affected (0.00 sec)
```

To verify that the index was created properly, use the `SHOW KEYS` command:

```
mysql> show keys from heap_test \G
*************************** 1. row ***************************
        Table: heap_test
   Non_unique: 1
     Key_name: name
 Seq_in_index: 1
  Column_name: name
    Collation: A
  Cardinality: NULL
     Sub_part: NULL
       Packed: NULL
         Null:
   Index_type: BTREE
      Comment:
1 row in set (0.00 sec)
```

By combining the flexibility of B-tree indexes and the raw speed of an in-memory table, query performance of the temp tables is hard to beat. Of course, if all you need are fast single-key lookups, the default hash indexes in Heap tables will serve you well. They are lightning fast and very space efficient.

The index data for Heap tables is always stored in memory—just like the data.

BDB Tables

MySQL's Berkeley DB (BDB) tables provide only B-tree indexes. This may come as a surprise to long-time BDB users who may be familiar with its underlying hash-based indexes. The indexes are stored in the same file as the data itself.

BDB's indexes, like those in MyISAM, also provide prefix compression. Like InnoDB, BDB also uses clustered indexes, and BDB tables require a primary key. If you don't supply one, MySQL creates a hidden primary key it uses internally for locating rows. The requirement exists because BDB always uses the primary key to locate rows. Index entries always refer to rows using the primary key rather than the record's physical location. This means that record lookups on secondary indexes are slightly slower then primary-key lookups.

InnoDB Tables

InnoDB tables provide B-tree indexes. The indexes provide no packing or prefix compression. In addition, InnoDB also requires a primary key for each table. As with BDB, though, if you don't provide a primary key, MySQL will supply a 64-bit value for you.

The indexes are stored in the InnoDB tablespace, just like the data and data dictionary (table definitions, etc.). Furthermore, InnoDB uses clustered indexes. That is, the primary key's value directly affects the physical location of the row as well as its corresponding index node. Because of this, lookups based on primary key in InnoDB are very fast. Once the index node is found, the relevant records are likely to already be cached in InnoDB's buffer pool.

Full-Text Indexes

A full-text index is a special type of index that can quickly retrieve the locations of every distinct word in a field. MySQL's provides full-text indexing support in MyISAM tables. Full-text indexes are built against one or more text fields (VARCHAR, TEXT, etc.) in a table.

The full-text index is also stored in a table's *.MYI* file. It is implemented by creating a normal two-part MyISAM B-tree index in which the first field is a VARCHAR, and the second is a FLOAT. The first field contains the indexed word, and the FLOAT is its local weight in the row.

Because they generally contain one record for each word in each indexed field, full-text indexes can get large rather quickly. Luckily, MySQL's B-tree indexes are quite efficient, so space consumed by full-text is well worth the performance boost.

It's not uncommon for a query like:

```
select * from articles where body = "%database%"
```

to run thousands of times faster when a full-text index is added and the query is re-written as:

```
select * from articles (body) match against ('database')
```

As with all index types, it's a matter of trading space for speed.

Index Limitations

There are many times when MySQL simply can't use an index to satisfy a query. To help you recognize these limitations (and hopefully avoid them), let's look at the four main impediments to using an index.

Wildcard matches

A query to locate all records that contain the word "buffy":

```
select * from pages where page_text like "%buffy%"
```

is bound to be slow. It requires MySQL to scan every row in the table. And it won't even find all occurrences, because "buffy" may be followed by some form of punctuation. The solution, of course, is to build a full-text index on the page_text field and query using MySQL's MATCH AGAINST syntax.

When you're dealing with partial words, however, things degenerate quickly. Imagine trying to find the phone number for everyone whose last name contains the string "son", such as Johnson, Ansona, or Bronson. That query would look like this:

```
select phone_number from phone_book where last_name like "%son%"
```

That seems suspiciously similar to the "buffy" example, and it is. Because you are performing a wildcard search on the field, MySQL will need to read every row, but switching to a full-text index won't help. Full-text indexes deal with complete words, so they're of no help in this situation.

If that's surprising, consider how you'd attempt to locate all those names in a normal phone book. Can you think of an efficient approach? There's really no simple change that can be made to the printed phone book that will facilitate this type of query.

Regular expressions

Using a regular expression has similar problems. Imagine trying to find all last names that end with either "ith," such as Smith, or "son" as in Johnson. As any Perl hacker would tell you, that's easy. Build a regular expression that looks something like (son|ith)$.

Translating that into MySQL, you might write this query:

```
select last_name from phone_book where last_name rlike "(son|ith)$"
```

However, you'd find that it runs slowly, and it does so for the same reasons that wildcard searches are slow. There's simply no generalized and efficient way to build an index that facilitates running arbitrary wildcard or regular-expression searches.

In this specific case, you can work around this limitation by storing reversed last names in a second field. Then you can reverse the sense of the search and use a query like this:

```
select last_name from phone_book where rev_last_name like "thi%"
union
select last_name from phone_book where rev_last_name like "nos%"
```

But that's efficient only because you're starting at the beginning of the string, which is really the end of the real string before it is reversed. Again, there's no general solution to this problem.

Note that a regular expression still isn't efficient in this case. You might be tempted to write this query:

```
select last_name from phone_book where rev_last_name rlike "^(thi|nos)"
```

You would be disappointed by its performance. The MySQL optimizer simply never tries to optimize regex-based queries.

Poor statistics or corruption

If MySQL's internal index statistics become corrupted or otherwise incorrect (possibly as the result of a crash or accidental server shutdown), MySQL may begin to exhibit very strange behavior. If the statistics are simply wrong, you may find that it no longer uses an index for your query. Or it may use an index only some of the time.

What's likely happened is that MySQL believes that the number of rows that match your query is so high that it would actually be more efficient to perform a full table scan. Because table scans are primarily sequential reads, they're faster than reading a large percentage of the records using an index, which requires far more disk seeks.

If this happens (or you suspect it has), try the index repair and analysis commands explained in the "Index Maintenance" section later in this chapter.

Too many matching rows

Similarly, if a table actually does have too many rows that really do match your query, performance can be quite slow. How many rows are too many for MySQL? It depends. But a good rule of thumb is that when MySQL believes more than about 30% of the rows are likely matches, it will resort to a table scan rather than using the index. There are a few exceptions to this rule. You'll find a more detailed discussion of this problem in Chapter 5.

Index Maintenance

Once you're done adding and dropping indexes, and your application is running happily, you may wonder about any ongoing index maintenance and administrative tasks. The good news is that there's no requirement that you do anything special, but there are a couple of things you may want to do from time to time.

Obtaining Index Information

If you're ever asked to help debug a slow query or indexing problem against a table (or group of tables) that you haven't seen in quite a while, you'll need to recover some basic information. Which columns are indexed? How many values are there? How large is the index?

Luckily, MySQL makes it relatively easy to gather this information. By using SHOW CREATE TABLE, you can retrieve the complete SQL necessary to (re-)create the table. However, if you care only about indexes, SHOW INDEXES FROM provides a lot more information.

```
mysql> SHOW INDEXES FROM access_jeremy_zawodny_com \G
*************************** 1. row ***************************
        Table: access_jeremy_zawodny_com
   Non_unique: 1
     Key_name: time_stamp
 Seq_in_index: 1
  Column_name: time_stamp
    Collation: A
  Cardinality: 9434851
     Sub_part: NULL
       Packed: NULL
         Null: YES
   Index_type: BTREE
      Comment:

1 rows in set (0.00 sec)
```

You may substitute KEYS for INDEXES in the query.

The table in the example has a single index named time_stamp. It is a B-tree index with only one component, the time_stamp column (as opposed to a multicolumn index). The index isn't packed and is allowed to contain NULL values. It's a non-unique index, so duplicates are allowed.

Refreshing Index Statistics

Over time, a table that sees many changes is likely to develop some inefficiencies in its indexes. Fragmentation due to blocks moving around on disk and inaccurate index statistics are the two most common problems you're likely to see. Luckily, it's easy for MySQL to optimize index data for MyISAM tables.

You can use the OPTIMIZE TABLE command to reindex a table. In doing so, MySQL will reread all the records in the table and reconstruct all of its indexes. The result will be tightly packed indexes with good statistics available.

Keep in mind that reindexing the table can take quite a bit of time if the table is large. During that time, MySQL has a write lock on the table, so data can't be updated.

Using the *myisamchk* command-line tool, you can perform the analysis offline:

```
$ cd database-name
$ myisamchk table-name
```

Just be sure that MySQL isn't running when you try this, or you run the risk of corrupting your indexes.

BDB and InnoDB tables are less likely to need this sort of tuning. That's a good thing, because the only ways to reindex them are a bit more time consuming. You can manually drop and re-create all the indexes, or you have to dump and reload the tables. However, using ANALYZE TABLE on an InnoDB table causes InnoDB to re-sample the data in an attempt to collect better statistics.

## CHAPTER 5

Query Performance

This chapter deals with an issue faced by every MySQL user sooner or later: speeding up slow queries. MySQL is a very fast database server, but its innate speed can carry your applications only so far. Eventually you need to roll up your sleeves, get your hands dirty, and figure out why your queries are slow—and ultimately figure out what needs to be done to get a response quickly.

We're frequently asked how we "figure this stuff out." It's really quite simple. Once you start to understand how MySQL does what it does, you'll begin to have an intuitive feeling for it, and query optimization will start to seem really easy. It's not always that easy, but with the proper background, you should end up able to figure out most optimization problems.

This chapter aims to provide a framework for understanding how MySQL works to resolve queries. With this foundation, you can continue through this chapter to the next, where the knowledge is applied to application design and server performance tuning.

We'll begin with an overview of how MySQL handles query processing. After that, we'll look at the optimizer's built-in features. Then we'll discuss identifying slow queries and finish up with a look at some of the hints you can provide to MySQL's query optimizer.

Query Processing Basics

How MySQL goes from receiving a query to sending the results back to a client is relatively straightforward. The work happens in several distinct stages. Let's walk through them.

Query Cache

You can enable the query cache (available as of MySQL 4.0.1) by setting query_cache_type to an appropriate value in *my.cnf*:

```
query_cache_type = 1
```

MySQL attempts to locate the results of any SELECT query in the query cache before bothering to analyze or execute it. It does this by hashing the query and using the hashed value to check for the results in the cache. MySQL uses the exact query text it receives, so the cache is sensitive to the most trivial variations.

As far as the cache is concerned, the query:

```
SELECT * FROM table1
```

is different from:

```
select * FROM table1
```

The same goes for variations in whitespace. MySQL doesn't trim extra space from the beginning or end of queries. This is rarely a problem because most repetitive queries are generated by applications rather than humans sitting at a keyboard.

To save some effort, MySQL cheats a bit. It only bothers to hash SELECT queries, since they're the only ones it makes any sense to cache. Unfortunately, older 4.0 versions of MySQL don't consider every SELECT query. The logic it uses simply checks the first three characters of your query, looking for SEL in a case-insensitive way.

As a result of this three-character "tunnel vision," any time you introduce whitespace or anything else at the beginning of the query, MySQL won't bother with the query cache. This can be a real problem in some applications. We know of a feed-processing system in which the developers uses comments to embed extra information at the beginning of each query:

```
/* <b>GetLatestStuff</b> */ SELECT * FROM sometable WHERE ...
```

The comment made is easier to identify the queries in an administrative tool that grabs the output of SHOW PROCESSLIST for display on a web page. Unfortunately, there's no way to tell MySQL to "try harder" when deciding whether a query is a SELECT, so these queries are never cached. Luckily, this problem is cured with a simple upgrade to MySQL 5.0.

It is possible to tell MySQL that it should *not* cache a given query, however. The way to dodge the query cache is to add the SQL_NO_CACHE hint to your query.

```
SELECT SQL_NO_CACHE * FROM mytable
```

This is helpful in controlling cache pollution. If your application has a set of queries that will never benefit from the query cache (perhaps because they run only once a day), there's no sense in caching them. Telling MySQL not to cache such queries leaves more room for storing the results of repetitive queries.

When the query cache is running in ondemand mode (set query_cache_type to 2 in *my.cnf*), MySQL does the work of trying to find a query in the cache only when it sees a SQL_CACHE hint in the query:

```
SELECT SQL_CACHE * FROM mytable
```

If the query's hashed value is found in the cache, MySQL sends the results from the cache to the client, bypassing any additional effort, just as expected.

The format of the results in the query cache is identical to the format used when sending them to a client. So there is very little overhead in retrieving results from the cache and sending them to a client. MySQL simply sends the data over the network. We'll look at query cache performance in Chapter 6.

Parsing, Analysis, and Optimization

Before MySQL can do anything interesting (or useful) with a noncached query, it must parse the query into its component parts. As part of that process, it verifies that the query is syntactically valid and gathers some basic information about the query:

- What type of query is this? Is it a SELECT, INSERT, UPDATE, or DELETE, or some other administrative command such as SET or GRANT?
- Which tables are involved? Are there any aliases used?
- What is the WHERE clause?
- Are there other hints or modifiers involved?

Once a query is broken down into more basic pieces, MySQL begins the more challenging work of figuring out what to do with it. This is where the *query optimizer* kicks in. The query optimizer's goal, simply put, is to find the most efficient way to execute a query given all the available information. Most of the time, this means the optimizer works to limit the number of records it must examine. It does this because the time associated with disk I/O is often (but not always) the governing factor that determines how long a query will take. Intuitively, this makes complete sense. It is an extension of the very same logic that explains why indexes are so helpful.

How the optimizer goes about making decisions is often regarded by people unfamiliar with MySQL internals as something like voodoo. Of course, it's not voodoo at all. MySQL has a set of rules and heuristics that have been evolving since its early days. These rules guide its decision-making process. But like any computer program that must deal with the infinite ways humans can assemble data and ask questions about it, the optimizer's not perfect. The rules and heuristics it uses work very well much of the time, but, on occasion, they do not.

The MySQL developers are constantly improving the optimizer—attempting to make it smarter and faster with each new release. Based on feedback from real-world users, they are always looking for ways to refine MySQL's ability to make the right decision. If you find a query that causes MySQL to make bad decisions, be sure to report it. Unreported problems are rarely fixed.

To make good decisions, MySQL tries to answer several important questions.

- Are there any indexes that are candidates for finding the rows quickly?
- Which index is best? If multiple tables are involved, which index is best for each table?
- Which tables depend on which other tables in the join?
- What's the optimal join order for the tables?

Of course, MySQL needs to make a decision very quickly and without actually testing all the options. Otherwise it might spend more time deciding how to execute the query than actually executing it!

The bulk of MySQL's effort centers around indexes and table join order. These aren't the only factors, but they're certainly the important ones. To get a better understanding of what MySQL is thinking about a SELECT query, it's best to look at the EXPLAIN output for the query.

Using EXPLAIN

So, what sort of knowledge can MySQL gather without expending a lot of effort and time? Let's look at a some queries against a news headline table—the sort of thing you might use to build a customizable news web site. The structure of the table is listed next. Rather than guessing what MySQL will probably do, we'll use its under-appreciated EXPLAIN command to help figure that out. In doing so, we'll see how adding an index or simply rephrasing a query can often better use an existing index and greatly improve performance.

```
mysql> describe Headline;
+------------+------------------+------+-----+---------+----------------+
| Field      | Type             | Null | Key | Default | Extra          |
+------------+------------------+------+-----+---------+----------------+
| Id         | int(10) unsigned |      | PRI | NULL    | auto_increment |
| Headline   | varchar(255)     |      |     |         |                |
| Url        | varchar(255)     |      | UNI |         |                |
| Time       | int(10) unsigned |      | MUL | 0       |                |
| ExpireTime | int(10) unsigned |      |     | 0       |                |
| Date       | varchar(6)       |      |     |         |                |
| Summary    | text             | YES  |     | NULL    |                |
| ModTime    | timestamp        | YES  |     | NULL    |                |
+------------+------------------+------+-----+---------+----------------+
8 rows in set (0.00 sec)
```

As you can tell, the Headline table contains information about news stories: title, summary, date, and so on. Headlines can be associated with multiple topics, which are defined in the Topic table. The T2H table maps topics to headlines and vice versa.

The relationship is many-to-many because a single headline may be associated with multiple topics.

When you write a query against a primary key or unique index, MySQL should know that there can be only a single match for each value. Indeed, this query is very fast:

```
mysql> SELECT Headline, Url FROM Headline WHERE Id = 13950120 \G
*************************** 1. row ***************************
Headline: Midwest Cash Grain PM - Soy off, USDA data awaited
     Url: http://biz.yahoo.com/rm/030328/markets_grain_cash_2.html
1 row in set (0.00 sec)
```

Just as it's obvious to you or me, MySQL knows that only one record can possibly match. Its strategy for finding the row is straightforward: simply check the primary index for a match. If it exists, fetch the row. To verify that, let's EXPLAIN it:

```
mysql> EXPLAIN SELECT Headline, Url FROM Headline WHERE id = 13950120 \G
*************************** 1. row ***************************
           id: 1
  select_type: SIMPLE
        table: Headline
         type: const
possible_keys: PRIMARY
          key: PRIMARY
      key_len: 4
          ref: const
         rows: 1
        Extra:
1 row in set (0.00 sec)
```

Just as expected, MySQL knows there's only one matching row. The rows value tells you so. What MySQL says here isn't always to be completely trusted, however, as you'll see in a little bit.

Of course, EXPLAIN is relating much more than how many rows to expect. Let's quickly review the information it provides:

id The ID of this table in the query. EXPLAIN produces one output record for each table in the query.

select_type
What is this table's role in the larger query? Possible values are SIMPLE, PRIMARY, UNION, DEPENDENT UNION, SUBSELECT, and DERIVED. As we look at the more complicated queries, the meaning will become clearer.

table
The name of the table MySQL will read records from.

type
What type of join will MySQL use? In this example, you see const because there was a constant value in the query. Other possible values are system, eq_ref, ref,

range, `index`, or `ALL`. We'll revisit this in more detail in the "Joins" section, later in this chapter.

possible_keys

> A list of the indexes (or NULL if none) MySQL can use to find rows in the table.

key

> The name of the index MySQL decides to use, after checking all possible indexes (listed in `possible_keys`) and choosing the best.

key_len

> The size of the key value (in bytes).

ref

> The columns or values that are used to match against the key.

rows

> The number of rows MySQL thinks it needs to examine to satisfy the query. If you frequently add and remove records from the table, running `ANALYZE TABLE` lets MySQL update the index statistics so it can make better estimates.

Extra

> Any extra information MySQL wishes to convey about the execution of this query. We'll see some examples of that shortly.

The simple case is just that—simple. Let's ask for a range of values instead.

```
mysql> SELECT Url FROM Headline WHERE id BETWEEN 13950120 AND 13950125;
+----------------------------------------------------------+
| Url                                                      |
+----------------------------------------------------------+
| http://biz.yahoo.com/rm/030328/markets_grain_cash_2.html |
| http://biz.yahoo.com/prnews/030328/cgf038_1.html         |
| http://biz.yahoo.com/bw/030328/285487_1.html             |
| http://biz.yahoo.com/rc/030328/turkey_hijack_5.html      |
| http://biz.yahoo.com/rm/030328/food_aid_iraq_1.html      |
+----------------------------------------------------------+
5 rows in set (0.00 sec)

mysql> EXPLAIN SELECT Url FROM Headline WHERE id BETWEEN 13950120 AND 13950125 \G
*************************** 1. row ***************************
           id: 1
  select_type: SIMPLE
        table: Headline
         type: range
possible_keys: PRIMARY
          key: PRIMARY
      key_len: 4
          ref: NULL
         rows: 3
        Extra: Using where
1 row in set (0.00 sec)
```

In this case, the type has switched from const to range to indicate that a search for more than one value. Similarly, ref is now NULL.

Every thing seems reasonable unless you look closely. When executed, the query returns five rows, but the rows says three. That's because the rows value is merely an estimate. It probably should have been called estimated_rows.

The estimate is based on the index MySQL is using. Based on the distribution of records across the possible key values, it simply approximates that there are three valid records between 13950120 and 13950125.

Also notice that the Extra column says Using where. That's MySQL's reassuring way of telling you that it's using the limitations specified in the WHERE clause to select records. It wasn't present in the first example because MySQL treats a single-row lookup using the primary key as special case.

What if we try fetching records based on a nonindexed column:

```
mysql> SELECT COUNT(*) FROM Headline WHERE ExpireTime >= 1112201600;
+----------+
| COUNT(*) |
+----------+
|     3971 |
+----------+
1 row in set (1.04 sec)

mysql> EXPLAIN SELECT COUNT(*) FROM Headline WHERE ExpireTime >= 1112201600 \G
*************************** 1. row ***************************
           id: 1
  select_type: SIMPLE
        table: Headline
         type: ALL
possible_keys: NULL
          key: NULL
      key_len: NULL
          ref: NULL
         rows: 302116
        Extra: Using where
1 row in set (0.00 sec)
```

The NULL value in the key column of the EXPLAIN output tell us that MySQL won't be using an index for this query. In fact, the NULL value in the possible_keys column tells us that there were no indexes to pick from at all. If this type of query is likely to be common, we can simply add an index and rerun the query (or the EXPLAIN) to verify that MySQL uses it.

```
mysql> ALTER TABLE Headline ADD INDEX (ExpireTime);
Query OK, 302116 rows affected (40.02 sec)
Records: 302116  Duplicates: 0  Warnings: 0

mysql> SELECT COUNT(*) FROM Headline WHERE ExpireTime >= 1112201600;
+----------+
```

```
| COUNT(*) |
+----------+
|     3971 |
+----------+
1 row in set (0.01 sec)

mysql> EXPLAIN SELECT COUNT(*) FROM Headline WHERE ExpireTime >= 1112201600 \G
*************************** 1. row ***************************
           id: 1
  select_type: SIMPLE
        table: Headline
         type: range
possible_keys: ExpireTime
          key: ExpireTime
      key_len: 4
          ref: NULL
         rows: 12009
        Extra: Using where; Using index
1 row in set (0.00 sec)
```

The query now runs in 0.01 seconds instead of 1.04. The EXPLAIN output looks much better, with the new ExpireTime index being used for a range search. Note again the discrepancy between rows (12009) and the actual row count (3971). In a case like this, it might be possible to improve the estimate that MySQL makes by running either ANALYZE TABLE or OPTIMIZE TABLE on the Headline table.

Also, notice that MySQL said Using index. That means this is an *index-only query*. MySQL is able to get all the data it needs from the ExpireTime index, so it doesn't bother fetching any of the rows from disk.

But what if you need to fetch multiple headlines, and you know their IDs? Should you use OR or IN(...)? Let's find out what MySQL can tell us, using the lowest and highest headline IDs as well as one in between:

```
mysql> SELECT Url FROM Headline WHERE Id IN(1531513, 10231599, 13962322);
+-----------------------------------------------+
| Url                                           |
+-----------------------------------------------+
| http://biz.yahoo.com/bond/010117/bf.html      |
| http://biz.yahoo.com/e/021101/yhoo10-q.html   |
| http://biz.yahoo.com/bw/030331/315850_1.html  |
+-----------------------------------------------+
3 rows in set (0.00 sec)

mysql> EXPLAIN SELECT Url FROM Headline WHERE Id IN(1531513, 10231599, 13962322) \G
*************************** 1. row ***************************
           id: 1
  select_type: SIMPLE
        table: Headline
         type: range
possible_keys: PRIMARY
          key: PRIMARY
      key_len: 4
```

```
          ref: NULL
         rows: 3
        Extra: Using where
1 row in set (0.00 sec)

mysql> SELECT Url FROM Headline WHERE Id = 1531513 OR Id = 10231599 OR Id =
13962322;
+-----------------------------------------------+
| Url                                           |
+-----------------------------------------------+
| http://biz.yahoo.com/bond/010117/bf.html      |
| http://biz.yahoo.com/e/021101/yhoo10-q.html   |
| http://biz.yahoo.com/bw/030331/315850_1.html  |
+-----------------------------------------------+
3 rows in set (0.03 sec)

mysql> EXPLAIN SELECT Url FROM Headline WHERE Id = 1531513 OR Id = 10231599 OR Id =
13962322 \G
*************************** 1. row ***************************
           id: 1
  select_type: SIMPLE
        table: Headline
         type: range
possible_keys: PRIMARY
          key: PRIMARY
      key_len: 4
          ref: NULL
         rows: 3
        Extra: Using where
1 row in set (0.00 sec)
```

Both queries execute very quickly, and their EXPLAIN output is the same. They're functionally the same. It's clear that either query may return anywhere from zero to three rows. We're querying based on a unique index (the primary key), so there isn't much for MySQL to think about. As it turns out, we happen to know that in this case, MySQL internally changed the multi-OR query to one that uses a single IN(...) list. However, it's clear that as the number of IDs increases, the query string will be smaller if you use the IN(..). A smaller query means less parsing overhead and better performance.

What if we use a subquery to fetch the URL for the highest numbered headline?

```
mysql> EXPLAIN SELECT Url FROM Headline WHERE Id IN (SELECT MAX(Id) FROM Headline);
```

After waiting five minutes, we killed the query. Either we did something wrong, or MySQL wasn't using the obvious approach to resolve this query. Hmm.

To find out, let's explain it.

```
mysql> EXPLAIN SELECT Url FROM Headline WHERE Id IN (SELECT MAX(id) FROM Headline) \G
*************************** 1. row ***************************
           id: 1
  select_type: PRIMARY
        table: Headline
```

```
          type: ALL
  possible_keys: NULL
            key: NULL
        key_len: NULL
            ref: NULL
           rows: 302116
          Extra: Using where
*********************** 2. row **************************
             id: 2
    select_type: DEPENDENT SUBSELECT
          table: Headline
           type: index
  possible_keys: NULL
            key: PRIMARY
        key_len: 4
            ref: NULL
           rows: 302116
          Extra: Using index
2 rows in set (0.00 sec)
```

Yikes!

MySQL isn't using any indexes! Notice that both possible_keys fields are NULL. Is this a bug? Perhaps, especially when you consider that the key field in the dependent subselect says that it selected the primary key. But it wasn't in the list of possible keys. And, worse yet, MySQL believes it must examine 302,116 rows to resolve a single-record lookup supposedly based on a primary key.

Of course, this testing was performed with MySQL 4.1.0 alpha, prerelease code in which the query optimizer hadn't been properly tuned to handle subselects well.* The point isn't that MySQL didn't do the right thing. No matter how well tuned it is, MySQL will make a bad decision once in a while. When it does, you need to be able to diagnose the problem and, in some cases, come up with a workaround.

So let's rewrite the query a bit to simplify things. We're using IN(...) in a query that can only return one row. So let's change that to an equality (=) test.

```
mysql> SELECT Url FROM Headline WHERE Id = (SELECT MAX(id) FROM Headline);
+----------------------------------------------+
| Url                                          |
+----------------------------------------------+
| http://biz.yahoo.com/bw/030331/315850_1.html |
+----------------------------------------------+
1 row in set (0.00 sec)

mysql> EXPLAIN SELECT Url FROM Headline WHERE Id = (SELECT MAX(id) FROM Headline) \G
*********************** 1. row **************************
             id: 1
    select_type: PRIMARY
```

---

* Subsequent tests with the 4.1.2 alpha version proved that the query optimizer no longer had this bug.

```
          table: Headline
           type: const
  possible_keys: PRIMARY
            key: PRIMARY
        key_len: 4
            ref: const
           rows: 1
          Extra:
************************** 2. row **************************
             id: 2
    select_type: SUBSELECT
          table: NULL
           type: NULL
  possible_keys: NULL
            key: NULL
        key_len: NULL
            ref: NULL
           rows: NULL
          Extra: Select tables optimized away
2 rows in set (0.00 sec)
```

A-ha! That did it. The query ran in a split second.

The EXPLAIN output is interesting too. MySQL noticed that we were attempting something very trivial and optimized away the second table. All those NULL values are MySQL's way of saying, "These simply don't matter."

But what if that hadn't worked? Or what if we're using an older MySQL that doesn't have subselects yet? Simple. We can rewrite the query as two SELECT statements and store the intermediate value in a variable on the server side so that no client-side state is required:

```
mysql> SELECT @max := MAX(Id) FROM Headline;
+-----------------+
| @max := MAX(Id) |
+-----------------+
|        13962322 |
+-----------------+
1 row in set (0.00 sec)

mysql> SELECT Url FROM Headline WHERE Id = @max;
+-------------------------------------------+
| Url                                       |
+-------------------------------------------+
| http://biz.yahoo.com/bw/030331/315850_1.html |
+-------------------------------------------+
1 row in set (0.00 sec)
```

We don't even need to explain those queries. Based on what we already know, they'll obviously be fast (and they are). Both are queries on primary keys and fetch single values.

And, for completeness, the most MySQL-like way to write that query is to use an ORDER BY and LIMIT:

```
SELECT Url FROM Headline ORDER BY Id DESC LIMIT 1;
```

Let's look at one last example. What if you query based on two different indexed fields? MySQL tries to select the index that will result in the fewest rows being examined. So the results will vary depending on your data and the values you choose.

```
mysql> SELECT COUNT(*) FROM Headline WHERE ExpireTime >= 1112201600 AND Id <=
5000000;
+----------+
| COUNT(*) |
+----------+
|     1175 |
+----------+
1 row in set (0.04 sec)

mysql> EXPLAIN SELECT COUNT(*) FROM Headline
    -> WHERE ExpireTime >= 1112201600 AND Id <= 5000000 \G
*************************** 1. row ***************************
           id: 1
  select_type: SIMPLE
        table: Headline
         type: range
possible_keys: PRIMARY,ExpireTime
          key: ExpireTime
      key_len: 4
          ref: NULL
         rows: 12009
        Extra: Using where
1 row in set (0.00 sec)
```

For this query, given the choice between the primary key field (Id) and the ExpireTime, MySQL decided to use ExpireTime. However, if the ExpireTime value is changed so that it matches many more rows, MySQL should favor the primary key:

```
mysql> EXPLAIN SELECT COUNT(*) FROM Headline WHERE ExpireTime >= 1012201600 AND Id <=
5000000 \G
*************************** 1. row ***************************
           id: 1
  select_type: SIMPLE
        table: Headline
         type: range
possible_keys: PRIMARY,ExpireTime
          key: PRIMARY
      key_len: 4
          ref: NULL
         rows: 13174
        Extra: Using where
1 row in set (0.00 sec)
```

As expected, it does.

Again, this decision-making process is all based on MySQL's notion of what the data looks like—how evenly distributed the values are. Different storage engines (InnoDB, MyISAM, BDB) use different methods to gather those statistics. As a result, you may find that some queries are executed differently if you convert your data to a different table type. Of course, running ANALYZE TABLE will also affect MySQL's statistics.

Joins

Things become slightly more complex when you're querying multiple tables. MySQL has to decide which order makes the most sense. Again, the goal it to read as few rows as possible, so it will consider each table and estimate how many rows it must read from each. In doing so, it also needs to understand the relationship among the tables. For example, with a query like this, it's clear that MySQL can't read the table order first:

```
SELECT customer.name, order.date_placed, region.name
FROM customer, order, region
WHERE order.customer_id = customer.id
AND customer.region_id = region.id
AND customer.name = 'John Doe'
```

The rows MySQL will need to retrieve from the order table depend on the customer table. So it must read customer before order. In fact, the same is true of region. So in this case, MySQL has to read customer records first. From there it will decide to read the remaining tables in whatever order it chooses.

Unfortunately, finding the optimal join order is one of MySQL's weakest skills. Rather than being clever about this problem, the optimizer simply tries to brute-force its way through. It tries every possible combination before choosing one. That can spell disaster in a some cases. We've seen at least one case in which MySQL took 29 seconds to decide how to execute a multitable join and then 1 second to actually execute it. In this particular case, there were over 10 tables involved. Since MySQL is considering all possible combinations, performance begins to degrade quite drastically as you go beyond a handful of tables. The exact number, of course, depends on how powerful CPUs are this year.

Execution

There's not a lot to say about query execution. MySQL simply follows its plan, fetching rows from each table in order and joining based on the relevant columns (hopefully using indexes). Along the way, it may need to create a temporary table (in memory or on disk) to store the results. Once all the rows are available, it sends them to the client.

Along the way, MySQL gathers some information and statistics about each query it executes, including:

- Who issued the query
- How long the process took
- How many rows were returned

That information will appear in the slow query log (discussed later in this chapter) if the query time exceeds the server's threshold, and the log is enabled. If the query is issued interactively, it will also appear after the query results.

Optimizer Features and Oddities

When testing queries, always remember to use realistic data. A common source of problems with MySQL is the query optimizer's handling of test data. It often does surprising things. If you don't know what it's doing and why (and it rarely tells you why), you may spend a lot of time tracking down a problem that really isn't there. Or, worse yet, you may embarrass yourself asking about it on the MySQL mailing list, only to learn that you've created the problem all on your own.

In general, MySQL uses an index when it is reasonably confident that doing so is *more efficient* than not doing so. This leads to false negatives during testing. The false negative tends to occur in the two situations that we'll now investigate.

Too Little Diversity

Even if you have a lot of data (thousands of rows or more), MySQL may choose to ignore your indexes some of the time if your data doesn't have sufficient diversity. Why might that happen? Imagine you have a table that contains historical climate data for most world cities:

```
CREATE TABLE weather
(
  city       VARCHAR(100) NOT NULL,
  high_temp  TINYINT      NOT NULL,
  low_temp   TINYINT      NOT NULL,
  the_date   DATE         NOT NULL,
  INDEX (city),
  INDEX (the_date),
)
```

Rather than loading all two million records, you load two years worth of data (1980 and 1981) to test. After some testing, you find that queries that need to access many of the records are using full table scans rather than the the_date index. For example, to find the average high temperature in 1980, you might write something like this:

```
SELECT AVG(high_temp) FROM weather
WHERE the_date BETWEEN '1980-01-01' AND '1980-12-31';
```

Having data from only 1980 and 1981 loaded, that query needs to examine 50% of the rows in the weather table. In such a case, MySQL decides that it is faster to simply scan the entire table.

How does it know? When you cross a certain threshold, it is slower to locate rows using an index than to read them sequentially. For MySQL, the cutoff point is roughly 30%. The number is chosen by the MySQL developers based on their extensive experience (and knowledge of the code) and is subject to change from release to release. The actual number is specific to each storage engine: InnoDB has a different threshold than MyISAM tables, and so forth.

The main reason index performance is worse in these circumstances goes all the way down to the hardware: disk seek performance. Indexes are always sorted, but the data on disk is not. Using an index means accessing the rows in index-sorted order rather than in the order they reside on disk. The end result is more time spent moving around the disk and less time reading data. Sequential reads are always going to be faster than random seeks. If you're lucky enough to be using a RAM disk, most of the overhead vanishes.

You can draw two conclusions from this knowledge. First, if a table really is going to remain very small, you may want to leave off the indexes. (Unique indexes are an exception to this rule. Without them you can't enforce a unique constraint on the table.) The second conclusion merely reinforces what we said earlier—always use a representative data set for your testing. It should be representative both in terms of size and diversity.

One special case that must be mentioned is that of index-only queries. If you happen to write a query that requires only columns contained within a single index, you'll be pleasantly surprised. MySQL is smart enough to realize that all the required data is present in the index, so it doesn't bother to fetch any of the rows from disk. This, obviously, provides you with excellent performance.

Index-Based Ordering

One of MySQL's weak points is sorting. It can usually fetch 15,000 rows in a heartbeat, but if you happen to need them in any particular order it may take quite a bit more time.[*]

The problem is really two-fold. First, sorting is simply more work, and work takes time. Aside from adding a faster CPU, there's no avoiding that fact. If you're not sorting on a computed field, your first instinct is likely to add an index on the sorting column. Unfortunately, that rarely helps. As you'll remember from Chapter 4,

---

[*] Of course, performance is always relative. we've seen queries that MySQL answered in 20 ms take 200 ms after adding an ORDER BY clause. For many applications, 200 ms is still quite fast.

MySQL uses at most one index per table per query. Odds are that you're already using an index on the table in question, so MySQL will not touch your new index.

The solution to the second problem also goes back to Chapter 4. Add the sorting column as a second part in the existing index. By doing so you get the best of both worlds. You'll have an index MySQL can use to quickly locate rows (just as before) *and* an index that provides order to the data. That removes the need for MySQL to make a sorting pass over the results.

Going back to the weather example, to speed up queries like this:

```
SELECT * FROM weather WHERE city = 'Toledo' ORDER BY the_date DESC
```

you'd change the index on city to an index on (city, the_date):

```
ALTER TABLE weather DROP INDEX city, ADD INDEX (city, the_date)
```

Remember that the order of columns is significant. The leftmost prefix rule dictates that city must appear first in the index to be used for that query.

Taking things a step further, you might then be tempted to remove the single index on the_date. Don't do it unless you're sure there are no queries using the_date in their WHERE clause. A query based on the_date can't be satisfied using the new index on (city, the_date) because the_date isn't a leftmost prefix in the index.

Impossible Queries

MySQL performs a basic logical analysis of the WHERE clause of every query. In doing so, it can often detect when you've asked for something that doesn't make any sense:

```
SELECT * FROM mytable WHERE id < 5000 and id > 30000
```

If it finds an impossible WHERE clause, it returns zero records, sparing the expense of running an otherwise pointless and possibly expensive query.

If you suspect that MySQL has optimized away an impossible WHERE clause, simply ask it to EXPLAIN the query. If you see a result like this:

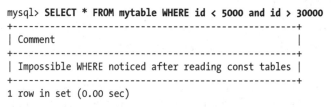

```
mysql> SELECT * FROM mytable WHERE id < 5000 and id > 30000
+-----------------------------------------------------+
| Comment                                             |
+-----------------------------------------------------+
| Impossible WHERE noticed after reading const tables |
+-----------------------------------------------------+
1 row in set (0.00 sec)
```

you'll know what it was thinking.

Aside from making a simple typo, it's unlikely that you'll run many queries like that. However, if you're building an application on top of MySQL and happen to make a typo or a serious logic error in the code, you can end up running lots of pointless queries before tracking down the problem. It's good to know that MySQL doesn't waste much time dealing with your illogical queries.

Full-Text Instead of LIKE

From Chapter 4, it's clear that full-text indexes are much faster than using a LIKE clause in your queries to search for a word or phrase. In the vast majority of cases, you should use a full-text index to tackle these types of problems.

However, there are times when this can be problematic. The query optimizer doesn't look very closely at full-text indexes when deciding which index to use for a table. In fact, if there's a usable full-text index, the optimizer will always prefer it regardless of how many rows it actually eliminates from the result set. Hopefully this will be fixed in a future version of MySQL.

Identifying Slow Queries

Figuring out which queries are slow is usually easier than figuring out *why* they're slow and making the necessary changes to fix them. The easiest way to track them is to let MySQL do some of the work for you. By enabling the *slow query log*, you instruct MySQL to log every query that takes longer than a specified number of seconds. In addition to the query, it also logs some other metadata.

Here's an example record from a slow query log:

```
# Time: 030303  0:51:27
# User@Host: user[user] @ client.example.com [192.168.50.12]
# Query_time: 25  Lock_time: 0  Rows_sent: 3949  Rows_examined: 378036
select ArticleHtmlFiles.SourceTag, ArticleHtmlFiles.AuxId from ArticleHtmlFiles left
join Headlines on ArticleHtmlFiles.SourceTag = Headlines.SourceTag and
ArticleHtmlFiles.AuxId = Headlines.AuxId where Headlines.AuxId is NULL;
```

While the log contains a lot of useful information, there's one very important bit of information missing: an idea of *why* the query was slow. Sure, if the log says 12,000,000 rows were examined and 1,200,000 sent to the client, you know why it was slow. But things are rarely that clear cut. Worse yet, you may find a slow query, paste it into your favorite MySQL client, and find that it executes in a fraction of a second.

You must be careful not to read too much information into the slow query log. When a query appears in the log, it doesn't mean that it's a bad query—or even a slow one. It simply means that the query took a long time *then*. It doesn't mean that the query will take a long time now or in the future.

There are any number of reasons why a query may be slow at one time but not at others:

- A table may have been locked, causing the query to wait. The Lock_time indicates how long the query waited for locks to be released.

- None of the data or indexes may have been cached in memory yet. This is common when MySQL is first started or hasn't been well tuned. Chapter 4 covers this in more detail.

- A nightly backup process was running, making all disk I/O considerably slower.
- The server may have been handling hundreds of other unrelated queries at that same time, and there simply wasn't enough CPU power to do the job efficiently.

The list could go on. The bottom line is this: the slow query log is nothing more than a partial record of what happened. You can use it to generate a list of possible suspects, but you really need to investigate each of them in more depth. Of course, if you happen to see the same query appearing in the log over and over, there's a very good chance you have a slow query on your hands.

MySQL also comes with *mysqldumpslow*, a Perl script that can summarize the slow query log and provide a better idea of how often each slower query executes. That way you don't waste time trying to optimize a 30-second slow query that runs once a day, while there are five other 2-second slow queries that run thousands of time per day.

Appendix B contains information on using `mytop` to perform real-time query monitoring, including slow queries.

Influencing MySQL with Hints

Many relational database servers implement some notion of hints—a simple syntax for providing additional information to the underlying SQL engine and query optimizer. Sometimes you may need to do this to work around a bug or improve performance. Let's have a quick look at the various hints that can influence MySQL's query processing. As you saw with the query cache, hints in MySQL often appear right after the SELECT keyword:

```
SELECT SQL_CACHE * FROM mytable ...
```

But as you'll see, that's not always the case.

If you're worried about code portability because your SQL may need to run on a database server other than MySQL, you can often enclose hints within comments so that they'll be ignored by other servers—or older versions of MySQL itself:

```
SELECT /*! SQL_CACHE */ * FROM mytable ...
```

Join Order

MySQL normally doesn't care about the order in which you list tables in your queries. It examines the possibilities and decides which table to read first, second, and so on. Once in a while, you might find that MySQL isn't handling a multitable join very well. After looking at the EXPLAIN output for the query, you realize that it's accessing the tables in a less than optimal order.

If you think you can do a better job of optimizing the join order than MySQL has done, you can use the STRAIGHT_JOIN hint in place of a comma or JOIN keyword in your query:

```
SELECT * FROM table1 STRAIGHT_JOIN table2 WHERE ...
```

Doing so forces MySQL to join the tables in the order they appear in your query, regardless of the order it would otherwise decide to use.

Index Usage

MySQL provides several index-related hints to cover cases when you'd like more control over the indexes it considers.

To provide a list of indexes you'd like MySQL to consider, ignoring all others, add USE INDEX after the table name in the query:

```
SELECT * FROM mytable USE INDEX (mod_time, name) ...
```

If you simply want MySQL to ignore one or more indexes, use IGNORE INDEX instead:

```
SELECT * FROM mytale IGNORE INDEX (priority) ...
```

To force MySQL to use a particular index, use FORCE INDEX in the query:

```
SELECT * FROM mytable FORCE INDEX (mod_time) ...
```

In doing so, you're telling MySQL to ignore any decisions it might otherwise have made about the best way to find the data you've asked for. It will disobey that request only if the index you specify can't possibly be used to resolve the query.

Result Sizes

A set of hints also exists to tell MySQL that you'd like the resulting rows to be handled in a particular way. Like most hints, you really shouldn't be using them unless you know they help. Overusing them will likely cause performance problems sooner or later.

When dealing with a large number of rows that may take a bit of time for the client to consume, consider using SQL_BUFFER_RESULT. Doing so tells MySQL to store the result in a temporary table, thus freeing up any locks much sooner.

The SQL_BIG_RESULT hint tells MySQL that there will be a large number of rows coming back. When MySQL sees this hint, it can make more aggressive decisions about using disk-based temporary tables. It will also be less likely to build an index on the temporary table for the purpose of sorting the results.

Query Cache

As noted at the beginning of this chapter, the query cache stores the results of frequently executed SELECT queries in memory for fast retrieval. MySQL provides opt-in and opt-out hints that can be used to control whether or not a query's results are cached.

By using SQL_CACHE, you ask MySQL to cache the results of this query. If the query_cache_type is set to 1, this hint has no affect because all SELECT queries are cached by default. If query_cache_type is set to 2, however, the cache is enabled, but queries are cached only on request. Using SQL_CACHE covers this case.

On the flip side, SQL_NO_CACHE asks MySQL not to cache the results of a query. Because this is an opt-out request, it works for query_cache_type 1 or 2.

Stupid Query Tricks

We can't end a chapter on query optimization without looking at some common tricks that can increase performance of some queries. While these are all rather specific, you may find techniques that can be applied in other circumstances.

Two Is Better Than One

Sometimes MySQL doesn't optimize a seemingly simple query the way you'd expect. A good example of this behavior occurred in a database used to track historical stock prices. There are two tables involved: SymbolHistory and Symbols.

As far as we're concerned, the Symbols table contains two important fields: Id and Symbol. The Id is an auto_increment primary key. Here's the PriceHistory table:

```
mysql> DESCRIBE PriceHistory;
+----------+---------+------+-----+------------+-------+
| Field    | Type    | Null | Key | Default    | Extra |
+----------+---------+------+-----+------------+-------+
| SymbolID | int(11) |      | PRI | 0          |       |
| Date     | date    |      | PRI | 0000-00-00 |       |
| Open     | float   |      |     | 0          |       |
| High     | float   |      |     | 0          |       |
| Low      | float   |      |     | 0          |       |
| Close    | float   |      |     | 0          |       |
| Volume   | float   |      |     | 0          |       |
+----------+---------+------+-----+------------+-------+
8 rows in set (0.01 sec)
```

It has a two-part index on (SymbolID, Date).

The Symbols table maps stock tickers to numeric identifiers. It also contains various other bits of metadata about each security. The PriceHistory table contains the historical price data. One of the most common queries run against the data is, "Show me all closing prices for a given stock sorted from newest to oldest."

To fetch the price history for IBM, the query looks like this:

```
mysql> EXPLAIN SELECT date_format(Date,'%Y%m%d') as Day, Close
    -> FROM Symbols, PriceHistory
```

```
    -> WHERE Symbols.ID=PriceHistory.SymbolID AND Symbols.Symbol = 'ibm'
    -> ORDER BY Date DESC \G
*********************** 1. row ***************************
        table: Symbols
         type: const
possible_keys: PRIMARY,Symbols_SymbolIDX
          key: Symbols_SymbolIDX
      key_len: 20
          ref: const
         rows: 1
        Extra: Using filesort
*********************** 2. row ***************************
        table: PriceHistory
         type: ref
possible_keys: PriceHistory_IDX
          key: PriceHistory_IDX
      key_len: 4
          ref: const
         rows: 471
        Extra: Using where
2 rows in set (0.01 sec)
```

Notice the Using filesort in the EXPLAIN output, which means MySQL will need to sort all the records based on the date. It turns out that the Date column is in the index, but MySQL can't use it directly for sorting because it's not the first part of a composite index. The result is a second pass over the rows to return them in the correct order. That sorting process can be slow when the query is run hundreds of times each minute on a large variety of stocks, some of which have thousands of records.

To improve the performance, we need to arrange it so that MySQL can query the PriceHistory and use the index on the Date column. The easiest way to do so is to break it up into two queries using a temporary variable, just like we did earlier to work around the lack of subselects:

```
mysql> SELECT @sid := Id FROM Symbols WHERE Symbol = 'ibm';
+------------+
| @sid := Id |
+------------+
|     459378 |
+------------+
1 row in set (0.02 sec)

mysql> EXPLAIN SELECT date_format(Date,'%Y%m%d') as Day, Close
    -> FROM PriceHistory WHERE SymbolID = @sid ORDER BY Date DESC \G
*********************** 1. row ***************************
        table: PriceHistory
         type: ref
possible_keys: PriceHistory_IDX
          key: PriceHistory_IDX
      key_len: 4
          ref: const
```

```
      rows: 7234
     Extra: Using where
1 row in set (0.00 sec)
```

An improvement like this can often mean the difference between a CPU-bound server handling 200 queries per second and a partially idle server handling 700 queries per second. The overhead associated with performing two queries instead of one is still usually less than that extra sorting pass.

Unions Instead of ORs

Earlier we used a query like this to demonstrate that MySQL handles the situation efficiently:

```
mysql> EXPLAIN SELECT COUNT(*) FROM Headline
    -> WHERE ExpireTime >= 1112201600 AND Id <= 5000000 \G
*************************** 1. row ***************************
           id: 1
  select_type: SIMPLE
        table: Headline
         type: range
possible_keys: PRIMARY,ExpireTime
          key: ExpireTime
      key_len: 4
          ref: NULL
         rows: 12009
        Extra: Using where
1 row in set (0.00 sec)
```

In this example, MySQL uses the ExpireTime index to fetch a set of rows. It then applies the rest of the WHERE clause to eliminate those rows with ID values less than or equal to 5,000,000.

But what if the AND is changed to an OR condition, and we change it from a COUNT(*) to something a bit more meaningful?

```
mysql> EXPLAIN SELECT * FROM Headline
    -> WHERE ExpireTime >= 1012201600 OR Id <= 5000000
    -> ORDER BY ExpireTime ASC LIMIT 10\G
*************************** 1. row ***************************
           id: 1
  select_type: SIMPLE
        table: Headline
         type: ALL
possible_keys: PRIMARY,ExpireTime
          key: NULL
      key_len: NULL
          ref: NULL
         rows: 302116
        Extra: Using where
1 row in set (0.00 sec)
```

Uh oh. MySQL has decided to perform a full table scan. Actually executing the full query (rather than just explaining it) takes almost three seconds. Let's think about why MySQL made this choice.

We know that MySQL will use only one index per table per query, and the Headline table has an index on Id as well as one on ExpireTime. So why didn't it pick either one?

No matter which index MySQL selects, it has to perform a full table scan to satisfy the other condition. Queries using OR conditions prevent MySQL from easily eliminating candidate rows. So rather than use one index to find some of the rows and then perform the table scan, MySQL decides that it's faster to simply use a table scan. This is slated to be fixed in MySQL 5.0.

In a well-normalized database, queries like the previous one tend not be very common. But when they do occur, they can be real performance killers. Luckily we can sometimes rewrite them using a UNION.

To do this, we'll break the query into two queries that can each use a single index. Then we'll merge and sort the results. The result looks like this:

```
(SELECT * FROM Headline WHERE ExpireTime >= 1081020749
ORDER BY ExpireTime ASC LIMIT 10)

UNION

(SELECT * FROM Headline WHERE Id <= 50000
ORDER BY ExpireTime ASC LIMIT 10)

ORDER BY ExpireTime ASC LIMIT 10
```

The first query should be able to use the ExpireTime index while the second one uses the Id index. We must make sure to ask for the total number of rows desired (10) in *both* queries. The outer ORDER BY and LIMIT clauses will take care of the final sorting and counting.

It turns out that the UNION-based query runs in 0.02 seconds. That's far faster than the query it replaces. Just to make sure we understand what MySQL does, let's explain it:

```
mysql> EXPLAIN (SELECT * FROM Headline WHERE ExpireTime >= 1081020749
    -> ORDER BY ExpireTime ASC LIMIT 10)
    -> UNION
    -> (SELECT * FROM Headline WHERE Id <= 50000
    -> ORDER BY ExpireTime ASC LIMIT 10)
    -> ORDER BY ExpireTime ASC LIMIT 10 \G
*************************** 1. row ***************************
           id: 1
  select_type: PRIMARY
        table: Headline
         type: range
possible_keys: ExpireTime
```

```
            key: ExpireTime
        key_len: 4
            ref: NULL
           rows: 40306
          Extra: Using where
*************************** 2. row ***************************
             id: 2
    select_type: UNION
          table: Headline
           type: range
  possible_keys: PRIMARY
            key: PRIMARY
        key_len: 4
            ref: NULL
           rows: 1
          Extra: Using where; Using filesort
2 rows in set (0.00 sec)
```

Not bad at all. The second query needs a file sort operation, but at least it will use an index to locate all the rows.

## CHAPTER 6

Server Performance Tuning

The operating system your MySQL server runs on and the server's configuration can be just as important to your server's performance as the indexes, schema, or queries themselves. In this chapter, we will help you understand how to tune your server to improve performance, as opposed to tuning schema or queries. We'll be looking at changes to your hardware, operating system, and MySQL configuration to see what effects they have on overall performance.

We assume that you've already made efforts to boost the performance of your queries. If you haven't done that already, stop now and read Chapters 4 and 5 to get a handle on optimizing your queries and your application code. Only then should you worry about server settings. Hardware is often not the solution to MySQL performance problems. Poorly optimized queries can slow you down far more than not having the latest CPU or SCSI disk. To put this in perspective, one of the MySQL AB trainers even says that changing hardware might, in the best cases, give you a 10-fold performance increase. But tuning queries (and schemas) can *often* give you 1000-fold performance increase. Seriously.

Some topics covered in this chapter are platform-specific. The authors' knowledge of the various platforms on which MySQL runs is limited. In many cases, you'll need to consult your local documentation for various operating system tools and specifics.

We start with an overview of the factors that limit performance and then look more in depth at RAID, hardware, and operating system issues. The chapter finishes with a discussion of techniques you can use to locate, identify, and fix bottlenecks.

Performance-Limiting Factors

Before we can begin to think about what to adjust on a busy MySQL server, it's best to get an understanding of the various factors that affect performance and, most importantly, *how* they can affect it. One of the single biggest problems that most MySQL users face is simply not understanding how to go about finding bottlenecks.

Disks

The fundamental battle in a database server is usually between the CPU(s) and available disk I/O performance; we'll discuss memory momentarily. The CPU in an average server is orders of magnitude faster than the hard disks. If you can't get data to the CPU fast enough, it must sit idle while the disks locate the data and transfer it to main memory.

The real problem is that a lot of the disk access is random rather than sequential: read 2 blocks from here, 10 from there, 4 from there, and so on. This means that even though your shiny new SCSI disks are rated at 80 MB/sec throughput, you'll rarely see values that high. Most of the time you'll be waiting for the disks to locate the data. The speed at which the heads move across the platter and fetch another piece of data is known as *seek time,* and it's often the governing factor in real-world disk performance.

The seek time consists of two factors. First is the amount of time required to move the head from one location to the next. When the head arrives at the new location, it often needs to wait for the disk platter to rotate a bit more so that it can read the desired piece of information. The disk's rotation speed, measured in RPMs, is the second factor. Generally speaking, the faster the platters rotate, the lower the disk's seek time will be. When you're shopping for your database server's disks, it's usually better to spend the extra cash for the 15,000-RPM model rather than saving a bit with the cheaper 10,000-RPM model. As a bonus, higher RPM drives provide greater transfer rates because they're reading data from a faster moving platter.

This all means that the first bottleneck you're likely to encounter is disk I/O. The disks are clearly the slowest part of the system. Like the CPU's caches, MySQL's various buffers and caches use main memory as a cache for data that's sitting on disk. If your MySQL server has sufficient disk I/O capacity, and MySQL has been configured to use the available memory efficiently, you can better use the CPU's power.

A common complaint against MySQL is that it can't handle really large tables. Assuming the people making that statement have even used MySQL, they likely encountered an I/O bottleneck they didn't know how to fix. MySQL worked great with a few hundred megabytes of data, but once loaded up with 60 GB, it became slow. The conclusion drawn was that MySQL was somehow inadequate.

Of course, there are some circumstances in which MySQL can become CPU-bound rather than I/O-bound: they're simply not as common. If you often ask MySQL to perform some computation on your data (math, string comparison, etc.), the CPU will work harder. When running a CHECK TABLE command, you'll likely find the CPU pegged. And, of course, queries that aren't using indexes really tax it as well.

Memory

To bridge the gap between blazingly fast CPUs and comparatively slow disks, we have memory. With respect to performance, it's in the middle—significantly faster than disks but still much slower than the CPU. The underlying operating system generally uses free memory to cache data read from and written to disk. That means if you frequently query the same small MyISAM table over and over, there's a very good chance you'll never touch the disk. Even though MySQL doesn't cache row data for MyISAM tables (only the index blocks), the entire MyISAM table is likely in the operating system's disk cache.

Modern CPUs are even substantially faster than main memory. To combat this mismatch, chip makers have designed multilevel caching systems. It's common for a CPU to contain level 1, level 2, and even level 3 caches. The caches use significantly faster and more expensive memory, so they're generally a fraction of the size of main memory; a 512-KB L2 cache is generous.

With that in mind, simply adding memory to your server will improve MySQL performance only if the operating system can make good use of it by caching even more disk blocks. If your database is 512 MB, and you already have 1 GB of memory, adding more memory probably won't help.

On the other hand, if you run more than just MySQL on the server, adding memory may help. Maybe that Java application server you've been running is eating up a lot of the memory that could otherwise cache disk access. Keep in mind that Linux, like most modern operating systems, considers caching disk I/O an optional feature. It doesn't reserve any memory for it. So when free memory is low, MySQL can really suffer because MyISAM tables expect the OS to do some read caching.

MySQL's buffers and caches

By adjusting how much memory MySQL uses, you can often realize significant performance improvements. To do that effectively, you first need to understand how MySQL uses memory. Most of the memory MySQL allocates is used for various internal buffers and caches. These buffers fall into two major groups: *global buffers* and *per-connection* buffers. As their name implies, global buffers are shared among all the connections (or threads) in MySQL.

The two most important global buffers are the MyISAM key buffer (key_buffer_size) and InnoDB's buffer pool (innodb_buffer_pool_size). The MyISAM key buffer is where MySQL caches frequently used blocks of index data for MyISAM tables. The less often MySQL needs to hit the disk to scan a table's index, the faster queries will be. If possible, consider making the key buffer large enough to hold the indexes for your most actively used tables—if not all your tables. By adding up the size of the .*MYI* files for the tables, you'll have a good idea how large to set the buffer.

MySQL doesn't cache rows for MyISAM tables—only indexes. InnoDB, on the other hand, caches index and row data together in its buffer pool. As you'll recall from Chapter 4, InnoDB uses clustered indexes. Because it stores the index and row data together, it's only natural to cache the index and row data in memory when possible.

Network

The performance of your network usually doesn't have much bearing on MySQL. In most deployments, clients are very near the servers—often connected to the same switch—so latency is low, and available bandwidth is quite high. But there are less common circumstances in which the network can get in the way.

Duplex mismatch is a common network configuration problem that often goes unnoticed until load begins to increase. When it does, by all appearances MySQL is sending results very slowly to clients. But when you check the server, you find the CPU is nearly idle, and the disks aren't working very hard either. For whatever reason, there's a lot of 100-Mbit Ethernet equipment that has trouble auto-sensing the proper settings. Be sure your server and switch agree on either half or full duplex operation.

Some MySQL deployments use Network Attached Storage (NAS) devices, such as a Network Appliance filer, rather than local disks for MySQL's data. The idea is that if the server dies, you can simply swap in a new one without having to worry about copying data or dealing with synchronization issues. (See Chapter 8 for more on this topic.) While that's all true, in dealing with a configuration it's critical that your network be as uncongested as possible. Ideally, you'll want to have a fast dedicated network path between your MySQL server and the storage server. Typically that means installing a second Network Interface Card (NIC) that is connected to a private network with your storage server.

In a replication setup consisting of a single master and many slaves, it's quite possible to saturate a single network interface on the master with all the traffic generated by the slaves. This isn't because of something MySQL does horribly wrong. It's really just a matter of scale. Imagine that you have 50 slaves replicating from the master. Under normal circumstances, each slave uses a relatively small amount of bandwidth—say 100 KB/sec. That adds up to 5 Mbit/sec of bandwidth required for 50 slaves. If you're using 100-Mbit Ethernet, that's not a big deal. But what if your master begins getting more inserts per second, or large inserts that contain BLOB fields? You may reach the point that each slave needs 800 KB/sec of bandwidth to keep up with the master's data stream. At that point, you're looking at 40 Mbit/sec of data on your 100-MBit network.

At that point you should begin to worry. One hundred Mbit/sec is the network's theoretical maximum bandwidth. In reality its capacity is quite a bit less that. Many network engineers use 50% utilization as a rule of thumb for capacity planning. Once

Buying Server Hardware

When you shop for new database hardware, either with the intention to build yourself or to buy from a big-name vendor, there are many details to consider. What's the difference between the $4,000 server sold by a big name vendor such as IBM, HP, or Dell, and the seemingly equivalent $2,300 unit that your favorite "white box" company is selling? There are several, and some affect MySQL performance. Let's have a look.

Memory speed

The CPU can access data faster if it's stored in PC3700 memory than older PC133 memory. Be sure to get the fastest system bus you can and memory to match. The less time the CPU spends waiting for data to arrive, the more work it can get done in a given amount of time. Server-class hardware often uses Error Checking and Correcting (ECC) memory that can detect flaws in memory that result from aging and outside factors such as radiation and cosmic rays.

CPU cache

Frequently accessed memory is cached by the CPU in its level 1, 2, or 3 cache. The larger cache you can get, the better.

Multiple I/O channels

More expensive "server class" systems often have multiple, separate I/O channels rather than a single shared bus. That means the data moving between main memory and your disk controller doesn't interfere with the data path between the CPU and your network card. Again, this means the CPU spends less time waiting for data to arrive or depart.

Unfortunately, this difference doesn't show up until a the system is under a fair amount of stress. If you take a normal white box system and a server class system and compare them with a simple benchmark, they may score the same. The white box might even score higher. But when they are under real-world production loads, the white box could perform miserably.

Redundant power

Having multiple power supplies won't make your server any faster. It will, however, allow the server to keep running if the primary supply dies. Given the choice between good performance and no performance, choose wisely. And, if you plug them into different power sources, you're protected in case a fuse or circuit breaker dies.

Hot-swappable disks

Hot-swappable RAID disks are a valuable feature not all servers provide. Not having them means that you can survive a disk failure, but you'll eventually need to shut down the machine to swap out the bad disk. The only way around this is if there's room for a spare disk (or *hot spare*) the RAID system can bring online in the event of a failure. When running a RAID array in "degraded" mode (missing a disk), you're either sacrificing performance, redundancy, or both. You probably don't want to do either one for very long!

—continued—

On a similar note, many name-brand servers provide battery-backed RAID controllers that ensure unwritten changes do get written to disk when power is restored. This boosts performance as well, because the writes can be considered completed when they are written to the controllers memory, rather than actually waiting for the physical disk writes to complete. Unfortunately, the caches provided by most vendors are relatively small.

Gigabit network or multiple network ports

Server-class hardware typically comes with better networking options than your run-of-the-mill desktop or laptop. Specifically you'll either see gigabit Ethernet or dual Ethernet ports (often 100 Mbit). Having multiple network ports may be useful when setting up replication, as you'll see in Chapter 7.

It can be very tempting, especially if buying a number of servers for a cluster, to consider skimping on "the little things" like how much CPU cache is onboard, or the speed of the memory, because those little things, over the cost of a couple hundred machines, can add up. Resist that urge, when you are building a singer server or replication master. It is one of the few times that "throwing money at it" can make your life significantly more pleasant down the road.

On the other hand, if you want to build the next Google, your goal is probably to buy the greatest number of inexpensive machines as possible and to scale by simply adding more of them later on.

they consistently see utilization that high, they begin thinking about how to break up the network to better isolate the traffic. The trouble is, that doesn't help much in this case. Because there's a single master, all slaves must read from it.

There are three possible solutions to this problem. First, you can take a load off the master by introducing a second tier of slaves that replicate from the master. They, in turn, serve as masters for the 50 slaves. See Chapter 7 for more information about multitiered replication architectures.

Another option is to add a second network card to the master and split the 50 slaves across multiple switches. Each of the master's NICs are connected to a different switch. The problem is that you'd need to remember which server is on which switch port and adjust the slave configuration appropriately.

A final solution is to compress the data stream between the master and slaves. This assumes that the data isn't already compressed and that the master has sufficient CPU power to handle compressing 50 outbound data streams while handling a high rate of inserts. Given the rate at which CPUs are evolving, this will soon be feasible. Chapter 7 discusses options for encrypting and compressing replication.

Performance can become an issue when your network links have relatively high latency. This is typically a problem when the client and server are separated by a great distance or by an inherently high-latency link, such as dial-up or satellite. Your goal should be to keep the clients and servers as close (in network sense) to each other as possible. If you can't do this, consider setting up slaves that are close to your most distant clients.

At first glance, this may not seem like a server-performance issue, but a high-latency or low-bandwidth network can really slow things down on the server side. When a client performs a large SELECT on a MyISAM table, it obtains a read lock on the data. Until the SELECT completes, the server won't release the lock and service any pending write requests for the table. If the client asking for the data happens to be far away or on a flaky or congested network, it will take a long time to retrieve the data and release the lock. The end result is that things get backed up on the server side even though the server has sufficient CPU and disk I/O to do the work.

RAID

Nobody likes to lose data. And since disks eventually die, often with little warning, it's wise to consider setting up a RAID (Redundant Array of Inexpensive[*] Disks) array on your database servers to prevent a disk failure from causing unplanned downtime and data loss. But there are many different types of RAID to consider: RAID 0, 1, 0+1, 5, and 10. And what about hardware RAID versus software RAID?

From a performance standpoint, some options are better than others. The faster ones will sacrifice something to gain that performance—usually price or durability. In all cases, the more disks you have, the better performance you'll get. Let's consider the benefits and drawbacks of each RAID option.[†]

RAID 0

Of all the RAID types, RAID 0, or *striping*, offers the biggest performance improvement. Writes and reads are both faster in RAID 0 than in any other configuration. Because there are no spare or mirrored disks, it's inexpensive. You're using every disk you pay for. But the performance comes at a high price. There's no redundancy at all. Losing a single disk means that your whole array is dead.

RAID 0 should be used only when you don't care about data loss. For example, if you're building a cluster of MySQL slaves, it's entirely reasonable to use RAID 0. You'll reap all the performance benefits, and if a server does die, you can always clone the data from one of the other slaves.

---

[*] The "I" in RAID has meant, at various times, either "Inexpensive" or "Independent." It started out as "Inexpensive," but started being referred to as "Independent" because drives weren't really all that inexpensive. By the time people actually started using "Independent," the price of disks had plummeted and they really were "Inexpensive." Murphy at work.

[†] For a more complete treatment of this topic, consult Derek Vadala's *Managing RAID on Linux* published by O'Reilly.

RAID 1

Moving up the scale, RAID 1, or *mirroring*, isn't as fast as RAID 0, but it provides redundancy; you can lose a disk and keep on running. The performance boost applies only to reads. Since all the data is on every disk in the mirrored volume, the system may decide to read data in parallel from the disks. The result is that in the optimal case it can read the same amount of data in roughly half the time.

Write performance, however is only as good as a single disk. It can even be half as good depending on whether the RAID controller performs the writes in parallel or sequential order. Also, from a price point of view, you're paying for twice as much space as you're using. RAID 1 is a good choice when you need redundancy but have space or budget for only two disks—such as in a 1-U rackmount case.

RAID 5

From a performance standpoint, RAID 5, which is striping (RAID 0) with distributed *parity blocks*, can be beneficial. There are two disks involved in every operation, so it's not substantially faster than RAID 1 until you have more than three disks total. Even then, its other benefit, size, shines through. Using RAID 5, you can create rather large volumes without spending a lot of cash because you sacrifice only a single disk. By using more smaller disks, such as eight 36-GB disks instead of four 72-GB disks, you increase the number of spindles in the array and therefore boost seek performance and throughput.

RAID 5 is the most commonly used RAID implementation. When funds are tight, and redundancy is clearly more important than performance, it's the best compromise available.

RAID 10 (also known as RAID 1+0)

To get the best of both worlds (the performance benefits of RAID 0 along with the redundancy of RAID 1), you need to buy twice as many disks. RAID 10 is the only way to get the highest performance on your database server without sacrificing redundancy. If you have the budget to justify it, you won't be disappointed.

JBOD

The configuration sometimes called "Just a Bunch of Disks" (JBOD) provides no added performance or redundancy. It's simply a combination of two or more smaller disks to produce a single, larger virtual disk.

Table 6-1 summarizes various RAID features.

Table 6-1. Summary of various RAID features

Level	Redundancy	Disks required	Faster reads	Faster writes
RAID 0	No	N	Yes	Yes
RAID 1	Yes	2[a]	Yes	No
RAID 5	Yes	N+1	Yes	No

Table 6-1. *Summary of various RAID features (continued)*

Level	Redundancy	Disks required	Faster reads	Faster writes
RAID 10	Yes	N*2	Yes	Yes
JBOD	No	N/A	No	No

[a] Typically, RAID 1 is used with two disks. but it's possible to use more than two. Doing so will boost read performance but doesn't change write performance.

Mix and Match

When deciding how to configure your disks, consider the possibility of multiple RAID arrays. RAID controllers aren't that expensive, so you might benefit from using RAID 5 or RAID 10 for your databases and a separate RAID 1 array for your transaction and replication logs. Some multichannel controllers can manage multiple arrays, and some can even bind several channel controllers together into a single controller to support more disks.

Doing this isolates most of the serial disk I/O from most of the random, seek-intensive I/O. This is because transaction and replication logs are usually large files that are read from and written to in a serial manner, usually by a small number of threads. So it's not necessary to have a lot of spindles available to spread the seeks across. What's important is having sufficient bandwidth, and virtually any modern pair of disks can fill that role nicely. Meanwhile, the actual data and indexes are being read from and written to by many threads simultaneously in a fairly random manner. Having the extra spindles associated with RAID 10 will boost performance. Or, if you simply have too much data to fit on a single disk, RAID 5's ability to create large volumes works to your advantage.

Sample configuration

To make this more concrete, let's see what such a setup might look like with both InnoDB and MyISAM tables. It's entirely possible to move most of the files around and leave symlinks in the original locations (at least on Unix-based systems), but that can be a bit messy, and it's too easy to accidentally remove a symlink (or accidentally back up symlinks instead of actual data!). Instead, you can adjust the *my.cnf* file to put files where they belong.

Let's assume you have a RAID 1 volume on which the following filesystems are mounted: */*, */usr*, and *swap*. You also have a RAID 5 (or RAID 10) filesystem mounted as */data*. On this particular server, MySQL was installed from a binary tarball into */usr/local/mysql*, making */usr/local/mysql/data* the default data directory.

The goal is to keep the InnoDB logs and replication logs on the RAID-1 volume, while moving everything else to */data*. These *my.cnf* entries can accomplish that:

```
datadir = /data/myisam
log-bin = /usr/local/mysql/data/repl/bin-log
```

```
innodb_data_file_path = ibdata1:16386M;ibdata2:16385M
innodb_data_home_dir = /data/ibdata
innodb_log_group_home_dir = /usr/local/mysql/data/iblog
innodb_log_arch_dir = /usr/local/mysql/data/iblog
```

These entries provide two top-level directories in *data* for MySQL's data files: *ibdata* for the InnoDB data and *myisam* for the MyISAM files. All the logs remain in or below */usr/local/mysql/data* on the RAID 1 volume.

Hardware Versus Software

Some operating systems can perform *software RAID*. Rather than buying a dedicated RAID controller, the operating system's kernel splits the I/O among multiple disks. Many users shy away from using these features because they've long been considered slow or buggy.

In reality, software RAID is quite stable and performs rather well. The performance differences between hardware and software RAID tend not to be significant until they're under quite a bit of load. For smaller and medium-sized workloads, there's little discernible difference between them. Yes, the server's CPU must do a bit more work when using software RAID, but modern CPUs are so fast that the RAID operations consume a small fraction of the available CPU time. And, as we stressed earlier, the CPU is usually not the bottleneck in a database server anyway.

Even with software RAID, you can use multiple disk controllers to achieve redundancy at the hardware level without actually paying for a RAID controller. In fact, some would argue that having two non-RAID controllers is better than a single RAID controller. You'll have twice the available I/O bandwidth and have eliminated a single point of failure if you use RAID 1 or 10 across them.

Having said that, there is one thing that can be done with hardware RAID that simply can't be done in software: write caching. Many RAID controllers can add battery-backed RAM that caches reads and writes. Since there's a battery on the card, you don't need to worry about lost writes even when the power fails. If it does, the data stays in memory on the controller until the machine is powered back up. Most hardware RAID controllers can also read cache as well.

IDE or SCSI?

It's a perpetual question: do you use IDE or SCSI disks for your server? A few years ago, the answer was easy: SCSI. But the issue is further muddied by the availability of faster IDE bus speeds and IDE RAID controllers from 3Ware and other vendors. For our purposes, Serial-ATA is the same as IDE.

The traditional view is that SCSI is better than IDE in servers. While many people dismiss this argument, there's real merit to it when dealing with database servers. IDE disks handle requests in a sequential manner. If the CPU asks the disk to read

---

four blocks from an inside track, followed by eight blocks from an outside track, then two more blocks from an inside track, the disk will do exactly what it's told; even if it's not the most efficient way to read all that data. SCSI disks have a feature known as Tagged Command Queuing (TCQ). TCQ allows the CPU to send several read/write requests to the disk at the same time. The disk controller then tries to find the optimal read/write pattern to minimize seeks.

IDE also suffers from scaling problems; you can't use more than one drive per IDE channel without suffering a severe performance hit. Because most motherboards offer only four IDE channels at most, you're stuck with only four disks unless you add an additional controller. Worse yet, IDE has rather restrictive cable limits. With SCSI, you can typically add 7 or 14 disks before purchasing a new controller. Furthermore, the constant downward price pressure on hard disks has affected SCSI as much as IDE.

On the other hand, SCSI disks still cost more than their IDE counterparts. When you're considering four or more disks, the price difference is significant enough that you might be able to purchase IDE disks and be able to afford another controller, possibly even an IDE RAID controller. Many MySQL users are quite happy using 3Ware IDE RAID controllers with 4–12 disks on them. It costs less than a SCSI option, and the performance is reasonably close to that of a high-end SCSI RAID controller.

RAID on Slaves

As we mentioned in the discussion of RAID 0, if you're using replication to create a cluster of slaves for your application, it's likely that you can save money on the slaves by using a different form of RAID. That means using a higher-performance configuration that doesn't provide redundancy (RAID 0), using fewer disks (RAID 5 instead of RAID 10), or using software rather than hardware RAID, for example. If you have enough slaves, you may not necessarily need the redundancy on the slaves. In the event that one slave suffers the loss of a disk, you can always synchronize it with another nearby slave to get it started again.

Operating System

From an operating system point of view, there are several things to consider when building a fast MySQL server. We'll discuss numerous filesystem issues, swap configuration, and threading performance.

Filesystems

The proliferation of freely available filesystems in the Linux world has lead to a regular stream of questions about the best filesystem choice for MySQL on Linux. In a way, it's not all that different from choosing the right storage engine for your tables. You need to consider the benefits and drawbacks of each, as well as your needs. Unlike switching table types, however, you can't change filesystems on the fly. And without creating a bit of a maintenance nightmare, you can't easily use one filesystem for some tables and another for the remaining ones.

It's worth pointing out that filesystem performance is a relatively minor issue most of the time. If switching filesystems gives you your largest performance gains, you've done so many other things right, you deserve a reward.

This section is admittedly Linux-centric. That's primarily because Linux is the operating system with the widest variety of choices, and it's also because Linux happens to be what the authors are most experienced with.

Journaling

The biggest difference among the filesystems is journaling. Journaling filesystems maintain a log (or journal) that is never cached. The journal is similar in concept to a write-ahead transaction log. Whenever the filesystem is updated, a record describing the transaction is appended to the log. Another idle thread actually processes these transactions by writing the new data to the filesystem and flagging each processed transaction as it is completed.

If the machine crashes, the filesystem performs a roll-forward recovery, much as InnoDB would. Upon reboot, it simply finishes processing updates from the journal. Incomplete transactions in the journal are discarded, so the filesystem's internal consistency is guaranteed. This significantly decreases the complexity of running a filesystem check, meaning much shorter reboot times in the event of a crash. Even though InnoDB provides its own journaling (in the form of a transaction log), using a journaling filesystem with InnoDB is still worthwhile because of the time saved during an unexpected reboot.

Older filesystems such as Linux's ext2 and Windows FAT16/FAT32 provide no journaling. In the event of an unclean shutdown, they need to perform consistency checks upon reboot. On Linux, you must wait for *fsck* to do the job. On Windows, *scandisk* is what you end up waiting for. Luckily Microsoft's NTFS does provide journaling and it's the standard filesystem on Microsoft's server operating systems, Windows NT, 2000, and XP. In the Macintosh world, OS X provides a journaling option for its HFS filesystem. Tru64 and AIX also provide their own journaling filesystem implementations.

FreeBSD currently has no journaling filesystems available, but it does offer an alternative to journaling, known as *soft updates*. Developed by BSD hacker Kirk McKusick, soft updates ensure that metadata changes are written to disk in such an order that the data is always consistent. Doing this eliminates the need for a separate log and most synchronous disk operations while boosting performance through aggregated disk operations. More information is available on Kirk's web site (*http://www. mckusick.com/softdep/*) and in the FreeBSD manual pages for *newfs* and *tunefs*.

Solaris users who need journaling have traditionally purchased a filesystem product from Veritas, but newer versions of Solaris provide a journaling filesystem that eliminates the need for third-party software.

Other features and tweaks

Many of the newer filesystems (those designed in the past 10 years or so) have other important features that affect performance. Their designers realized that disk sizes were steadily increasing, and intensive new applications (high-volume databases, streaming video, etc.) could benefit from rethinking filesystem design. As a result, we have a good selection of high performance filesystems to choose from today. See the next section "Choosing a filesystem" for more details.

The two most notable enhancements in these newer filesystems are support for large directories and better management of fragmentation and free space. Large directory support means that operations on directories that contain thousands of files aren't appreciably slower than operations on smaller directories. This becomes an issue for MySQL only when you have a MySQL database that contains a large number of MyISAM tables. Since each table is composed of three files, the number of files can grow quickly.

Free-space management and fragmentation affect systems on which there are lots of MyISAM tables that change frequently (lots of deletes, inserts, and updates). Some filesystems are smarter than others about allocating contiguous blocks of disk space for files. This helps to reduce fragmentation, which means fewer disk seek operations when operating on the tables.

Choosing a filesystem

Choosing a filesystem for MySQL is a matter of considering your needs, the available filesystems, and your comfort level with them. Here we present a brief description of the options on modern Linux systems:

ext2

> The ext2 filesystem has been around Linux since the early days. It doesn't offer many advanced features, but it is time-tested and known for being very lightweight and reliable.

ext3

> ext3 evolved out of a desire to add journaling support to the ext2 filesystem. You can think of ext3 as simply that—ext2 with journaling added on. Most of ext2's limitations (such as poor performance with large directories) still exist in ext3.

One interesting byproduct of the ext3 implementation is that you can actually switch the ext3 journal on and off using *tunefs*. With the journal disabled, an ext3 filesystem effectively becomes an ext2 filesystem again.

ReiserFS

ReiserFS, originally created by Hans Reiser, has proven to be quite popular in the Linux world. It was built from the ground up as a modern filesystem. It handles large directories exceptionally well and has a very reliable journaling implementation. As of this writing, ReiserFS Version 3 is in widespread use, and ReiserFS Version 4 is being tested among kernel developers and other adventurous souls.

XFS

Ported by SGI from their IRIX operating system, XFS was designed to handle large filesystems with an emphasis on consistent performance. SGI was interested in creating a filesystem that held up under the type of heavy loads that are generated by high-end streaming media applications.

JFS

Like SGI, JFS came from another large technology company. IBM has been shipping JFS on their AIX platform for many years. Like SGI, IBM focused on performance and reliability when building JFS.

Table 6-2 summarizes the features implemented by various Linux filesystems.

Table 6-2. Linux filesystem features

Filesystem	Journaling	Large directories
ext2	No	No
ext3	Yes (optional)	No (patch available)
ReiserFS	Yes	Yes
XFS	Yes	Yes
JFS	Yes	No

FreeBSD

On FreeBSD, there are really only two filesystem types to choose from: UFS and UFS2. The main difference between them is that UFS2 can handle over 1 TB of data, and it has built-in access control list (ACL) and extended attribute support. Aside from the size differences, none of the differences really affect database users. If you have large directories, the UFS_DIRHASH kernel option may help. It creates in-memory hash tables for large directories, and it doesn't affect the on-disk layout.

Do you need a filesystem at all?

Traditional high-end database servers often don't use a filesystem at all. Instead, the database server bypasses the filesystem interface entirely and communicates directly

---

with the disks. This raw access method puts the burden of managing space, fragmentation, and read/write requests on the database server itself.

The historical rationale for bypassing the filesystem is that early operating systems didn't place much emphasis on filesystem performance. As long as they stored and retrieved data reliably, most people were happy. Another reason is that volume managers didn't really exist, so the operating systems of the day had no good way to combine the server's whopping 10-MB disks into a single, larger disk. When databases routinely exceeded the size of a single disk, vendors had little choice but to implement their own low-level storage.

Nowadays, modern disks are orders of magnitude larger, modern servers provide RAID, and modern operating systems often have volume managers that make adding more space a trivial operation. Despite these advances, many DBAs still use raw partitions rather than filesystems. Users coming from other database systems often ask about MySQL's ability to use raw disks, expecting it to boost performance even more. Not to be outdone, MySQL's InnoDB storage engine can use raw partitions for its tablespaces.

To take advantage of this capability, you must leave InnoDB's home directory unset and specify that the data-file paths point to raw devices:

```
innodb_data_home_dir=
innodb_data_file_path=/dev/sdb1:18Graw;/dev/sdc1:18Graw
```

However, you must first initialize the partitions. To do so, use newraw instead of raw the first time and start MySQL. InnoDB will the initialize the partitions. Watch the MySQL log file for completion, shut down MySQL, change newraw to raw, and start MySQL again.

From a performance standpoint, tests have shown a very small (2–5%) performance improvement using raw partitions. When you use raw partitions, you can no longer use any of your favorite command-line tools (*ls*, *du*, etc.) to investigate the storage. Furthermore, backups are more complicated when using raw disks. Your choice of backup tools is greatly reduced because most deal with filesystems rather than raw disk partitions.

Swap

In an ideal world, your server would never swap. Swapping is usually an indication that you don't have enough memory or that things are configured improperly—maybe MySQL's key buffer is too large, or you're starting too many unused services at boot time. Maybe it's the operating system itself. Some operating systems make a habit of swapping when there's still free memory available.

Some versions of the 2.4 Linux kernel, for example, are known for being a bit too aggressive with swapping. Linux has generally tried to use all available free memory for caching disk access. From the virtual memory subsystem's point of view, free memory is wasted memory. Early versions (2.4.0–2.4.9) were okay, as are later versions (2.4.18 onward). But the middle versions (2.4.10–2.4.17) were known for being a bit too aggressive. On a dedicated MySQL server, with a key buffer of 1 GB and 2 GB of total RAM, it was not uncommon to see Linux swap out parts of the key buffer while performing a table scan, only to swap it back in moments later. Needless to say, this had a very negative affect on performance. The only solution in such a case is to turn off swap entirely or upgrade to a newer kernel. Luckily, most other operating systems haven't suffered from this problem. Even though most systems are well behaved, some MySQL administrators advocate turning swap off as a preventative measure.

Threading

As a multithreaded server, MySQL is most efficient on an operating system that has a well implemented threading system. Windows and Solaris are excellent in this respect. Linux, as usual, is a bit different. Traditionally, Linux has had a slightly unusual threading implementation—using cloned processes as threads. It performs well under most circumstances, but in situations with thousands of active client connections, it imposes a bit of overhead.

More recent work on the Linux scheduler and alternative threading libraries have improved the situation. The Native POSIX Thread Library (NPTL) is shipped by default in RedHat Linux Version 9.0. Other distributions have just begun adopting it as well.

Another popular free operating system, FreeBSD, has threading problems that are much worse. Versions prior to 5.2 provide rather weak native threading. In some circumstances, I/O-intensive threads are able to get an unfair amount of CPU time, thus keeping other threads from executing as quickly as they should. Given the I/O-intensive nature of some database queries, this has a rather devastating affect on MySQL.

If upgrading isn't an option, build MySQL from the FreeBSD ports collection, and be sure to enable support for LinuxThreads. Doing so causes MySQL to use an alternative threading that's more like that available in Linux 2.4. Each thread is actually a process that, thanks to FreeBSD's rfork( ) call, has shared access to MySQL's global buffers. The overhead of this approach may sound like an issue, but it's really quite efficient. Many of Yahoo's hundreds of MySQL servers are using LinuxThreads on FreeBSD quite effectively.

The section "Solving Kernel Bottlenecks" later in this chapter discusses how MySQL's thread cache can help reduce the overhead associated with creating and destroying threads.

Techniques

With all the basic theory and recommendations covered, it's time to get down to business. When you notice your server is slow, what can you do about it? How do you locate the bottlenecks? What tools are available? What's the thought process?

The first step is to identify the type of bottleneck at the operating-system level. Using standard operating system tools, try to determine which of the server's resources are being taxed. Using *top*, *vmstat*, or the Windows Task Manager, check the machine's CPU utilization. If it's at or near 100%, it's obviously CPU-bound. Use *top* to verify which processes are responsible for the bulk of the CPU utilization. (If you don't have much experience with operating-system performance tools, consult a qualified system administrator.)

If MySQL is indeed consuming lots of CPU time, there are several techniques you can employ in an attempt to reduce the CPU load. See the section "Solving CPU Bottlenecks" later in this chapter. If the processes using the bulk of the CPU time aren't *mysqld*, you clearly have to solve a problem unrelated to MySQL. Perhaps it's a runaway process or simply something that should be moved to another machine. Either way, it's not a MySQL issue, so the problem is "solved" from our point of view.

If the CPU is very busy but there doesn't appear to be any obvious process or group of processes using a large amount of CPU time, look at the division between system and user time. If there's an unusually high amount of time being spent on system (kernel) tasks, that *may* be a sign of a MySQL configuration problem or something completely unrelated. See "Solving Kernel Bottlenecks" later in this chapter for an example of why MySQL might be working the kernel too hard.

If the CPU is relatively idle because it's frequently waiting for the disks, see the next section, "Solving I/O Bottlenecks." You'll know this because of the higher than normal numbers you see with *vmstat* and/or *iostat*. If the CPU is waiting on disk I/O because of swapping activity, however, go to the section "Solving Memory Bottlenecks."

Solving I/O Bottlenecks

Disk (I/O) bottlenecks tend to be the most common MySQL performance problem. They're typically caused by inefficient queries—meaning that MySQL has to read too many rows to locate the data you're interested in. Usually that means your queries aren't using an index, or they're using an index that's not terribly effective for this particular query. Before going much further, be sure you've reviewed Chapter 5.

Diagnosing a query that's not using an index is relatively easy. If you've enabled the slow query log (see the section "Identifying Slow Queries" in Chapter 5) and set log-long-format, MySQL automatically logs any query that doesn't use an index. You really need to start with that query: use EXPLAIN and do simple benchmarks when you have more than one way to write a given query.

After you've looked at any slow queries and fixed them, the next things to look at are more subtle issues. In some cases, queries do use an index and run relatively fast, so MySQL never considers them to be slow, but it's actually the wrong index from a performance point of view. There may be an alternative index MySQL can use to further decrease the I/O required.

Wrong index

Finding queries that use the wrong index can be more of a challenge. It requires an intimate understanding of your data and the queries being run against it. A real-world example may help to illustrate how subtle the problem can be.

Jeremy uses the mod_log_sql Apache module to record all his web site hits into a MyISAM table named access_jeremy_zawodny_com. The table is roughly 1.3 GB in size, contains over 6 million records, and looks like this:

```
+------------------+----------------------+------+-----+---------+-------+
| Field            | Type                 | Null | Key | Default | Extra |
+------------------+----------------------+------+-----+---------+-------+
| agent            | varchar(255)         | YES  | MUL | NULL    |       |
| bytes_sent       | int(10) unsigned     | YES  |     | NULL    |       |
| child_pid        | smallint(5) unsigned | YES  |     | NULL    |       |
| cookie           | varchar(255)         | YES  |     | NULL    |       |
| request_file     | varchar(255)         | YES  |     | NULL    |       |
| referer          | varchar(255)         | YES  |     | NULL    |       |
| remote_host      | varchar(50)          | YES  | MUL | NULL    |       |
| remote_logname   | varchar(50)          | YES  |     | NULL    |       |
| remote_user      | varchar(50)          | YES  |     | NULL    |       |
| request_duration | smallint(5) unsigned | YES  |     | NULL    |       |
| request_line     | varchar(255)         | YES  |     | NULL    |       |
| request_method   | varchar(6)           | YES  |     | NULL    |       |
| request_protocol | varchar(10)          | YES  |     | NULL    |       |
| request_time     | varchar(28)          | YES  |     | NULL    |       |
| request_uri      | varchar(255)         | YES  | MUL | NULL    |       |
| server_port      | smallint(5) unsigned | YES  |     | NULL    |       |
| ssl_cipher       | varchar(25)          | YES  |     | NULL    |       |
| ssl_keysize      | smallint(5) unsigned | YES  |     | NULL    |       |
| ssl_maxkeysize   | smallint(5) unsigned | YES  |     | NULL    |       |
| status           | smallint(5) unsigned | YES  |     | NULL    |       |
| time_stamp       | int(10) unsigned     | YES  | MUL | NULL    |       |
| virtual_host     | varchar(50)          | YES  |     | NULL    |       |
+------------------+----------------------+------+-----+---------+-------+
```

There are separate indexes on four columns: agent, time_stamp, request_uri, and remote_host. The intention is to provide an efficient way to produce statistics based on time, user agent (browser), the document fetched (request_uri), or the client (remote_host). Notice the indexes on each of those columns.

Most queries ran very quickly, but one particular query was problematic. It seemed to run longer than expected. After repeated execution and watching *vmstat* output, it became clear that a lot of time was spent waiting on the disk. The query attempts to find out which documents a given client has requested during a particular time range—usually a single day. It is run once for every client that requested anything in the past day. The request looks like this:

```
select request_uri from access_jeremy_zawodny_com
  where remote_host = '24.69.255.236'
    and time_stamp >= 1056782930
    and time_stamp <= 1056869330
order by time_stamp asc
```

Running the query through EXPLAIN proved to be quite interesting:

```
mysql> explain select request_uri from access_jeremy_zawodny_com
    ->     where remote_host = '24.69.255.236'
    ->       and time_stamp >= 1056782930
    ->       and time_stamp <= 1056869330
    -> order by time_stamp asc \G
*************************** 1. row ***************************
        table: access_jeremy_zawodny_com
         type: ref
possible_keys: time_stamp,remote_host
          key: remote_host
      key_len: 6
          ref: const
         rows: 4902
        Extra: Using where; Using filesort
1 row in set (0.00 sec)
```

MySQL chose to use the index on remote_host. But it doesn't always make that choice. Sometimes it decides to use the index on time_stamp. Here's an example:

```
mysql> explain  select request_uri from access_jeremy_zawodny_com
    ->     where remote_host = '67.121.154.34'
    ->       and time_stamp >= 1056782930
    ->       and time_stamp <= 1056869330
    -> order by time_stamp asc \G
*************************** 1. row ***************************
        table: access_jeremy_zawodny_com
         type: range
possible_keys: time_stamp,remote_host
          key: time_stamp
      key_len: 5
          ref: NULL
         rows: 20631
        Extra: Using where
1 row in set (0.01 sec)
```

The only difference between those two queries is the IP address we're looking for. In each case, MySQL's query optimizer estimates the number of rows it will need to read to satisfy the query using each possible index. In the first example, it decides that there are fewer records with a remote_host of 24.69.255.236 than there are records in the specified 24-hour time range. In the second example, it does just the opposite, deciding the time range will result in fewer rows to read.

By experimenting with various IP addresses, it doesn't take long to find one for which MySQL makes the wrong choice. It chooses the remote_host index when using the time_stamp index is actually faster—even though the remote_host requires reading the fewest rows.* How is that possible?

The underlying assumption is that all rows cost roughly the same amount of time to read. But this is a case in which that's not always true. Consider how the data will be stored in this MyISAM table. Apache is logging requests to the table all the time and has been doing so for over a year. Rows are never removed, so the data is already sorted by timestamp in the table and on disk (assuming minimal fragmentation).

Once you have a nontrivial amount of information in a table like this, the rules change a bit. If we assume that the records for a given IP address are evenly distributed among the millions of records, it's clear that using the remote_host index *may* result in many more disk seeks. And since disk seeks are slower than reading consecutive blocks from disk, it follows that MySQL may be doing less work (evaluating fewer rows) but the disk is doing more work—using precious seek time that may slow down other queries too.

In logging applications when you're frequently querying based on a time range as well as another indexed field, this problem is quite common and has no good generalizable solution. If you have some insight into your data and can add it to the software that writes the queries, that can help a lot. The software could be configured to tell MySQL which index to use. For example, if your software knows that a given IP address shows up only very infrequently recently, it can force MySQL to use the time_stamp range:

```
SELECT ... USE_INDEX(time_stamp) ...
```

It's not the ideal solution, but it is quite effective when used appropriately.

Temporary tables

Another problem that doesn't show up in the slow query log is an excessive use of disk-based temporary tables. In the output of EXPLAIN, you'll often see Using temporary. It indicates that MySQL must create a temporary table to complete the query. However, it doesn't tell you whether that temporary table will be in memory or on disk. That's controlled by the size of the table and MySQL's tmp_table_size variable.

---

* Using a USE INDEX specification in the query, you can test the performance of either index.

If the space required to build the temporary table is less than or equal to `tmp_table_size`, MySQL keeps it in memory rather than incur the overhead and time required to write the data to disk and read it again. However, if the space required exceeds `tmp_table_size`, MySQL creates a disk-based table in its `tmpdir` directory (often */tmp* on Unix systems.) The default `tmp_table_size` size is 32 MB.

To find out how often that happens, compare the relative sizes of the `Created_tmp_tables` and `Created_tmp_disk_tables` counters:

```
mysql> SHOW STATUS LIKE 'Created_tmp_%';
+-------------------------+-------+
| Variable_name           | Value |
+-------------------------+-------+
| Created_tmp_disk_tables | 18    |
| Created_tmp_tables      | 203   |
| Created_tmp_files       | 0     |
+-------------------------+-------+
```

If you create a lot of disk-based temporary tables, increase the size of `tmp_table_size` if you can do so safely. Keep in mind that setting the value too high may result in excessive swapping or MySQL running out of memory if too many threads attempt to allocate in-memory temporary tables at the same time. Otherwise, make sure that `tmpdir` points to a very fast disk that's not already doing lots of I/O.

As a last resort, consider using a tmpfs (or ramdisk, or mdmfs, or whatever your OS calls memory-backed filesystems) and setting $TMPDIR to point there when starting MySQL.

Caching

If your queries are already optimized and using the most efficient indexes, it's still possible to run into I/O bottlenecks at some point. Simply running too many queries, no matter how efficient they are, can become too much for the disk(s) to keep up with. If so, it's time to consider caching.

The easiest thing to do is make sure you're using the MySQL query cache. Available since MySQL 4.0, the query cache keeps the results of frequently executed SELECTs in memory so that MySQL doesn't need to perform any disk I/O at all. See the section "Query Cache" in Chapter 5 for more information.

Taking things a step further, you might consider application-level caching. If there's data that doesn't change frequently at all, query for it once in a while and store it in memory or on local disk until you requery for it.

Spread the load

If you've already covered the causes listed earlier and implemented the suggestions, it's likely that you need to spread the I/O load more effectively. As described earlier, installing disks with faster RPMs and lower seek times may help. Using RAID (especially RAID 0, RAID 5, or RAID 10) will spread the work across multiple disks, possibly eliminating or reducing the bottleneck.

Another option, if you have multiple disks and can't easily configure RAID, is to attempt to balance the disk I/O manually. Spend some time with *iostat* or *systat* (depending on your OS) to discover where the bulk of the I/O is going. If you have all your MySQL data on a single disk, you can try moving pieces to another disk. If the majority of activity is focused on a small group of tables, consider moving them to a separate disk.

Another approach is to separate predominantly random I/O from that which is mostly serial. Store logs such as the binary logs, replication relay logs, and InnoDB transaction logs, on a separate disk from the actual data files. It's ultimately a game of trial and error. As with benchmarking, keep a close eye on the numbers and try not to change too many things at once.

Finally, replication is always an option. If you've simply outgrown the capacity of a single machine, it's often the least disruptive solution. See Chapter 7 to learn all about replication.

Solving CPU Bottlenecks

CPU bottlenecks in MySQL can be difficult to track down. Unlike some database servers, MySQL currently doesn't provide per-query statistics about the amount of time spent actually doing work versus waiting for disk I/O to complete.

Luckily it doesn't have to be a complete guessing game. If you see a query in the slow query log and suspect that it may be CPU-bound, simply benchmark it. Pull out a copy of MySQL super-smack, and run it a few thousand times in a row. Then, in another window, watch *top*, *vmstat*, or your favorite system monitoring tool. If the CPU quickly hits 100% utilization even with a relatively low number of concurrent queries, the query is very likely CPU-bound.

If you find yourself staring at a very large list of slow queries, how do you decide which ones to start analyzing? Easy: look for those that examine a large number of rows (thousands, tens of thousands, or more), and focus on those that use any of MySQL's built-in data-manipulation functions. Common suspects are those that:

- Format or compare dates
- Encrypt data or compute hashes
- Perform complex comparisons, such as regular expressions

You'll often find that something as simple as computing an MD5 hash over millions of values per hour is using too much CPU time. By moving the logic into the application servers that query that database, you'll free up CPU time for work that only MySQL can do efficiently.

If you can't easily ask MySQL to do less work by moving logic into the application layer, you always have the option of throwing hardware at the problem. You can do this in one of two ways. You might simply upgrade the CPUs in your server or add more CPUs if there's room. Alternatively, you may find it less expensive and more scalable to add new servers, replicate the data to them, and spread the load among them. There's nothing wrong with using Moore's Law to your advantage once in a while.

High CPU utilization with MyISAM tables isn't *always* bad. It may mean that you are doing queries on tables that have been entirely cached in the operating system's cache. This may or may not be a bad thing. It's certainly better than reading from disk, but each time MySQL has to ask the OS for a block of data, that's CPU time that could be better spent processing the rest of the query. Moving to InnoDB or BDB tables lets MySQL cache table data itself, so it doesn't have to ask the OS for records.

Solving Memory Bottlenecks

Tuning memory usage on MySQL servers can be a delicate balancing act. As explained earlier, MySQL has some global memory buffers in addition to a number of per-thread buffers. The trick is to balance the performance gains that come from having large global buffers against the need to service a particular number of concurrent users. At a minimum, you should have enough memory available to handle MySQL's global buffers plus the per-thread buffers multiplied by the maximum number of concurrent connections you will use.

Expressed mathematically, that is:

```
min_memory_needed = global_buffers + (thread_buffers * max_connections)
```

where `thread_buffers` includes the following:

```
sort_buffer
myisam_sort_buffer
read_buffer
join_buffer
read_rnd_buffer
```

and `global_buffers` includes:

```
key_buffer
innodb_buffer_pool
innodb_log_buffer
innodb_additional_mem_pool
net_buffer
```

We say that's the minimum memory required because ideally you'd like some left over for the operating system itself to use. In the case of MyISAM tables, "spare" memory will often be put to use caching records from MyISAM data (.*MYD*) files.

In addition to any memory the threads may allocate in the process of handling queries, the threads themselves also require a bit of memory simply to exist. The thread_ stack variable controls this overhead. On most platforms, 192 KB is the default value.*

A likely problem is typified by an all-too-common scenario. Imagine you have a server with 1 GB of memory hosting a mix of MyISAM and InnoDB tables—mostly MyISAM. To get the most bang for your buck, you configure a 512-MB key_buffer after watching the key efficiency in mytop (see Appendix B) and a 256-MB innodb_ buffer_pool after checking the buffer pool and memory statistics from SHOW INNODB STATUS (see Appendix A). That leaves 256 MB that is used to cache data files at the operating system level as well as the per-thread buffers that are allocated on an as-needed basis. The MySQL server handles a relatively small number of concurrent users, maybe 20–50 most of the time, and the per-thread buffer settings are all left at their default sizes.

Things work very well until a few new applications are built that also use this MySQL server. These new applications need a significant number of concurrent connections. Instead of 20–50 connections on average, the server is handling 300–400. When this happens, the odds of several connections needing to allocate a per-thread buffer (such as the sort_buffer) at the same time increase quite a bit.

This can lead to a particularly nasty series of events. If a large number of threads need to allocate additional memory, it's probably because the server is handling a heavy query load. That can cause MySQL to allocate so much memory that the operating system begins swapping, which causes performance to degrade further, which means that each query takes longer to complete. With queries running more slowly, the odds of more threads needing memory increases. It's a vicious spiral.

The only solution is to restore balance between the system's memory and MySQL's memory needs. That means doing one of the following.

- Add more memory
- Decrease max_connections
- Decrease some of the per-thread buffer sizes

---

* If you happen to be using LinuxThreads on FreeBSD, the value is hardcoded in the LinuxThreads library. Changing MySQL's thread_stack setting will have no effect. You must recompile the library to change the stack size.

Be proactive. Monitor memory use on your servers. Do the math to ensure that in the worst case (hitting `max_connections` and each thread allocating additional memory), you'll still have a bit of breathing room.

Solving Kernel Bottlenecks

Though it's not common, you may find that MySQL doesn't appear to be using an overwhelming amount of CPU time, yet the machine is rather busy. There's little idle CPU. Upon looking at it more closely, you find that quite a bit of the time is spent in "system" rather than "user" or "idle." That's likely a sign that MySQL is doing something unusual to exercise the kernel—usually creating and destroying threads.

This happened at Yahoo! during the launch of a new web site. In September 2002, engineers were scrambling to create a September 11th memorial web site known as *remember.yahoo.com.*[*] On it, anyone could create a memorial "tile" by selecting a graphic and adding a customized message. The tile was then viewable by anyone visiting the site. To get the job done as quickly as possible, it was constructed using standard open source tools, including FreeBSD, Apache, PHP, and MySQL

The architecture was relatively straightforward, but we'll simplify it a bit to focus on the main point. A group of frontend web servers was configured to connect to a slave server by way of a hardware load balancer. Using the slave connection, the server could pull the information necessary to display the tiles. When a visitor created a tile, however, the web server needed to connect to the master to insert several records. The master was a beefier machine: dual 1.2-GHz CPUs, 2 GB of RAM, and a SCSI hardware RAID 5 disk array.

At its peak, there were roughly 25–30 web servers that needed to work with the master. Each server was configured to run roughly 30–40 Apache processes. That meant the master would need to support over 1,000 concurrent clients. Knowing that could tie up substantial resources on the master, the designers opted for a simplified approach. Unfortunately, the web application (written in PHP) was configured to use persistent connections. So, to keep connection numbers down on the master, the `wait_timeout` was set very low—to roughly 10 seconds.

By and large, it worked. Idle connections were dropped after 10 seconds. The number of connections on the master remained below 200, leaving lots of resources free. But there was a problem: the CPUs in the master were quite busy. Most of the time there was less than 10% idle time, and nearly 50% of the CPU time was being spent on system (rather than user) tasks.

---

[*] The entire site was conceived, designed, built, and launched in roughly two weeks using the spare time of handful of Yahoo's engineers.

After an hour or so of head-scratching, looking at system logs and the output of SHOW STATUS, a light finally flickered on in Jeremy's head. The value of Threads_created was very large and increasing at an alarming rate. The kernel was so busy creating and destroying threads that it was eating into MySQL's ability to use the CPUs effectively.

With that realization, the solution was easy. Increasing the thread_cache from its default value of 0 to roughly 150 resulted in an instant improvement. The system CPU time dropped to roughly 10%, thus freeing up quite a bit of CPU time for MySQL to use. As it turns out, MySQL didn't need it all, so the machine ended up with 20% idle time—breathing room.

## CHAPTER 7

Replication

MySQL use often grows organically. In the corporate world, a single application developer may build the company's next killer app on top of MySQL. This initial success with MySQL development typically breeds more projects and more success. As the amount of data you manage using MySQL grows, you'll certainly appreciate its ability to handle large amounts of data efficiently. You may even find that MySQL has become the de facto standard backend storage for your applications.

At the same time, you may also begin to wish for an easy way to copy all the data from one MySQL server to another. Maybe you need to share data with a remote office in your organization, or you might just like to have a "hot spare" available in case your server dies. Fortunately, MySQL has a built-in replication system. You can easily configure a second server as a *slave* of your *master*, ensuring that it has an exact copy of all your data.

In this chapter, we'll examine all aspects of MySQL replication. We begin with an overview of how replication works, the problems it solves, and the problems it doesn't solve. We then move on to the ins and outs of configuring replication. After that we'll consider the various architectures you can construct using various numbers of masters and slaves. We'll continue with a discussion of administrative issues, including maintenance, security, useful tools, and common problems. Finally, we'll look ahead to some planned changes and improvements for MySQL's replication.

 MySQL Versions 3.23.xx and 4.0.x have slightly different replication implementations. Much of the discussion in this chapter applies to both versions. There are sections that apply to only one, however, and they are explicitly noted.

Replication Overview

Database replication has an undeserved reputation for being complex to set up and prone to failure. The early versions of MySQL replication were difficult to configure because the process was inadequately documented. In its most basic form, replication consists of two servers: a master and a slave. The master records all queries that change data in its *binary log*. The slave connects to the master, reads queries from the master's binary log, and executes them against its local copy of the data.

Before peering under the hood, let's look at the types of problems replication does and doesn't solve. If you're reading this in the hopes of deploying replication to cure a problem, this section may help you decide whether you're on the right track.

Problems Solved with Replication

Replication isn't perfect, but it can be quite useful in solving several classes of problems in the areas of scalability and backups.

Data distribution

Need to maintain a copy of your data 10,000 miles away? Replication makes it trivial to do so. As long as you have decent connectivity between two sites, you can replicate a MySQL database. Think of this as scaling geographically.

In fact, it's possible to use replication over a network connection that isn't "always on," such as traditional dial-up using PPP. You can simply let the slave fail and reconnect (it'll keep trying for a long time). Or you can use one of the SLAVE STOP commands (described later) to disable the slave's replication when no connection is available. The master doesn't mind if a slave disconnects for a few hours and then reconnects. But you can't let the slave go for too long without reconnecting to the master, because the older record of changes will eventually be purged to keep the master from running out of disk space.

Of course, you can also use replication between two servers that sit next to each other. Any time you need multiple up-to-date copies of your MySQL data, replication is often the easiest solution. You can even replicate data between two MySQL servers on the same machine, which is often a good way to test a new version of MySQL without using a second machine.

Load balancing

If you use MySQL on a large data warehousing application or a popular web site, odds are that your server is running many more read queries (SELECT) than write queries (INSERT, UPDATE, and DELETE). If that's the case, replication is an excellent way to support basic load balancing. By having one or more slave servers, you can spread most of the work among several servers.

The trick, of course, is coming up with an effective way to spread the queries among the available slaves so they get roughly equal workloads. One simple approach is to use round-robin DNS. Assign multiple IP addresses for a hostname such as *db-slave*.

example.com, and your application will connect to one at random each time it opens a new connection to MySQL.*

A more sophisticated approach involves the same solutions that are used in web server load balancing. Network load-balancing products from Foundry Networks, Cisco, Nortel, and others work just as well for MySQL as they do for web sites.† The same is true of software solutions such as the Linux Virtual Server (LVS) project (*http://www.linuxvirtualserver.org/*).

Load-balancing techniques are covered in greater detail in Chapter 8.

Backup and recovery

Backing up a busy MySQL server can be difficult when your clients demand access to the data 24 hours a day. Rather than deal with the complexity of implementing a backup process that minimizes the impact on your clients, you might find it easier simply to configure a slave server and back it up instead. Because the slave will have an exact copy of the data, it's just as good as backing up the master. Plus you'll never impact the clients who are using the master. You might even decide that you don't necessarily need or want to back up the data as long as you have the "hot spare" slave database available in the case of problems with the master.

Chapter 9 covers backup and recovery techniques in more detail.

High availability and failover

Using replication, you can avoid making MySQL (or the system hosting it) a single point of failure in your applications. Although there's no out-of-the-box, automated failover solution for MySQL, you can achieve a good degree of high availability using some relatively simple techniques.

Using a creative DNS setup, you can insulate your applications from having to know which server is the master and minimize the effort involved in switching to a slave when the master fails.

Let's suppose you have two MySQL servers, *db1.example.com* and *db2.example.com*. Rather than hardcoding the name of the master in your applications, you can set up *db.example.com* as a CNAME (or alias) in DNS for your master. By using a very low Time To Live (TTL) on the DNS record, you can ensure that clients will not cache the information longer than necessary.

In the event your master goes down, simply update your DNS to point db.example. com at the new master. As soon as the TTL expires, your applications will pick up the new information and connect to the proper server. There will be some time during

---

* Some operating systems don't randomize this very well.

† That's not entirely true, as you'll soon see.

which the applications can't contact MySQL, but that time will be relatively brief if you use a low enough TTL.[*]

If you'd like to eliminate entirely the need to use DNS, you can play similar games using IP addresses. Because it's trivial to add and remove additional IP addresses from a server, a scheme like this may serve you well:

- Use an IP address for each role, such as 192.168.1.1 for the master and an address in the 192.168.1.100–192.168.120 range for each slave.
- Make sure each machine has its own primary IP address in addition to the role-based IP address.
- When the master goes down, any of the slaves can be scripted to pick up the IP address and immediately take over.
- The master should be set so that if it ever loses its master address or goes down, it doesn't automatically pick up the address again (i.e., it assumes someone else will).

See the "High Availability" section of Chapter 8 for more on the topic.

Problems Not Solved with Replication

Replication doesn't solve every problem. Performance can become an issue with replication because every slave still needs to execute the same write queries as the master. In a very write-heavy application, slaves need to be at least as powerful as the master. If you attempt to use replication to set up a load-balancing system, you may be disappointed. It may be more productive to implement a partitioning system with multiple masters—one for each partition of the data.

Also, there's no guarantee that a slave will be completely in sync with the master at any given moment. If the load on a slave is relatively high, the slave may fall behind and need time to catch up.

Network bandwidth and latency can also become an issue. If the slave is far away from the master (in a network sense) and there isn't sufficient bandwidth, a slave may be able to keep up with the master's query load, but it won't be able to get data fast enough to do so.

Let's look at two specific examples that illustrate problems not easily solved with replication.

---

[*] Be careful not to set it too low, however. The DNS resolvers shipped with some operating systems have been known to simply ignore TTLs that are deemed to be too low. When in doubt, test the implementation before depending on it to work.

Real-time data transmission

MySQL's replication isn't the ideal vehicle for transmitting real-time or nearly real-time data such as a stock quote feed or an online auction site. In those applications, it's important that the user sees up-to-date data no matter which database server they use.

The only way to combat MySQL's lack of any latency guarantee is to implement your own monitoring system. It needs to use some sort of heartbeat to verify that each server has a reasonably up-to-date copy of the data. In the event that a server falls too far behind, the monitoring system needs to proactively remove it from the list of active servers until it can catch up.

Of course, you can also build your application in such a way that it updates all the slaves with the newest data. However, that can add a lot of complexity and may not be worth the effort. You'd end up writing a lot of code to handle the exceptional conditions, such as when a single server falls behind or is intermittently inaccessible. Testing and debugging all those situations can be very time-consuming and difficult.

As Derek went over this, he thought, "Wouldn't it be cool if MySQL could provide a query response that signified, 'Go ask another server, I'm really busy right now'?" This would allow clients to automatically find willing servers in a multihost DNS rotation.

For example, the client wants to connect to *db.example.com* (which is *db1*, *db2*, and *db3*). It connects (randomly) to *db2*, and the server answers the query with "I'm busy; go ask someone else," whereupon the client knows enough to try *db1* or *db3*. Because the client library would be connecting to the same virtual server, it could transparently disconnect from the busy server and connect to some other (hopefully less busy) server.

As a result, all you would need is some automated way for a slave server to know how far behind they are and to shut themselves off from queries when they get too far behind, and you'd have some protection. Of course, this could also be subject to a cascading failure. If all the slaves are very busy, the last thing you'd want is for them to start removing themselves from the pool of available servers. Continue on to Chapter 8 for a deeper discussion of these issues.

Online ordering

An ordering system is different from a real-time stock quote feed or an auction site in a couple of important ways. First, the ratio of reads to writes is likely to be much lower. There isn't a constant stream of users running read-only queries against the data. Also, when users are running read queries, they're often part of a larger transaction, so you can't send those read queries to a slave. If you did, the slave might not have the correct data yet. Transactions aren't written to the binary log and therefore sent to slaves until they first commit on the master. A slave will contain only committed transactions.

Replication can still be very useful for an order processing system. It's reasonable to use a slave for running nightly reports and queries that don't need the most recent data.

Replication Performance

Having considered the problems that replication does and doesn't solve, you may still be a bit unsure about using it. Maybe replication is fast enough to get the job done, despite the lack of any performance guarantees built into the system. Wouldn't it be nice to have a general idea of how fast replication really is?

That's exactly what we wanted to know when we first began using replication—partly for our own sanity and partly because we knew a lot of people would soon be interested in MySQL replication. The first question they'd ask is, "How fast is it?" To answer that question, we devised the following simple test to measure the practical minimum replication latency in a particular environment.

A Perl script opened two database connections, one to the master and one to the slave. The master and slave were on the same 100-Mbit switched Ethernet network. The script then inserted a record into the master and immediately attempt to retrieve it from the slave. If the record wasn't available, the script immediately retried. We kept the records intentionally small, containing just an auto-increment column and a VARCHAR field into which we inserted the current time.

The results were encouraging. Of the 1,000 records inserted, 950 of them were available on the first attempt. That left 50 records that required at least a second try. Of those 50, 43 were available on the second attempt. The remaining 7 were there on the third try. The test was quick and very unscientific, but it can help to set realistic expectations.

Configuring Replication

With the theory out of the way, let's get our hands on some servers and configure a master and slave. We'll cover two scenarios. In the first, we'll assume that you have a fresh installation of MySQL on the master and slave, with no data on either server aside from the default test and mysql databases. Later, we'll examine the ways you can configure replication on a running master with minimal hassle and interruptions for your users.

On a New Server

Configuring replication on a new server is a straightforward process. The tasks you need to perform are:

1. Create a replication account on each server.
2. Add configuration entries in *my.cnf* on each server.
3. Restart the master and verify the creation of a binary log.
4. Restart the slave and verify that replication is working.

That's it. Four steps.

For the sake of clarity, we'll use the hostnames *master* and *slave* for our master and slave, respectively.

Account creation

When the slave connects to the master, it must authenticate itself just like any other MySQL client, so it needs a username and password. We'll create an account named *repl* with a password of c0pyIT! on both the master and slave.

Why create the account on the slave? Should the master ever fail, you'll want the slave to become the new master. When the old master is repaired, it can be put back online as a slave of the new master (which is the old slave). If the account didn't exist on the new master, the new slave wouldn't be able to replicate.

So, on each server let's create the account and give it only the minimum privileges necessary for replication: REPLICATION SLAVE and REPLICATION CLIENT. (In MySQL 3.23 you'd use USAGE and FILE.)

```
mysql> GRANT REPLICATION SLAVE, REPLICATION CLIENT ON *.* TO
repl@"192.168.1.0/255.255.255.0" IDENTIFIED BY 'c0pyIT!';
Query OK, 0 rows affected (0.00 sec)
```

After creating the account, verify that the settings are correct:

```
mysql> SHOW GRANTS FOR repl;
+-------------------------------------------------------------------------------+
|Grants for repl@"192.168.1.0/255.255.255.0"                                    |
+-------------------------------------------------------------------------------+
| GRANT REPLICATION SLAVE, REPLICATION CLIENT ON *.* TO 'repl'@'...' IDENTIFIED BY ...|
+-------------------------------------------------------------------------------+
1 row in set (0.00 sec)
```

If that command returns no rows or doesn't list the privileges, double-check that you entered the GRANT command properly.

Configuration file entries

The next step is to update the *my.cnf* file on each server. You need to tell the master to enable binary logging and to tell the slave about its master, login credentials, and so on.

Finally, each server needs to be assigned an ID number, known as a *server ID*. As you'll see later, the server ID is recorded in each server's binary log entries so that any other server can know which server first executed and logged a query. The server ID can be any number in the range 1–4294967295.*

So, on the master, make sure the following lines are present in the [*mysqld*] section of the *my.cnf* file:

```
log-bin
server-id = 1
```

The `log-bin` option tells MySQL to enable binary logging. By default, MySQL places the log file in its data directory. To place the logs elsewhere, you can supply a path and filename:

```
log-bin = /var/db/repl/log-bin
```

The slave requires a bit more information than the master. Add the following lines to its *my.cnf* file:

```
server-id = 2
master-host = master.example.com
master-user = repl
master-password = cOpyIT!
master-port = 3306
```

The slave's settings are self-explanatory. It just needs to know how to contact the master and authenticate itself. Later we'll look at some optional replication settings that can also appear in *my.cnf*.

Restart master

With the settings on the master, it's time to stop and start MySQL and verify that the binary log appears. No replication-specific method is necessary; simply stop and restart MySQL using your normal scripts that handle MySQL when the machine boots and shuts down.

If you didn't specify a path and filename after `log-bin` in your *my.cnf* file, MySQL writes the log files in your data directory. Otherwise, the logs are written in the location you specified.

You should find a binary log file with a *.001* extension. By default, the filename will be *hostname-bin*. On the host *master.example.com*, the first log file will be *master-bin.001*.

---

* A server ID of 1 is assumed if not explicitly assigned.

If you haven't run any write queries yet, the file will be less than 100 bytes in size. Each log file contains a short header and some meta information.

If you then execute a few write queries, you should notice the size of the binary log file increasing. If not, check the error log for hints about what might have gone wrong.

You can use the *mysqlbinlog* utility to examine the data stored in a binary log file. It reads the entries and prints out the SQL for each one. It also prints some comments that contain other helpful information. For example, running it on a fresh log produces output like this:

```
$ mysqlbinlog master-bin.001
# at 4
#020922 14:59:11 server id 1  log_pos 4        \
  Start: binlog v 3, server v 4.0.4-beta-log created 020922 14:59:11
```

The first comment indicates that this entry is at offset 4 in the log. The second comment indicates when the log was created, the server ID, the log version, and the server version.

Restart slave

With the master logging properly, a simple restart of the slave should be sufficient to get replication running. When a MySQL server is started, it checks to see whether it should connect to a master and begin (or continue) replicating queries. Upon connecting to the master, MySQL logs a message in its error log to indicate whether the connection succeeded or failed:

```
021103 13:58:10  Slave I/O thread: connected to master 'repl@master:3306',
  replication started in log 'log-bin.001' at position 4
```

This entry indicates that the slave has connected to the master and begun reading the binary log file *master-bin.001* at position (or offset) 4, that of the first query.

Run some write queries on the master and verify that the data on the slave reflects those changes. Once the slave is happily replicating from the master, it can continue to do so indefinitely.

On an Existing Server

Setting up replication on a new server is easy. A few config file entries and a couple of restarts are all you need. On an existing server, however, there's a bit more work to do because you can't simply point a new slave at a master and ask it to clone all the existing data.[*]

---

[*] There are plans to fix that in a future version of MySQL.

There are a couple of ways to do get the job done. We'll look at two specific solutions in a moment. First, let's outline the work that needs to be done; we'll deal then with common solutions.

What needs to happen

Normally, to enable replication, you have to add binary logging to your server, which means subsequently restarting the server. If you happen to have binary logging already enabled, you don't have to restart the server. As described earlier, you'll need to add at least two lines to the server's *my.cnf* file:

```
log-bin
server-id = 1
```

Optionally, specify a full path and base filename for the binary logs:

```
log-bin = /var/db/repl/binary-log
```

The other task involves getting a copy of all the data from the master and putting it on the new slave. But there's a twist. The data given to the slave must correspond to the exact moment in time the binary log begins. Said another way, the binary log should contain *all* the queries that are executed on the master after the snapshot was taken and *none* of the queries from before the snapshot.

If the binary log contains queries that are already reflected in the data given to the slave, the slave has no way to know that. Consequently, it reexecutes the queries, possibly producing strange errors or otherwise making the data inconsistent with what is on the master.

If the binary log misses a few queries that weren't reflected in the slave's copy of the data, it won't see those queries. This can cause strange and hard-to-diagnose problems. Maybe records that were supposed to have expired are still there, or perhaps there's data on the master that doesn't appear on the slave.

Getting the initial data from the master to the slave may be complicated. If you're using only MyISAM tables and can afford to shut down the master for enough time to copy all the data, it will be easy. Otherwise, you'll need to perform an online copy or dump of the data.

Snapshot or backup, then copy

The easiest way to get the necessary data is to perform a snapshot (online backup) or a more traditional offline backup and then copy the data to the slave. Using archive tools such as *tar* or *zip*, or your traditional backup software, shut down MySQL and copy the contents of the data directory to your slave; then extract the data on the slave.

This method works well if you intend to replicate all the data and can shut down MySQL for the time required to make a copy of the data. If, however, you can't afford to have MySQL offline for more than a few seconds, there's an alternative approach: restart the server once after making the config file changes and then perform an online snapshot of the data.

A snapshot works well only for MyISAM tables. InnoDB and BDB tables are best backed up when MySQL isn't running at all. A snapshot also requires a read lock on the data for the duration of the snapshot. So you'll be able to service read requests during the snapshot process, but all writers will be blocked.

To perform the actual snapshot, you can write your own script to do the job, or you can use *mysqlhotcopy* or *mysqlsnapshot*. If you roll your own script, you need to ensure that the binary log is reset before the locks are released. The easiest way to do that is by executing FLUSH TABLES WITH READ LOCK and then RESET MASTER (or FLUSH MASTER in versions older than 3.23.26).

Chapter 9 covers backups as well as the *mysqlhotcopy* and *mysqlsnapshot* utilities.

Online table copies

Another approach is to use MySQL's command:

```
LOAD TABLE mytable FROM MASTER
```

Doing so instructs a slave to load an entire table from the master. By writing a relatively simple script, you can instruct the slave to clone all the tables it needs using a series of those commands.

The usefulness of this technique is relatively limited, however. Like the previous option, it requires a master that isn't being updated. In an environment in which there are frequent updates to the master, this technique is simply not viable. Furthermore, the slave copies only the data from the master. It then reconstructs the indexes locally, for which large amounts of data can take hours or even days.

Online copy and synchronize (MySQL 4.x only)

MySQL 4.0 introduced the LOAD DATA FROM MASTER command. It combines the previous two approaches by first obtaining a read lock on all the master's tables, then loading each table one by one using the LOAD TABLE mechanism.* It respects any slave-side database or table filtering. Once it completes the loading process, it releases the locks on the master and begins replicating.

While this option is very appealing, it suffers from the same limitations as scripting the LOAD TABLE command yourself. It is much slower than using a master snapshot. It also requires that you grant the repl user SUPER and RELOAD privileges on the master. Finally, it works only with MyISAM tables.

---

* This doesn't include the tables in the mysql database. Put another way, LOAD DATA FROM MASTER doesn't clone users and permissions from the master.

Under the Hood

What really happens during replication? What does the binary log contain? What's different in Version 4.0? To help answer those questions, let's get deeper into the details and then walk through the steps that MySQL performs during replication. We'll start with an insert on the master and follow it to completion on the slave. We'll also look at how MySQL 3.23 and 4.x differ.

Replication in 3.23

MySQL's original replication code provides basic replication services. The master logs all write queries to the binary log. The slave reads and executes the queries from the master's binary log. If the two are ever disconnected, the slave attempts to reconnect to the master.

If you follow a query from start to finish, here's what's happening behind the scenes:

1. The client issues a query on the master.
2. The master parses and executes the query.
3. The master records the query in the binary log.
4. The slave reads the query from the master.
5. The slave parses and executes the query.
6. The slave performs a sanity check, comparing its result with the master's. If the query failed on the slave but succeeded on the master, replication stops. The reverse is also true. If the query partially completed on the master but succeeds on the slave, the slave stops and complains.
7. The slave updates the *master.info* file to reflect the new offset at which it is reading the master's binary log.
8. The slave waits for the next query to appear in the master's binary log. When one appears, it starts over at Step 4.

That's a relatively simple arrangement. The master simply logs any queries that change data. The slave reads those queries from the master, one by one, and executes each of them. If there are any discrepancies between the results on the master and the slave, the slave stops replicating, logs an error, and waits for human intervention.

The simplicity of this system has problems, however. If the master and slave are separated by a slow network, the speed at which replication can occur becomes bounded by the network latency. Why? Because the process is highly serialized. The slave runs in a simple "fetch query, execute query, fetch query, ..." loop. If the "fetch query" half of the loop takes more than a trivial amount of time, the slave may not be able to keep up with the master during very heavy workloads. The master may be able to execute and log 800 queries per second, but if the slave requires 25 msec to fetch each query over the network, it can replicate no more than 40 queries per second.

This can be problematic even with a fast network connection. Suppose the master executes a query that takes five minutes to complete. Maybe it's an UPDATE that affects 50 million records. During the five minutes the slave spends running the same query, it isn't pulling new queries from the master. By the time it completes the query, it's effectively five minutes behind the master, in terms of replication. It has a fair bit of catching up to do. If the master fails during that five-minute window, there's simply no way for the slave to catch up until the master reappears. Some of these problems are solved in 4.0.

Replication in 4.0

To solve the problem of slaves falling behind because of slow queries or slow networks, the replication code was reworked for Version 4.0. Instead of a single thread on the slave that runs in a "fetch, execute, fetch, ..." loop, there are two replication threads: the *IO thread* and the *SQL thread*.

These two threads divide the work in an effort to make sure the slave can always be as up to date as possible. The IO thread is concerned only with replicating queries from the master's binary log. Rather than execute them, it records them into the slave's *relay log.** The SQL thread reads queries from the local relay log and executes them.

To put this in context, let's look at the step-by-step breakdown for replication in MySQL 4.0:

1. The client issues a query on the master.
2. The master parses and executes the query.
3. The master records the query in the binary log.
4. The slave's IO thread reads the query from the master and appends it to the relay log.
5. The slave's IO thread updates the *master.info* file to reflect the new offset at which it is reading the master's binary log. It then returns to Step 4, waiting for the next query.
6. The slave's SQL thread reads the query from its relay log, parses it, and then executes it.
7. The slave's SQL thread performs a sanity check, comparing its result with the master's. If the query failed on the slave but succeeded on the master, replication stops.
8. The slave's SQL thread updates the *relay-log.info* file to reflect the new offset at which it is reading the local relay log.
9. The slave's SQL thread waits for the next query to appear in the relay log. When one appears, it starts over at Step 6.

---

* To keep things simple, the relay log file uses the same storage format as the master's binary log.

While the steps are presented as a serial list, it's important to realize that Steps 4–5 and 6–9 are running as separate threads and are mostly independent of each other. The IO thread never waits for the SQL thread; it copies queries from the master's binary log as fast as possible, which helps ensure that the slave can bring itself up to date even if the master goes down. The SQL thread waits for the IO thread only after it has reached the end of the relay log. Otherwise it is working as fast as it can to execute the queries waiting for it.

This solution isn't foolproof. It's possible for the IO thread to miss one or more queries if the master crashes before the thread has had a chance to read them. The amount of data that could be missed is greatly reduced compared to the 3.23 implementation, however.

Files and Settings Related to Replication

There are several files and configuration options related to replication in this chapter. Without going into a lot of detail on any one of them (that's done elsewhere), the files fall into three categories: log files, log index files, and status files.

Log files

The log files are the binary log and the relay log. The binary log contains all write queries that are written when the log is enabled. The `log-bin` option in *my.cnf* enables the binary log. Binary log files must be removed when they're no longer needed because MySQL doesn't do so automatically.

The relay log stores replicated queries from a MySQL 4.0 slave (from the master's binary log) before it executes them. It's best thought of as a spool for queries. The relay log is enabled automatically in 4.0 slaves. The `relay-log` option in *my.cnf* can customize the name and location of the relay log's base filename:

```
relay-log = /home/mysql/relay.log
```

Like the binary log, MySQL always appends a sequence number to the base name, starting with 001. Unlike the binary log, MySQL takes care of removing old relay logs when they are no longer needed. MySQL 3.23 servers don't use relay logs.

Log index files

Each log file has a corresponding index file. The index files simply list the names of the log files on disk. When logs are added or removed, MySQL updates the appropriate index file.

You can add settings to *my.cnf* to specify the log index filenames and locations:

```
log-bin-index = /var/db/logs/log-bin.index
relay-log-index = /var/db/logs/relay-log.index
```

Never change these settings once a slave is configured and replicating. If you do, MySQL uses the new values when it is restarted and ignores the older files.

Status files

MySQL 3.23 and 4.0 slaves use a file named *master.info* to store information about their master. The file contains the master's hostname, port number, username, password, log file name, position, and so on. MySQL updates the log position and log file name (as necessary) in this file as it reads queries from the master's binary log. While you should never need to edit the file, it's worth knowing what it is used for.

The `master-info-file` option in *my.cnf* can be used to change the name and location of the *master.info* file:

```
master-info-file = /home/mysql/master-stuff.info
```

However, there's rarely a need to do so.

MySQL 4.0 slaves use an additional status file for the SQL thread to track its processing of the relay log, in much the same way the *master.info* file is used. The `relay-log-info-file` setting can be used to change the filename and path of this file:

```
relay-log-info-file = /home/mysql/logs/relay-log.info
```

Again, you won't need to change the default.

Filtering

There may be times when you don't need to replicate *everything* from the master to the slave. In such situations you can use the various replication filtering options to control what is replicated. This is well covered in the MySQL documentation, so we'll just recap the important parts.

There are two sets of configuration options for filtering. The first set applies to the binary log on the master and provide per-database filtering:

```
binlog-do-db=dbname
binlog-ignore-db=dbname
```

Any queries filtered on the master aren't written to its binary log, so the slave never sees them either.

The second set of options applies to the relay log on the slave. That means the slave still has to read each query from the master's binary log and make a decision about whether or not to keep the query. The CPU overhead involved in this work is minimal, but the network overhead may not be if the master records a high volume of queries.

Here is the second set of options:

```
replicate-do-table=dbname.tablename
replicate-ignore-table=dbname.tablename
replicate-wild-do-table=dbname.tablename
replicate-wild-ignore-table=dbname.tablename
replicate-do-db=dbname
replicate-ignore-db=dbname
replicate-rewrite-db=from_dbname->to_dbname
```

As you can see, the slave options are far more complete. They not only offer per-table filtering but also allow you to change the database or table names on the fly.

Replication Architectures

Though MySQL's replication system is relatively simple compared to some commercial databases, you can use it to build arbitrarily complex architectures that solve a variety of problems. In this section we'll look at some of the more popular and exotic configurations. We'll also review how MySQL's replication design makes this possible.

The Replication Rules

Before looking at the architectures, it helps to understand the basic rules that must be followed in any MySQL replication setup:

- Every slave must have a unique server ID.
- A slave may have only one master.
- A master may have many slaves.
- Slaves can also be masters for other slaves.

The first rule isn't entirely true, but let's assume that it is for right now, and soon enough you'll see why it isn't always necessary. In any case, the rules aren't terribly complex. Those four rules provide quite a bit of flexibility, as the next sections illustrate.

Sample Configurations

Building on the four rules, let's begin by constructing simple replication configurations and discussing the types of problems they solve. We'll also look at the types of configurations that don't work because they violate the second rule. We'll use the simple configuration as a building block for arbitrarily complex architectures.

Each configuration is illustrated in a figure that includes the server ID of each server as well as its role: master, slave, or master/slave.

Master with slaves

The most basic replication model, a single master with one or more slaves, is illustrated in Figure 7-1. The master is given server ID 1 and each slave has a different ID.

This configuration is useful in situations in which you have few write queries and many reads. Using several slaves, you can effectively spread the workload among many servers. In fact, each of the slaves can be running other services, such as Apache. By following this model, you can scale horizontally with many servers. The only limit you are likely to hit is bandwidth from the master to the slaves. If you have

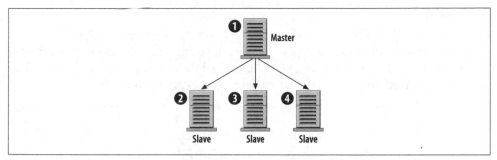

Figure 7-1. Simple master/slave replication

20 slaves, which each need to pull an average of 500 KB per second, that's a total of 10,000 KB/sec (or nearly 10 Mbits/sec) of bandwidth.

A 100-Mbit network should have little trouble with that volume, but if either the rate of updates to the master increases or you significantly increase the number of slaves, you run the risk of saturating even a 100-Mbit network. In this case, you need to consider gigabit network hardware or an alternative replication architecture, such as the pyramid described later.

Slave with two masters

It would be nice to use a single slave to handle two unrelated masters, as seen in Figure 7-2. That allows you to minimize hardware costs and still have a backup server for each master. However, it's a violation of the second rule: a slave can't have two masters.

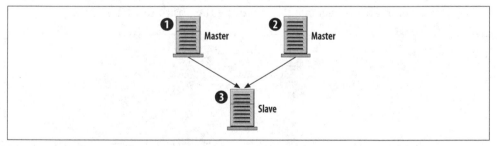

Figure 7-2. A slave can't have two masters

To get around that limitation, you can run two copies of MySQL on the slave machine. Each MySQL instance is responsible for replicating a different master. In fact, there's no reason you couldn't do this for 5 or 10 distinct MySQL masters. As long as the slave has sufficient disk space, I/O, and CPU power to keep up with all the masters, you shouldn't have any problems.

Dual master

Another possibility is to have a pair of masters, as pictured in Figure 7-3. This is particularly useful when two geographically separate parts of an organization need write access to the same shared database. Using a dual-master design means that neither site has to endure the latency associated with a WAN connection.

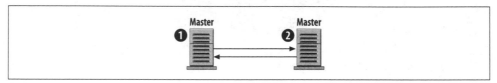

Figure 7-3. Dual master replication

Furthermore, WAN connections are more likely to have brief interruptions or outages. When they occur, neither site will be without access to their data, and when the connection returns to normal, both masters will catch up from each other.

Of course, there are drawbacks to this setup. The section, "Safe Multi-Master Replication," later in this chapter, discusses some of the problems associated with a multi-master setup. However, if responsibility for your data is relatively well partitioned (site A writes only to customer records, and site B writes only to contract records) you may not have much to worry about.

A logical extension to the dual-master configuration is to add one or more slaves to each master, as pictured in Figure 7-4. This has the same benefits and drawbacks of a dual-master arrangement, but it also inherits the master/slave benefits at each site. With a slave available, there is no single point of failure. The slaves can be used to offload read-intensive queries that don't require the absolutely latest data.

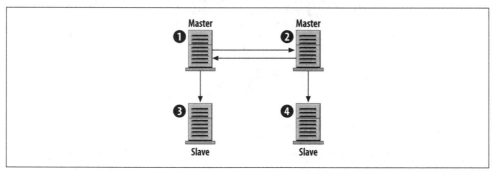

Figure 7-4. Dual master replication with slaves

Replication ring (multi-master)

The dual-master configuration is really just a special case of the master ring configuration, shown in Figure 7-5. In a master ring, there are three or more masters that form a ring. Each server is a slave of one of its neighbors and a master to the other.

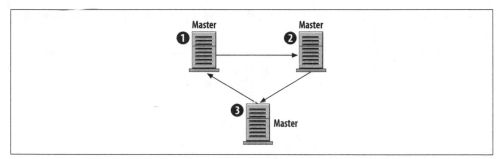

Figure 7-5. A replication ring or multi-master replication topology

The benefits of a replication ring are, like a dual-master setup, geographical. Each site has a master so it can update the database without incurring high network latencies. However, this convenience comes at a high price. Master rings are fragile; if a single master is unavailable for any reason, the ring is broken. Queries will flow around the ring only until they reach the break. Full service can't be restored until all nodes are online.

To mitigate the risk of a single node crashing and interrupting service to the ring, you can add one or more slaves at each site, as shown in Figure 7-6. But this does little to guard against a loss of connectivity.

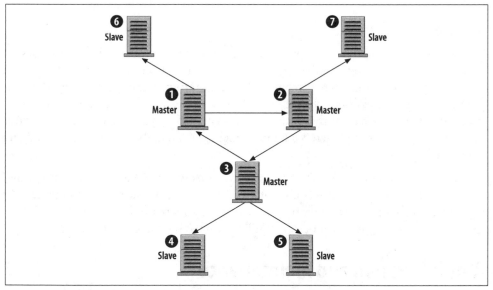

Figure 7-6. A replication ring with slaves at each site

Pyramid

In large, geographically diverse organizations, there may be a single master that must be replicated to many smaller offices. Rather than configure each slave to contact the master directly, it may be more manageable to use a pyramid design as illustrated in Figure 7-7.

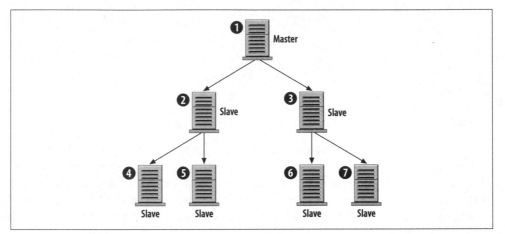

Figure 7-7. Using a pyramid of MySQL servers to distribute data

The main office in Chicago can host the master (1). A slave in London (2) might replicate from Chicago and also serve as a local master to slaves in Paris, France (4), and Frankfurt, Germany (5).

Design your own

There's really no limit to the size or complexity of the architectures you can design with MySQL replication. You're far more likely to run into practical limitations such as network bandwidth, management and configuration hassles, etc. Using the simple patterns presented here, you should be able to design a system that meets your needs. And that's what all this really comes down to: if you need to replicate your data to various locations, there's a good chance you can design a good solution using MySQL.

You can often combine aspects of the architectures we've looked at. In reality, however, the vast majority of needs are handled with less complicated architectures. As load and traffic grows, the number of servers may increase, but the ways in which they are organized generally doesn't. We'll return to this topic in Chapter 8.

Administration and Maintenance

Configuring replication isn't something you do every day (unless you're writing a book about MySQL, of course.) Once replication is set up and running, you're likely just to let it run. But there are a few administrative tasks you'll likely need to deal with at some point. You should, of course, consider automating them as much as possible.

Monitoring

Replication increases the complexity of monitoring MySQL's health. Are all the slaves replicating? Have the slaves encountered errors? How far behind is the slowest slave?

As you may have come to expect, MySQL provides all the data necessary to answer those questions (and many questions you probably haven't even considered), but extracting and understanding the data is something it won't do for you. In the section "Tools," later in this chapter, we'll try to provide some details to help you make sense of all the data MySQL provides, which should help you understand the tools that are helpful in processing that data.

Master status

Using the SHOW MASTER STATUS command, the master will tell you about its replication status:

```
mysql> SHOW MASTER STATUS \G
*************************** 1. row ***************************
            File: binary-log.004
        Position: 635904327
    Binlog_do_db:
Binlog_ignore_db:
1 row in set (0.00 sec)
```

The output includes the current binary log filename and the position (or offset) into the binary log where the next query will be written. The other two fields correspond to the binlog-do-db and binlog-ignore-db filtering options in the server's *my.cnf* file. If you are filtering binary log records on the master, one or both of these will list the database names affected by your filters.

You can also ask the master which binary logs still exist on disk:

```
mysql> SHOW MASTER LOGS;
+----------------+
| Log_name       |
+----------------+
| binary-log.001 |
| binary-log.002 |
| binary-log.003 |
| binary-log.004 |
+----------------+
4 rows in set (0.02 sec)
```

But the output is quite limited. It would be helpful to know the sizes and ages of the files as well. MySQL is doing little more than reading and displaying the contents of the *log-bin.index* file. To get more information, you need to log on to the server and examine the files by hand.

Slave status

There is significantly more information available on the slave side of replication, mostly because the slaves have more information to keep track of. To start, the SHOW SLAVE STATUS command provides a good summary of the information from both the *master.info* and *relay-log.info* files:

```
mysql> SHOW SLAVE STATUS \G
*************************** 1. row ***************************
          Master_Host: master.example.com
          Master_User: repl
          Master_Port: 3306
        Connect_retry: 15
      Master_Log_File: binary-log.004
  Read_Master_Log_Pos: 635904807
       Relay_Log_File: relay-log.004
        Relay_Log_Pos: 846096118
Relay_Master_Log_File: binary-log.004
     Slave_IO_Running: Yes
    Slave_SQL_Running: Yes
      Replicate_do_db:
  Replicate_ignore_db:
           Last_errno: 0
           Last_error:
         Skip_counter: 0
    Exec_master_log_pos: 635904807
       Relay_log_space: 846096122
1 row in set (0.00 sec)
```

In addition, there is some other metadata in the output. The Last_errno and Last_error fields provide information about the most recent replication-related error, if any. The Relay_log_space tells you how much space the relay log is consuming.

The two most important fields are Slave_IO_Running and Slave_SQL_Running. They tell you if the IO and slave threads are running.

Replication heartbeat

Watching the values produced by SHOW MASTER STATUS and SHOW SLAVE STATUS can give you a rough idea of how up to date a slave is. The trouble with relying on that information is that you're only looking at bytes. You can determine how many more bytes of log data the slave needs to execute before it is current. However, that doesn't tell you how many queries need to be executed. There's no good way to figure that out, short of running the binary log through *mysqlbinlog* and counting queries.

It is possible to determine how out of date the slave is with some degree of accuracy by implementing a simple heartbeat system. The heartbeat principle is easy. At a fixed interval, say 20 seconds, a process on the master inserts a record with the latest timestamp into a table. On the slave, a corresponding process reads the most recent record every 20 seconds. Assuming that the system clocks on both machines are in sync, you can tell how far behind the slave is to within 20 seconds of accuracy.

See the *write_heartbeat* and *read_heartbeat* scripts in the "Tools" section for a sample implementation.

Log Rotation

Binary log files accumulate on the server until they are explicitly removed. The SHOW MASTER LOGS command tells you how many logs there are at any given time. To remove one or more logs, use the PURGE MASTER LOGS TO ... command. It removes all the logs up to but not including the given log name.

Here's an example:

```
mysql> SHOW MASTER LOGS;
+----------------+
| Log_name       |
+----------------+
| binary-log.001 |
| binary-log.002 |
| binary-log.003 |
| binary-log.004 |
+----------------+
4 rows in set (0.02 sec)

mysql> PURGE MASTER LOGS TO 'binary-log.004';
```

The command tells MySQL to remove *binary-log.001*, *binary-log.002*, and *binary-log.003*. Be careful not to remove logs too quickly. If a slave is offline for a significant period of time, there's a chance that it still needs one or more of the logs you removed. If you're in doubt, run SHOW SLAVE STATUS on each slave to verify which log it is using.

To automate this process, see the purge_binary_logs script in the "Tools" section.

Changing Masters

Sooner or later you'll need to point your slaves at a new master. Maybe the old one is being replaced with a newer, faster computer; perhaps there was a failure, and you are promoting a slave to master. In MySQL 3.23 and 4.0, you need to inform the slaves about their new master. A future version of MySQL is supposed to include a fail-safe replication feature that automates the process.

A planned changing of masters is a straightforward process. (In the event of a master failure, it may not be so easy.) You simply need to issue the CHANGE MASTER TO ... command on each slave. In doing so, you inform the slave of the new master's parameters—the same ones specified in the *my.cnf* file. The slave will begin replicating from its new master, and MySQL will also update the *master.info* with the new information.

Using the right values

As usual, the devil is in the details. How do you decide which values to use? What if you get them wrong?

First, let's consider the easy case. If you are in control of the situation, the process is easy. Follow these steps:

1. Disconnect all clients (not slaves) from the master.
2. Make sure the new master is completely caught up.
3. Execute RESET MASTER on the new master.
4. Make sure each slave is caught up.
5. Shut down the old master.
6. Let all clients connect to the new master.
7. Issue a CHANGE MASTER TO ... command on each slave, pointing it to the new master.

The RESET MASTER command tells the master to flush all its binary logs and start fresh. By starting with a clean slate on the new master, there's no guesswork involved in determining the right log position. Since it's a brand new log, we know the position is 4, because each binary log has a 4-byte header that consumes positions 0–3.

The complete CHANGE MASTER TO ... command looks like this:

```
mysql> CHANGE MASTER TO
    -> MASTER_HOST='newmaster.example.com',
    -> MASTER_USER='repl',
    -> MASTER_PASSWORD='MySecret!',
    -> MASTER_PORT=3306,
    -> MASTER_LOG_FILE='log-bin.001',
    -> MASTER_LOG_POS=4;
```

If, on the other hand, the master crashes and you can't bring it back online in a reasonable amount of time, things aren't so clear-cut. If you have only one slave, of course, there's no decision to make. You use the slave. But if you have multiple slaves, you need to determine which one is the most up to date.

By examining the output of SHOW SLAVE STATUS on each slave, you can easily determine which one is closest to matching the master at the time it crashed. Once you know the log name and position, you can construct a CHANGE MASTER TO ... command to run on the remaining slaves.

In doing so, however, you'll likely cause some the slaves to be slightly out of sync with their new master. To illustrate why, assume that each query is assigned an increasing unique ID number. The original master had just executed query 500 when it crashed. The "most up-to-date" slave, the new master, had executed query 496. That means that your best slave is missing four queries, and there's no way to recover them unless your application logs every query it writes, which is unlikely.

Now, let's assume that there are two more slaves, *slave2* and *slave3*; *slave2* executed query 490, and *slave3* executed query 493. You have a choice. You can either point both slaves at the new master's current position (query 496) or you can try to figure the corresponding offsets for each slave in the new master's binary log. That will take more time, but it means you lose less data.

To find the matching log position for each slave, you need to have the binary log enabled on each slave. Use the *mysqlbinlog* command (described in the "Tools" section) to locate the last query executed. Then locate exactly the same query in the new master's binary log. Once you find the query, you'll have the offset you need. The output of *mysqlbinlog* always includes the offset in a comment right before the query. For example:

```
$ mysqlbinlog log-bin.001
...
# at 683
#021103 18:36:33 server id 1  log_pos 683   Query  thread_id=288 exec_time=0
error_code=0
SET TIMESTAMP=1036377393;
insert into test1 values (8);
```

The # at 683 line lists the position of the insert into test1 values (8) query in the log.

Tools

In this section, we'll look at some tools that can make dealing with replication a bit easier. A couple of the tools come straight out of the MySQL distribution, while others are home-grown and often ripe for improvement. The home-grown tools can serve as a starting point for solving your specific needs; such tools are available (and kept up to date) at *http://highperformancemysql.com*.

mysqlbinlog: Viewing data in logs

The *mysqlbinlog* utility has been mentioned several times in this chapter. It is used to decode the binary formats used by the binary log and relay log. Given a log file, it outputs the SQL queries contained in the log. Furthermore, it precedes each query with several pieces of metadata as comments.

```
$ mysql log-bin.001
...
# at 683
#021103 18:36:33 server id 1  log_pos 683   Query  thread_id=288 exec_time=0
error_code=0
SET TIMESTAMP=1036377393;
insert into test1 values (8);
```

The first line contains the offset (or position) of the query in the log. The second line begins with a date and timestamp followed by the server ID of the server that first executed the query. The log position is repeated on this line and followed by the event type.

Finally, there's the ID of the thread that executed the query, followed by the time the query took to execute (in seconds) and the error code generated by the query.

You can use *mysqlbinlog* to pull the logs from a remote server by specifying a hostname, username, and password. Using the -o command-line option, you can specify the offset from which you'd like to start reading. For example:

```
$ mysqlbinlog -h slave3.example.com -u root -p -o 35532 log-bin.032
```

check_repl: Ensuring that replication takes place

As discussed earlier, it's important to check that your slaves are replicating properly when you expect them to. The following script connects to the local MySQL server and makes sure that replication is running by examining the output of SHOW SLAVE STATUS and checking for the both the 3.23.xx and 4.x values:

```perl
#!/usr/bin/perl -w

## On a slave server, check to see that the slave hasn't stopped.

use strict;
use DBIx::DWIW;

my $conn = DBIx::DWIW->Connect(
    DB     => "mysql",
    User   => "root",
    Pass   => "password",
    Host   => "localhost",
) or exit;

my $info = $conn->Hash("SHOW SLAVE STATUS");

if (exists $info->{Slave_SQL_Running} and $info->{Slave_SQL_Running} eq 'No')
{
    warn "slave SQL thread has stopped\n";
}
elsif (exists $info->{Slave_IO_Running} and $info->{Slave_IO_Running} eq 'No')
{
    warn "slave IO thread has stopped\n";
}
elsif (exists $info->{Slave_Running} and $info->{Slave_Running} eq 'No')
{
    warn "slave has stopped\n";
}
```

This script makes no effort to repair a problem; it simply reports when something is wrong. Without knowing why the failure occurred, it's probably not wise to blindly restart replication. To skip the problem query and restart replication, see the next section.

fix_repl: Skipping a bad query to continue replication

In the event that replication has stopped on a slave, you should tell the slave to skip the problem query and continue, unless the problem warrants further investigation. No restart of MySQL is necessary.

In MySQL 3.23.xx, execute:

```
SET SQL_SLAVE_SKIP_COUNTER=1
SLAVE START
```

In Versions 4.0.0–4.0.2, execute:

```
SET SQL_SLAVE_SKIP_COUNTER=1
SLAVE START SQL_THREAD
```

In Version 4.0.3 and beyond, execute:

```
SET GLOBAL SQL_SLAVE_SKIP_COUNTER=1
SLAVE START SQL_THREAD
```

Yuck. If you're using a mixture of 3.23.xx and 4.0.x servers, it may be difficult to remember the exact syntax for each version. It's much easier to have a copy of the following *fix_repl* script on hand to do the hard work for you:

```perl
#!/usr/local/bin/perl -w
#
# fix mysql replication if it encounters a problem

$|=1;        # unbuffer stdout

use strict;
use DBIx::DWIW;

my $host = shift || 'localhost';
my $conn = DBIx::DWIW->Connect(
    DB   => "mysql",
    User => "root",
    Pass => "pa55word",
    Host => $host,
) or die "Couldn't connect to database!";

print "checking $host ... ";

my $info = $conn->Hash("SHOW SLAVE STATUS");
my $version = $conn->Scalar("SHOW VARIABLES LIKE 'Version'");
my $fix_cmd;
my $start_cmd;

# 3.23
if ($version =~ /^3\.23/ and $info->{Slave_Running} eq 'No')
{
    $fix_cmd = "SET SQL_SLAVE_SKIP_COUNTER = 1";
    $start_cmd = "SLAVE START";
}
```

```
# 4.0.0 - 4.0.2
elsif ($version =~ /^4\.0\.[012]/ and $info->{Slave_SQL_Running} eq 'No')
{
    $fix_cmd = "SET SQL_SLAVE_SKIP_COUNTER = 1";
    $start_cmd = "SLAVE START SQL_THREAD";
}

# 4.0.3 - 4.0.xx, 4.1.xx.  Don't know what 5.0 will be like.
elsif ($version =~ /^4\.[01]\./ and $info->{Slave_SQL_Running} eq 'No')
{
    $fix_cmd = "SET GLOBAL SQL_SLAVE_SKIP_COUNTER = 1";
    $start_cmd = "SLAVE START SQL_THREAD";
}

# things are okay or unknown version?
else
{
    print "GOOD\n";
    exit;
}

print "FIXING ... ";
$conn->Execute($fix_cmd);
$conn->Execute($start_cmd);
print "DONE\n";

exit;
```

Be careful with this technique. Blindly skipping queries on a slave may cause it to become out of sync with the master. If the query is failing due to a duplicate key error, it's probably safe, but you should investigate how that happened in the first place.

purge_binary_logs: Reclaiming space used by binary logs

To make log rotation easier, you can use something like the following *purge_binary_logs* Perl script. It connects to the specified server and checks to see how many binary logs are sitting around. If there are more than the specified threshold, it removes any extras.

```
#!/usr/bin/perl -w

## On a slave server, purge the replication logs if there are too many
## sitting around sucking up disk space.

use strict;
use DBIx::DWIW;

my $MIN_LOGS = 4; ## keep main log plus three old binary logs around

my $conn = DBIx::DWIW->Connect(
    DB   => "mysql",
    User => "root",
```

```
        Pass => "password",
        Host => 'localhost',
    );

    die "Couldn't connect to database!" if not $conn;

    ## see if there are enough to bother, exit if not
    my @logs = $conn->FlatArray("SHOW MASTER LOGS");
    exit if (@logs < $MIN_LOGS);

    ## if so, figure out what the last one we want to keep is, then purge
    ## the rest
    my $last_log = $logs[-$MIN_LOGS];
    print "last log is $last_log\n" unless $ENV{CRON};
    $conn->Execute("PURGE MASTER LOGS TO '$last_log'");

    exit;
```

Depending on your needs, there's a lot of room for improvement in this script. It would be nice if the script took command-line arguments so you wouldn't need to hardcode the hostname, password, and so on. It would also be nice if the script could check the sizes of the log files. If a master is restarted very frequently, using the number of log files as a metric probably isn't as useful as checking the volume of log data. However, the script can't be run remotely if it checked log file sizes, because it needs to examine the files directly.

A valuable but difficult addition would be for the script to remove logs only if it can tell that all slaves had already read them. That requires knowing all the slaves and contacting each one to verify its progress in the replication process.

mysqldiff: Replication sanity checks

As with anything new, you may not trust replication right away. To help convince yourself that it is really doing what it should do, it's good to perform spot checks on the data, making sure that the slaves have exactly the data they should have.

This checking can be done to varying degrees of paranoia:

- Simple metadata checks: make sure each table on the slaves contains the same number of rows that the same master table does.
- Verify all or some of the data by comparing rows on the master and slaves.
- Perform application-specific checks by running custom queries and comparing the results across servers.

The first check is quite easy to implement with a bit of Perl code:

```
#!/usr/bin/perl -w

use strict;
use DBIx::DWIW;
```

```perl
$|=1;        # unbuffer stdout

my $db_user = 'root';
my $db_pass = 'password';
my $db_name = 'test';
my $master  = 'master.example.com';

my @slaves = qw(
    slave1.example.com
    slave2.example.com
    slave3.example.com
);

my %master_count;

for my $server ($master)
{
    print "Checking master... ";
    my $conn = DBIx::DWIW->Connect(User => $db_user, Host => $server,
        Pass => $db_pass, DB => $db_name) or die "$!";

    for my $table ($conn->FlatArray("SHOW TABLES"))
    {
        my $count = $conn->Scalar("SELECT COUNT(*) FROM '$table'");
        $master_count{$table} = $count;
    }
    print "OK\n";
}

for my $server (@slaves)
{
    print "Checking $server... ";
    my $conn = DBIx::DWIW->Connect(User => $db_user, Host => $server,
        Pass => $db_pass, DB => $db_name) or die "$!";

    for my $table ($conn->FlatArray("SHOW TABLES"))
    {
        my $count = $conn->Scalar("SELECT COUNT(*) FROM '$table'");

        if ($count != $master_count{$table})
        {
            print "MISMATCH (got $count on $table, expecting $master_count{$table}\n";
        }
    }
    print "OK\n";
}

exit;
```

The script connects to the master and gets the number of rows in each table of the given database. Then it connects to each slave and checks to see that the counts match. If they don't, it issues a MISMATCH warning.

This framework can easily be extended to handle multiple databases, perform more specific checks, and even attempt to take corrective action. It is even ready to handle multiple masters.

write_heartbeat: Generating a periodic health check heartbeat

The following script can implement a heartbeat monitoring system as described earlier. To use it, create a database named MySQL_Admin and a table named Heartbeat with the following structure:

```
CREATE TABLE Heartbeat
(
    unix_time    INTEGER   NOT NULL,
    db_time      TIMESTAMP NOT NULL,
    INDEX        time_idx(unix_time)
)
```

The unix_time field holds the timestamp that is explicitly inserted into the table. The db_time field is set automatically by MySQL. By keeping track of both times and inserting new records instead of simply running an UPDATE on a single record, you maintain historical data in the event someone wants to graph or analyze it.

Let's look the script to add records:

```
#!/usr/bin/perl -w

use strict;
use DBIx::DWIW;

my $conn = DBIx::DWIW->Connect(
    DB   => "MySQL_Admin",
    User => "root",
    Pass => "password",
    Host => 'localhost',
) or die;

my $unix_time = time();
my $sql = "INSERT INTO Heartbeat (unix_time, db_time) VALUES ($unix_time, NULL)";
$conn->Execute($sql);

exit;
```

Running the script at a fixed interval generates a heartbeat that can be used by the read_heartbeat script to monitor replication latency.

read_heartbeat: Measuring replication log using heartbeat

The companion to *write_heartbeat* reads the most recent timestamp from the database and computes how far behind the slave might be. Remember that we can't know this time exactly unless the heartbeat records are generated every second, which is probably overkill for most installations.

```
#!/usr/bin/perl -w

use strict;
use DBIx::DWIW;

my $conn = DBIx::DWIW->Connect(
    DB   => "MySQL_Admin",
    User => "root",
    Pass => "password",
    Host => 'localhost',
) or die;

my $sql = "SELECT unix_time, db_time FROM Heartbeat
           ORDER BY unix_time DESC LIMIT 1";

my $info = $conn->Hash($sql);
my $time = $info->{unix_time};
my $delay = time() - $time;

print "slave is $delay seconds behind\n";

exit;
```

This script can also be extended to do far more than report on latency. If the latency is too great, it can send email or page a DBA.

Common Problems

Breaking MySQL's replication isn't difficult. The same simple implementation that makes it easy to set up also means there are many ways to stop, confuse, and otherwise disrupt it. In this section, we'll look at common problems, how they manifest themselves, and what can be done to solve or even prevent them.

Slave Data Changes

It should go without saying that manually changing data on a slave is usually a very bad idea. The same holds true for programmatically changing slave data. By accidentally making changes to data on a slave, you can easily introduce data inconsistencies that may cause replication to fail. It may take hours, days, weeks, or even months for the problem to surface, and when it does, you'll be hard pressed to explain what's going on.

Before MySQL 4.0.14 there was no way to tell MySQL not to allow any changes that don't originate from replication. Instead, the best solution in versions prior to 4.0.14 has an ironic aspect to it: you need to make a change on all the slaves, removing the permissions (or even the accounts) of users who can change data.

But that solution is problematic for other reasons. You'd probably forget about the change after a while. Then, late one night, the master would fail and you would need to promote a slave to master. You'd have to spend a bit of time trying figure out why applications are mysteriously failing.

As of Version 4.0.14, adding `read-only` to the slave's configuration file allows the slave to process write queries only via replication.

It's worth remembering that MySQL is very trusting when it comes to replication. The slave threads don't switch identities to run each query as the same user that originally executed it on the master. Instead, the slave thread runs with the equivalent of root access on the slave. It can, by design, change any data it needs to change. The trust comes from the fact that the slaves never verify that a particular user has the necessary privileges to run a query that appears in the binary log. It blindly trusts the master and that the master's logs haven't been tampered with.

Nonunique Server IDs

This has to be one of the most elusive problems you can encounter with MySQL replication. If you accidentally configure two slaves with the same server ID they'll appear to work just fine if you're not watching closely. But if you watch their error logs carefully or watch the master with *mytop* (covered in Appendix B), you'll notice something very odd.

On the master, you'll see only one of the two slaves connected at a given moment. Usually all slaves are connecting and replicating all the time. On the slave you'll see frequent disconnect/reconnect messages appearing in the error log, but none of those messages will lead you to believe that the server ID of one slave might be misconfigured.

The only real harm in this situation is that the slaves can't replicate very quickly. Because the slaves (not the master) keep track of their replication progress, there's no need to worry about giving one query to the first slave, one to the other slave, and so on. Both slaves get all the data; they just get it much more slowly.

The only solution to this problem is to be careful when setting up your slaves. If you see symptoms like this, double check the configuration of each slave to ensure that it has the server ID you expect it to. You may find it helpful to keep a master list of slave-to-server-ID mappings so that you don't lose track of which ID belongs to each slave. Consider using numeric values that have some sort of meaning in your setup, such as the last octet of each machine's IP address.

Log Corruption or Partial Log Record

The second most elusive problem occurs when a binary log somehow becomes corrupted. When that happens, the slave will typically fail with an error message like:

```
Error in Log_event::read_log_event(): '...', data_len=92,event_type=2
```

If that ever happens, there's little you can do. The slave is often confused enough that you can't simply try to skip the query and go to the next one. The only solution is to resync with the master and start over.

How does this happen? It's difficult to say. As long as the software is working properly, it could be a hardware or driver problem. Jeremy once saw a system have this problem repeatedly before he found that it had faulty RAM installed. We have heard of it happening on systems with disk controllers that don't have reliable drivers.

Bulk-Loading Data

While you can write code to load a lot of data into MySQL quickly, nothing beats the performance of using MySQL's LOAD DATA INFILE and LOAD DATA LOCAL INFILE commands to read data in from a flat file. In fact, the *mysqlimport* command-line tool uses LOAD DATA INFILE behind the scenes.

In all 3.23.xx versions of MySQL, replicating the LOAD DATA INFILE command is problematic. The contents of the file aren't stored in the binary log; only the query is, so the file must exist on the master until all slaves have copied it (they will do so automatically when they need it). If the file is removed prematurely, slaves can't copy the file, and replication will fail.

The LOAD DATA LOCAL INFILE command isn't affected. When the LOCAL option is specified, the *mysql* client reads the file from the client and generates the appropriate SQL to insert the data.

To avoid this problem, it's best either to load the data remotely using the latter syntax or to import the data programmatically. Either option ensures that the inserting is done via normal SQL statements that will all be properly logged.

Starting with Version 4.0, MySQL doesn't have this limitation. When a LOAD DATA INFILE command is issued, MySQL actually copies the entire file into the binary log. Slaves don't need to pull a copy of the original file from the master's disk.

Nonreplicated Dependencies

If you perform binary log filtering on either the master or the slave, it's quite easy to inadvertently break replication. For example, you may want to have a production database called production and a staging database called staging. The idea is to do all the necessary testing, development, and retesting in the staging database. When all the interim work is complete, you copy the data into the production database.

If the slave ignores queries from the staging database because of a filtering rule like the following, you'll probably end up frustrated:

```
replicate-do-db = production
```

You might try to run a query like this one to populate one of the production tables:

```
INSERT INTO production.sales SELECT * FROM staging.sales
```

This query works fine on the master, but the slaves will all fail because they don't have copies of the staging database. In fact, there's no easy way to make it work. Any attempt to reference the staging database is doomed to fail.

The only real solution in a case like this is to export all the data from the staging database and import it into the production database. You can do this programmatically if you want fine control over the process, or you can simply use *mysqldump* to dump the data to a text file and reimport it using *mysql*.

Missing Temporary Tables

This is really a special case of the previous example, but it warrants special attention because the real cause is a bit different. Instead of a filtering problem, this is a problem of restarting the slave at the wrong time.

Temporary tables replicate just fine, but if a series of queries that create and use a temporary table are interrupted on a slave by a restart or by stopping and starting replication, replication will fail.

Temporary tables are, by definition, temporary. When the server is restarted, they vanish. When the thread vanishes (such as with a SLAVE STOP or SLAVE STOP SQL_ THREAD command), any temporary tables created by that thread vanish.

There is no good solution for this problem. On the application side, it's best if temporary tables are created as late as possible, which helps minimize the time between the creation of the table and when it is actually needed. But even this solution only decreases the likelihood of the problem occurring.

You can avoid temporary tables completely, but that may involve time-consuming application changes. You'd have to ensure that the nontemporary tables created by your application always have unique names and that they are dropped when appropriate.

Because they are transient, this problem also affects Heap tables. They are always dropped explicitly, however so they vanish only when a slave is restarted. Stopping and restarting replication on the slave doesn't affect Heap tables.

Binary Log Out of Sync with Transaction Log

We know that MySQL records queries in the binary log after it executes them. We also know that MySQL writes transactions to the binary log after they have been committed. What happens if MySQL crashes, or someone pulls the plug in the microseconds after a transaction has been committed but before it writes the transaction to the binary log?

The result is that the master will contain the results of having completed the transaction, but the slaves will never see it. Ever. The transaction may have been a simple insert, or it could have been something as dramatic as a DROP TABLE command.

There is currently no workaround for this problem. Luckily MySQL crashes are rare. Make sure the power cables are plugged in tightly!

Slave Wants to Connect to the Wrong Master

If you change the hostname of your master, it's important to tell slaves using the CHANGE MASTER command:

```
mysql> CHANGE MASTER TO MASTER_HOST='newmaster.example.com';
```

You can't simply shut down the slave, edit the *my.cnf* file, and start it back up. MySQL always uses the *master.info* file if it exists, despite the settings contained in the *my.cnf* file.*

Alternatively, you can manually edit the *master.info* file, replacing the old hostname with the new one. The danger in relying on this method is that the *master.info* file can be deprecated, replaced, or radically changed in a future version of MySQL. It's best to stick to the documented way of doing things.

The Future of Replication

To solve some of MySQL's current shortcomings and to provide the infrastructure for handling problems that MySQL hasn't yet seen, a number of future enhancements have been proposed for MySQL. Let's look at them briefly.

Eliminating the Snapshot

With MySQL's current implementation, it's difficult to add a slave to a master after the master has been running for a long period of time. Many of the original binary logs have probably been removed to save space. Without all the logs, you can't simply configure the slave and point it at the master.

Even if you have all the binary logs on the master, it may take days, weeks, or even months for a slave to execute all the queries and finally catch up to the master. If you're looking to add slaves in a hurry, this clearly isn't the way to do it.

In either case, the ideal solution is simply to configure the new slave and tell it to begin replicating. Behind the scenes, the slave contacts the master and requests copies of the all the tables it needs, probably using a mechanism similar to LOAD TABLE

---

* This is, in my opinion, an easy-to-fix bug, but the MySQL maintainers don't agree. The workaround is to always use the CHANGE MASTER TO command for configuring slaves.

FROM MASTER. The master will need a way to track all changes to tables between the time that the slave begins and finishes copying the tables. Upon completion of the copy, the slave receives all the necessary changes and begins replicating from the binary log.

An alternative is for all of MySQL's storage engines to implement a versioning scheme similar to InnoDB's. When a new slave connects and begins to copy the tables, it can get a snapshot from that moment in time. When the copy is complete, the slave can begin replicating from the binary log position corresponding to the moment when the snapshot was marked.

Fail-Safe Replication

When a master fails, you must select a new master and instruct all the slaves to connect to the new master and begin replicating. Not only is that process prone to errors, it can be time-consuming too. Ideally, MySQL should handle failover automatically.

The proposed solution involves each slave registering itself with the master so that the master can keep track of it. Not only will the master know which servers are slaves, it can also keep track of how up to date each slave is. The slaves, in turn, will also keep track of who all the other slaves are.

In the event that the master fails, the slaves can elect a master based on the available information. Ideally, they will find the slave that was the most up to date when the master went down.

Safe Multi-Master Replication

Today it's possible to use replication in a multi-master architecture, as depicted earlier (see Figure 7-3). The major drawback to doing so, however, is that you can't rely on AUTO_INCREMENT columns to function properly.

Each MyISAM table has a single counter that controls the next AUTO_INCREMENT value. Once that value has increased, it can't easily be decreased. If inserts are timed properly, they cause data to become inconsistent between the two masters.

Imagine the following events occurring on two servers, *master1* and *master2*:

1. Both servers start with an empty orders table.
2. *master1* inserts a record for customer 58, which is assigned ID 1.
3. *master2* inserts a record for customer 1232, which is assigned ID 1.
4. *master2* replicates *master1*'s insert, adding the record for customer 58 and trying to assign it an ID of 1. That fails and results in a duplicate key error.
5. *master1* replicates *master2*'s insert, adding the record for customer 1232 and trying to assign it an ID of 1. That fails and results in a duplicate key error.

Each master was given an insert by some client before it had replicated the other master's insert. The result is that both masters are out of sync.

The current solution is to avoid using AUTO_INCREMENT fields completely and assign primary keys through some other means. You might use an MD5 hash of some values in the record, or perhaps use another library to generate a globally unique identifier (GUID).

Let's look at the two proposed solutions for the future.

Multipart auto-increment unique keys

The first is to use MyISAM's multipart auto-increment unique keys. Rather than using a single column as a primary key, you'd set up a table like this:

```
CREATE TABLE orders (
    server_id       INTEGER UNSIGNED NOT NULL,
    record_id       INTEGER UNSIGNED NOT NULL AUTO_INCREMENT,
    stuff           VARCHAR(255)     NOT NULL,
    UNIQUE mykey (server_id, record_id)
);
```

Notice that the record_id is an AUTO_INCREMENT field and is the second part of a two-part unique key. When you insert NULL into the record_id column, MySQL will consider the value of server_id when automatically generating a value.

To illustrate this, notice the following:

```
mysql> insert into orders values (1, NULL, 'testing');
Query OK, 1 row affected (0.01 sec)

mysql> insert into orders values (1, NULL, 'testing');
Query OK, 1 row affected (0.00 sec)

mysql> insert into orders values (2, NULL, 'testing');
Query OK, 1 row affected (0.00 sec)

mysql> select * from orders;
+-----------+-----------+---------+
| server_id | record_id | stuff   |
+-----------+-----------+---------+
|         1 |         1 | testing |
|         1 |         2 | testing |
|         2 |         1 | testing |
+-----------+-----------+---------+
3 rows in set (0.03 sec)
```

MySQL, in effect, allows you to select from multiple AUTO_INCREMENT sequences based on the prefix you use. By adding a function such as SERVER_ID( ) to MySQL and rewriting the previous queries, you can use AUTO_INCREMENT with multi-master replication safely.

```
mysql> insert into orders values (SERVER_ID( ), NULL, 'testing');
Query OK, 1 row affected (0.01 sec)
```

```
mysql> insert into orders values (SERVER_ID( ), NULL, 'testing');
Query OK, 1 row affected (0.00 sec)

mysql> insert into orders values (SERVER_ID( ), NULL, 'testing');
Query OK, 1 row affected (0.00 sec)
```

There are three problems with this approach. First, it works only for MyISAM tables. An ideal solution works across all table types. Another issue is that all slaves require some special logic. Today, when a slave reads the binary log of a master, it knows the master's server ID as well as its own, but it doesn't really do anything with the master's server ID. In this solution, the slave has to actually use the master's server ID any time that it replicated a query that involved the mythical SERVER_ID( ) function. That makes the replication logic a bit trickier on the slaves.

You could work around the lack of a SERVER_ID( ) function by simply using the actual server ID in your SQL statements. If you know you're talking to server 12, write the query accordingly:

```
mysql> insert into orders values (12, NULL, 'testing');
Query OK, 1 row affected (0.01 sec)
```

But there's the rub. You need to know, in advance of each query, what the server's ID is. Granted, the server's ID doesn't change, but if you're accessing one of many servers via a load balancer or don't have a persistent connection, the server you're talking to may change often. So you'd have to deal with the overhead of obtaining the server's ID whenever you need it.

```
mysql> show variables like 'server_id';
+---------------+-------+
| Variable_name | Value |
+---------------+-------+
| server_id     | 102   |
+---------------+-------+
1 row in set (0.00 sec)
```

Finally, and most importantly, using two columns as the primary key just doesn't feel natural. It feels like a hack or a workaround. If this solution became widespread, others problems might arise. For example, setting up foreign-key relationships would be troublesome. Putting aside the fact that InnoDB doesn't even support multipart auto-increment unique keys, how would you define a foreign-key relationship with multipart keys?

Partitioned auto-increment fields

The second solution is to make auto-increment fields a bit more complex. Rather than simply using a 32-bit integer that starts at 1 and keeps counting, it might make sense to use more bits and partition the key-space based on the server ID. Currently, server IDs are 32-bit values, so by using a 64-bit auto-increment value, the two can be combined. The high 32 bits of the value would be the server ID of the server that originally generated the record, and the low 32 bits would be the real auto-increment value.

Internally, MySQL needs to treat the 64-bit auto-increment value a lot like the multipart auto-increment unique keys previously discussed. The value generated for the low 32 bits is dependent on the value of the high 32 bits (the server ID). The benefit is that from the user's point of view, it's a single column and can be used just like any other column. Insert statements are no more complex; all the magic is conveniently under the hood, where it belongs.

There are some downsides to this approach, however. The most apparent issue is that there would be large gaps in the values. For the sake of simplicity, MySQL can always subtract 1 from the server ID when generating the high bits of the auto-increment value. This allows values to continue starting at 1 when the server ID is 1. However, as soon as a second server is introduced, with server ID 2, it inserts values starting from 4,294,967,297 (2^{32} + 1) and counting up from there.

Another problem is that columns will require more space on disk (both in the data and index files). BIGINT columns are already 8 bytes (64 bits) wide. Adding another 4 bytes (32 bits) for the server ID portion of the auto-increment value means a 50% increase in the space required. That may not sound like a lot, but an application that requires 64-bit values in the first place is likely to be storing billions of rows. Adding an additional 4 bytes to a table containing 10 billion rows means storing an additional 40 GB of data!

It makes sense to break compatibility with existing MySQL versions (which use 32-bit server IDs) and reduce the size of the server ID to 8 or 16 bits. After all, with even 8 bits available, you can have up to 255 unique servers in a single replication setup; with 16 bits, that jumps to 65,535. It's unlikely anyone will have that many servers in a single replication setup.[*]

---

[*] Perhaps Google will decide to run MySQL on their growing farm of 100,000+ Linux servers. They'd need more than 8 bits.

## CHAPTER 8

Load Balancing and High Availability

After you've set up replication and have a number of MySQL slaves available to handle your needs, the next problem you're likely to face is how to route the traffic. For the most part, the problem is quite similar to traditional HTTP load balancing. But since the MySQL protocol isn't HTTP, there are some important differences that emerge when you get into the nitty-gritty of load balancing MySQL.

The material in this chapter assumes that your MySQL servers are on different machines from your application servers. If you've set up a local MySQL slave on each of your web or application servers, there's no need to worry about MySQL load balancing. Instead, you need a load-balancing solution for the web or application server.

We'll start with a quick overview of load balancing from both a network and application perspective, and we'll discuss how load-balancing benefits MySQL deployments. Then we move to some of the issues specific to load balancing MySQL in various configurations, notably health checks and balancing algorithms.

In the limited scope of this book, there's no way to cover all issues surrounding load balancers and high availability of your systems. For more information on the topic we suggest Tony Bourke's *Server Load Balancing*, also published by O'Reilly.

Load Balancing Basics

The basic idea behind load balancing is quite simple. You have a farm or cluster of two or more servers, and you'd like them to share the workload as evenly as possible. In addition to the backend servers, a load balancer (often a specialized piece of hardware) handles the work of routing incoming connections to the least busy of the available servers. Figure 8-1 shows a typical load-balancing implementation for a large web site. Note that one load balancer is used for HTTP traffic and another for MySQL traffic.

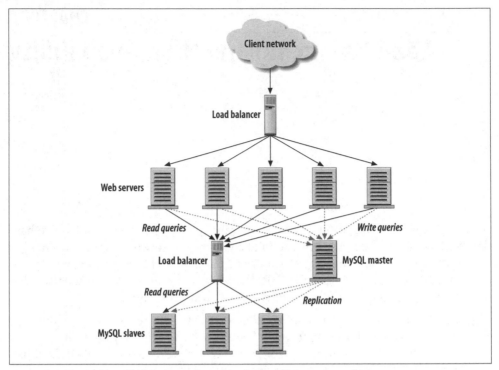

Figure 8-1. Typical load-balancing architecture for a read-intensive web site

There are four common goals or objectives in load balancing:

Scalability

In an ideal configuration, increasing capacity is as simple as adding more servers to the farm. By doing this properly, you can achieve linear scalability (for read-intensive applications) with relatively inexpensive equipment and guarantee good performance for your clients. Of course, not all applications scale this way, and those that do may require a more complex setup. We discuss those later in this chapter.

Efficiency

Load balancing helps to use server resources more efficiently because you get a fair amount of control over how requests are routed. This is particularly important when your cluster is composed of machines that aren't equally powerful. You can ensure that the less powerful machines aren't asked to do more than their fair share of the work.

Availability

With a cluster of MySQL slaves in place, the loss of any one server doesn't need to affect clients. They all have identical copies of the data, so the remaining servers can shoulder the increased load. This level of redundancy is similar to using RAID 1 across multiple hard disks.

Transparency

> Transparency means that clients don't need to know about the load-balancing setup. They shouldn't care how many machines are in your cluster or what their names are. As far as they're concerned, there's one big virtual server that handles their requests.

Achieving all four goals is critical to providing the type of reliable service that many modern applications demand.

Software Solutions

If you're not interested in a hardware solution for load balancing, you might consider a language-specific load-balancing API. In the Java world, for example, Clustered JDBC (C-JDBC) provides a transparent layer on top of JDBC that handles load-balancing SELECT queries behind the scenes. For more information, see the C-JDBC web site (*http://c-jdbc.objectweb.org/*) Some Java application servers also support pools-of-pools specifically for clustering purposes.

Perl DBI users are encouraged to look at the `DBIx::DBCluster` module on their nearest CPAN mirror.

For a language-independent solution, the Open Source SQL Relay package (available from *http://sqlrelay.sourceforge.net/*) may be more appropriate. It supports most popular compiled and scripting languages, connection pooling, access controls, and more.

Differences Between MySQL and HTTP Load Balancing

If you're already familiar with HTTP load balancing, you may be tempted to run ahead and set up something similar for MySQL. After all, MySQL is just another TCP-based network service that happens to run on port 3306 rather that port 80, right? While that's true, there are some important differences between HTTP and MySQL's protocol as well as differences between the ways that database servers and web servers tend to be used.

Requests

To begin with, the connect-request-response cycle for MySQL is different. Most web servers and web application servers accept all connections, process a request, respond, and then disconnect almost immediately.* They don't perform any fancy authentication. In fact, most don't even bother with a reverse lookup of an inbound

---

* With the increased adoption of HTTP/1.1, the disconnect may not occur right away, but the delay is still quite short in comparison to a typical MySQL server.

IP address. In other words, the process of establishing the connection is very lightweight.

The actual request and response process is typically lightweight too. In many cases, the request is for a static HTML file or an image. In that case, the web server simply reads the file from disk, responds to the client with the data, and logs the request. If the content is dynamic, the PHP, Java, or Perl code that generates it is likely to execute very quickly. The real bottlenecks tend to be the result of waiting on other backend services, such as MySQL or an LDAP server. Sure, there can be poorly designed algorithms that cause the code to execute more slowly, but the bulk of web-based applications tend to have relatively thin business-logic layers. They also tend to push nearly all the data storage and retrieval off to MySQL.

Even when there are major differences from request to request, the differences tend to be in the amount of code executed. But that's exactly where you want the extra work to be done. The CPU is far and away the fastest part of the computer. Said another way, when you're dealing with HTTP, all requests are created equal—at least compared to a database server.

As you saw early on in this book, the biggest bottleneck on a database server usually isn't CPU; it's the disk. Disk I/O is an order of magnitude slower than the CPU, so even occasionally waiting for disk I/O can make a huge difference in performance. A query that uses an index that happens to be cached in memory may take 0.08 seconds to run, while a slightly different query that requires more disk I/O may take 3 seconds to complete.

On the database side, not all requests are created equal. Some are far more expensive than others, and the load balancer has no way of knowing which ones are expensive. That means that the load balancer may not be *balancing* the load as much as it is crudely *distributing* the load.

Partitioning

Another feature that's common in load-balanced web application architectures is a caching system. When users first visit a web site, the web server may assign a session ID to the user, then pull quite a bit of information from a database to construct the user's preferences and profile. Since that can be an expensive operation to perform on every request, the application code caches the data locally on the web server—either on disk or in memory—and reuse it for subsequent visits until the cache expires.

To take advantage of the locally cached data, the load balancer is configured to inspect that user's session ID (visible either in the URL or in a site-wide cookie) and use it to decide which backend web server should handle the request. In this way, the load balancer works to send the same user to the same backend server, minimizing the number of times the user's profile must be looked up and cached. Of course, if the server goes offline, the load balancer will select an alternative server for the user.

Such a partitioning system eliminates the redundant caching that occurs if the load balancer sent each request to a random backend server each time. Rather than having an effective cache size equal to that of a single server, you end up with an effective cache size equal to the sum of all the backend servers.

MySQL's query cache can benefit from such a scheme. If you've dedicated 512 MB of memory on each slave for its query cache, and you have 8 slaves, you can cache up to 4 GB of different data across the cluster. Unfortunately, it's not that easy. MySQL's network protocol doesn't have a way to expose any hints to the load balancer. There are no URL parameters or cookies in which to store a session ID.

A solution to this problem is to handle the partitioning of queries at the application level. You can split the 8 servers into 4 clusters of 2 servers each. Then you'd decide, in your application, whether a given query should go to cluster 1, 2, 3, or 4. You'll see more of this shortly.

Connection pooling

Many applications use connection-pooling techniques; these techniques seem especially popular in the Java world and in PHP using persistent connections via *mysql_pconnect( )*. While connection pooling works rather well under normal conditions, it doesn't always scale well under load because it breaks one of the basic assumptions behind load balancing. With connection pooling, each client maintains a fixed or variable number of connections to one or more database servers. Rather than disconnecting and discarding the connection when a session is complete, the connection is placed back into a share pool so that it can be reused later.

Load balancing works best when clients connect and disconnect frequently. That gives the load balancer the best chance of spreading the load evenly; otherwise the transparency is lost. Imagine you have a group of 16 web servers and 4 MySQL servers. Your web site becomes very busy, and the MySQL servers begin to get bogged down, so you add 2 more servers to the cluster. But your application uses connection pooling, so the requests continue to go to the 4 overworked servers while the 2 new ones sit idle.

In effect, connection pooling (or persistent connections) work against load balancing. It's possible to compromise between the two if you have a connection-pooling system that allows the size of the pool to change as the demand increases and decreases. Also, by setting timeouts relatively low (say, five minutes instead of six hours), you can still achieve a level of load balancing while taking advantage of persistent database connections.

You can also enforce this on the MySQL side by setting each server's wait_timeout to a relatively low number. (This value tells MySQL how long a connection may remain idle before it is disconnected.) Doing so encourages sessions to be reestablished when needed, but the negative affects on the application side are minimal. Most MySQL APIs allow for automatic reconnection to the server any time you attempt to reuse a closed connection. If you make this change, consider also adjusting the thread_cache as described in the section "Solving Kernel Bottlenecks" in Chapter 6.

We don't mean to paint connection pooling in a negative light. It certainly has its uses. Every worthwhile Java application server provides some form of connection pooling. As mentioned earlier, some provide their own load-balancing or clustering mechanisms as well. In such systems, connection pooling *combined with* load balancing is a fine solution because there's a single authority mediating the traffic to the database servers. In the PHP and *mysql_pconnect( )* world, there often is not.

Multi-Master Load Balancing

While the main focus of this chapter is on the load balancing of MySQL slaves, it's entirely possible to use a load balancer to spread the workload among several masters. Assuming you followed the advice in the"Safe Multi-Master Replication" section of Chapter 7, there's little difference in the setup required.

There are different reasons for using slaves and for using multiple masters. When you use multiple masters, you'll still get transparency and redundancy; however, scalability and efficiency don't really apply because in a multi-master setup, every master must still execute every write query sooner or later.

By having several masters behind a load balancer, you can better handle brief surges in traffic that can otherwise overwhelm a single server. During that time, each master fall farther and farther behind on the updates it receives from the other(s), but when the traffic returns to a normal level, the masters will catch up with each other and return to a state of equilibrium.

It's very important to realize that this model doesn't work well for all applications. In this type of setup, there is no "one true source" of definitely correct information. That can cause subtle "bugs" in your application(s); for example, if you need to know if a record exists, you need to ask both servers.

Configuration Issues

To route the connection to a server, the load balancer must select a target server. To do this, it takes two pieces of information into account. First, it needs to know which servers are available. At any time, one or more of the backend servers can be offline (for maintenance, as the result of a crash, etc.). To keep track of the servers, the load balancer periodically checks each one's health.

Once the load balancer has a list of candidate servers, it must decide which should get the next connection. This process can take a number of factors into account, including past performance, load, client address, and so on. Let's look at both issues in more detail.

Health Checks

Load balancers need to perform a health check for each real server to ensure that it's still alive, well, and willing to accept new connections. When load-balancing a web server, this is often a trivial matter. The load balancer is configured to connect to TCP port 80 and request a *status file* such as */health.html*. If the server gets a 2xx response code back, it assumes the server is fine. If not, it may stop sending new requests to the server until it becomes healthy again.

A nice side benefit of asking for a specific file, rather than simply looking for any response on port 80, is that a server can be removed from the cluster without taking it offline: simply remove or rename the file.

Most load balancers provide a great deal of control over the parameters used when testing cluster hosts. Options may include the frequency of checks, the duration of check timeouts, and the number of unhealthy responses required to remove a server from the cluster. See your load balancer's documentation for details.

Determining health

So what constitutes a good health check for MySQL? Unfortunately, there's no single answer to that question.

It depends on how sophisticated your load balancer is. Some load balancers can verify only that each server is responding on the necessary TCP port. They'll generally connect to TCP port 3306 (or whichever port you're using) and assume the server is unhealthy if the connection is refused or if it has to wait too long for a response.

Some load balancers are more flexible. They might give you the option of scripting a complicated health check or of running the health check against a different port than normal. This provides a lot of flexibility and control. For example, you can run a web server (such as Apache) on the server and configure the load balancer to check a status file, just as you would for standard HTTP load balancing. You can exploit this indirect kind of check by making the status file a script (PHP, Perl, etc.) or Java servlet that performs arbitrarily complex logic to decide whether the server is really healthy.* The arbitrarily complex logic can be as simple as running a SELECT 1 query,

---

* Provided, of course, that the arbitrarily complex logic doesn't take arbitrarily long to execute. The load balancer won't wait forever.

or as complicated as parsing the output of SHOW SLAVE STATUS to verify that the slave is reasonably up to date.

If your load balancer offers this degree of flexibility, we highly recommend taking advantage of it. By taking control over the decision-making process, you'll have a better idea of how your cluster will respond in various situations. And after testing, if you're not happy with the results, simply adjust the logic and try again.

What types of things might you check for? This goes back to the question we're trying to answer: what makes a healthy MySQL server, from the load balancer's point of view?

A good health check also depends on your application needs and what's most important. For example, on a nearly real-time dynamic web site like Yahoo! News, you might put more emphasis on replication. If a slave gets busy enough handling regular queries that it becomes sluggish and ends up more than 30 seconds behind on replication, your code can return an unhealthy status code. The load balancer then removes the slave from the list of available servers until the health check passes again. Presumably the reduced demand on the server will allow it to quickly catch up and rejoin the cluster. (See the "Monitoring" section in Chapter 7 for ideas about detecting slow slaves.)

Of course, the success of this algorithm depends on how smart your scripts are. What if the slow server doesn't get caught up? And what if the additional demand that the remaining servers must bear causes them to fall behind? There's a very real chance that one by one, they'll start deciding they too are unhealthy. Before long, the problem cascades until you're left with a cluster of unhealthy servers sitting behind a load balancer that doesn't know where to send connections anymore.

At Yahoo! Finance, we've seen individual servers that try to be smart and end up creating even bigger problems because they didn't have the whole picture. Anticipating the problem mentioned in the previous paragraph, the code that performed health checks introduced yet another level of checking. Each server knew all the other members of the cluster. The health check included code to make sure that there were enough servers left. If a server determined that too many other servers were already down, it would elect to keep handling requests. After all, a slow site is better than no site at all.

But our implementation still wasn't smart enough; the servers still went down in a cascade. The reason turned out to be a simple race condition. The code performed a series of checks, but it did them in the wrong order. The code first checked to see that a sufficient number of other servers were healthy. It then went on to make sure MySQL wasn't too far behind on replication. The problem was that several servers could be doing the health check at exactly the same time. If that happened, it was possible for all servers to believe that all other servers were healthy and proceed to declare themselves unhealthy.

There are numerous solutions to the problem. One is to add a simple sanity check. Each server can, after declaring itself unhealthy, check to make sure that the situation hasn't radically changed. Another option is to appoint a single server in each cluster as the authority for determining who is and isn't healthy. While it introduces a single point of failure (what if this server dies?), it means there are fewer chances for race conditions and similar problems.

To summarize, some load balancers provide you with a lot of flexibility and power. Be careful how you use it. If you elect to take control of the decision-making process (and add complexity to it), be sure that the code is well tested. Ask a few peers to review it for you. Consider what will happen in unusual situations.

Connection limits

In normal operations, the load balancer should distribute connections relatively evenly among your severs. If you have eight backend servers, any one of them will handle roughly one eighth of the connections at a given time. But what happens when several backend servers go down at the same time? Because the rest of the cluster must bear the load, you need to ensure that the se servers are configured to handle it.

The most important setting to check is `max_connections`. In this circumstance, you'll find that if `max_connections` is set too low, otherwise healthy MySQL servers start refusing connections even if they're powerful enough to handle the load. Many installations don't set the `max_connections` option, so MySQL uses its built-in default of 100. Instead, set `max_connections` high enough that this problem can't happen. For example, if you find that each server typically handles 75 connections, a reasonable value for `max_connections` might be 150 or more. That way, even if half the backend servers failed, you're application won't fail to connect.

Next-Connection Algorithms

Different load balancers implement different algorithms to decide which server should receive the next connection. Some call these scheduling algorithms. Each vendor has different terminology, but this list should provide an idea of what's available:

Random
> Each request is directed to a backend server selected at random from the pool of available servers.

Round-robin
> Requests are sent to servers in a repeating sequence: A, B, C, A, B, C, etc.

Least connections
> The next connection goes to the server with the fewest active connections.

Fastest response

The server that has been handling requests the fastest receives the next connection. This tends to work well when the backend servers are a mix of fast and slow machines.

Hashed

The source IP address of the connection is hashed, thereby mapping it to one of the backend servers. Each time a connection request comes from the same client IP address, it is sent to the same backend server. The bindings change only when the number of machines in the cluster does.

Weighted

Several of the other algorithms can be weighted. For example, you may have four single-CPU machines and four dual-CPU machines. The dual-CPU machines are roughly twice as powerful as the single-CPU machines, so you tell the load balancer to send them twice as many requests—on average.

Which algorithm is right for MySQL? Again, it depends. There are several factors to consider and some pitfalls to avoid. One of the pitfalls is best illustrated with an example.

The consequences of poor algorithm choice

In September 2002, Yahoo! launched a one-week memorial site for those affected by the September 11, 2001 terrorist attacks. This site was described in Chapter 6. The *remember.yahoo.com* site was heavily promoted on the Yahoo! home page and elsewhere. The entire site was built by a small group of Yahoo! employees in the two weeks before the site's launch on September 9.

Needless to say, the site got a lot of traffic. So much, in fact, that Jeremy spent a couple of sleepless nights working to optimize the SQL queries and bring new MySQL servers online to handle the load. During that time the MySQL servers were running red hot. They weren't handling many queries per second (because they are poorly optimized) but they were either disk-bound, CPU-bound, or both. A server was slowest when it first came online because MySQL's key buffer hadn't yet been populated, and the operating system's disk cache didn't have any of the relevant disk blocks cached. They needed several minutes to warm up before taking their full query load.

The situation was made worse by the fact that the load balancer hadn't been configured with this in mind, and nobody realized it until very late in the process. When a server was reconfigured and brought back online, it was immediately pounded with 30–50 new queries. The machine became completely saturated and needed several minutes to recover. During the recovery time, it was nearly unresponsive, with the CPU at 100%, a load average over 25, and the disk nearly maxed out.

After quite a bit of theorizing and poking around, someone thought to question the load-balancer configuration. It turned out that it was set on a least-connections scheduling algorithm. That clearly explained why a new machine was bombarded with new connections and rendered useless for several minutes. Once the load balancer was switched to a random scheduling algorithm, it became much easier to bring down a slave, adjust the configuration, and put it back online without becoming completely overwhelmed.

The moral of the story is that the connection algorithm you select may come back to bite you when you least expect it (and can least afford it). Consider how your algorithm will work in day-to-day operations as well as when you're under an unusually high load or have a higher than normal number of backend servers offline for some reason.

We can't recommend the right configuration for your needs. You need to think about what will work best for your hardware, network, and applications. Furthermore, your algorithm choices are limited by the load balancing hardware or software you're using. When in doubt, test.

Cluster Partitioning

As noted earlier, Figure 8-1 is a common setup for many web sites. While that architecture provides a good starting point, the time may come when you want to squeeze more performance out of your replication setup. Partitioning is often the next evolutionary step as the system grows. In this section, we'll look at several related partitioning schemes that can be applied to most load-balanced MySQL clusters.

Role-Based Partitioning

Many applications using a MySQL backend do so in different roles. Let's consider a large community web site for which users register and then exchange messages and participate in discussions online. From the data storage angle, several features must be implemented for the site to function. For example, the system must store and retrieve records for individual users (their profiles) as well as messages and message-related metadata.

At some point, you decide to add a search capability to the site. Over the past year, you've accumulated a ton of interesting data, and your users want to search it. So you add full-text indexes to the content and offer some basic search facilities. What you soon realize is that the search queries behave quite a bit differently from most of the other queries you run. They're really a whole new class of queries. Rather than retrieving a very small amount of data in a very specific way (fetching a message based on its ID or looking up a user based on username), search queries are more intensive; they take more CPU time to execute. And the full-text indexes are quite a bit larger than your typical MyISAM indexes.

In a situation like this, it may make sense to split up the responsibility for the various classes of queries you're executing. Users often expect a search to take a second or two to execute, but pulling up a post or a user page should always happen instantly. To keep the longer-running search queries from interfering with the "must be fast" queries, you can break the slaves into logical subgroups. They'll all still be fed by the same master (for now), but they will be serving in more narrowly focused roles.

Figure 8-2 shows a simple example of this with the top half of the diagram omitted. There need not be two physically different load balancers involved. Instead, think of those as logical boxes rather than physical. Most load-balancing hardware can handle dozens of backend clusters simultaneously.

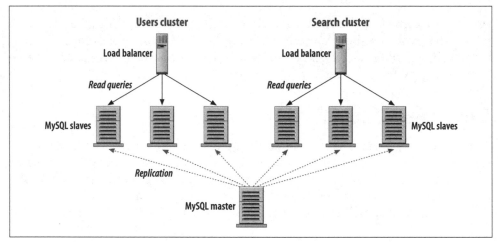

Figure 8-2. Partitioning based on role

With this separation in place, it's much easier to match the hardware to the task at hand. Queries sent to the user cluster are likely to be I/O bound rather taxing the CPU. They're mainly fetching a few random rows off disk over and over. So maybe it makes sense to spend less money on the CPUs and invest a bit more in the disks and memory (for caching). Perhaps RAID 0 is a good choice on these machines.

The search cluster, on the other hand, spends far more CPU time looking through the full-text indexes to match search terms and ranking results based on their score. The machines in this group probably need faster (or dual) CPUs and a fair amount of memory.

This architecture is versatile enough to handle workload splitting for a variety of applications. Anytime you notice an imbalance among the types of queries, consider whether it might be worthwhile to split your large cluster into a cluster made up of smaller groups based on a division of labor.

Data-Based Partitioning

Some high-volume applications have surprisingly little variety in the types of queries they use. Partitioning across roles isn't effective in these cases, so the alternative is to partition the data itself and put a bit of additional logic into the application code. Figure 8-3 illustrates this.

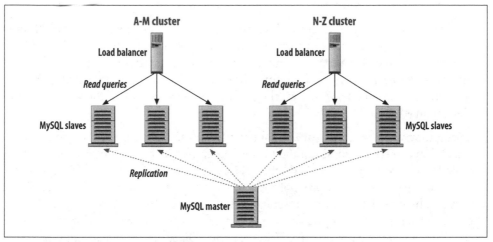

Figure 8-3. Partitioning based on data

In an application that deals with fetching user data from MySQL, a simple partitioning scheme is to use the first character of the username. Those beginning with letters A–M reside in the first partition. The other partition handles the second half of the alphabet. The additional application logic is simply a matter of checking the username before deciding which database connection to use when fetching the data.

The choice of splitting based on an alphabetic range is purely arbitrary. You can just as easily use a numeric representation of each username, sending all users with even numbers to one cluster and all odd numbers to the other. Volumes have been written on efficient and uniform hashing functions that can be used to group arbitrarily large volumes of data into a fixed number of buckets. Our goal isn't to recommend a particular method but to suggest that you look at the wealth of existing information and techniques before inventing something of your own.

Filtering and Multicluster Partitioning

Assuming that the majority of activity is read-only (that is, on the slaves), the previous partitioning solutions scale well as the demand on a high-volume application increases. But what happens when a bottleneck develops on the master? The obvious solution is to upgrade the master. If it is CPU-bound, add more CPU power. If it's I/O bound, add faster disks and more of them.

There's a flaw in that logic, however. If the master is having trouble keeping up with the load, the slaves will be under at least as much stress. Remember that MySQL's replication is query based. The volume of write queries handled by the slaves is usually identical to that handled by the master. If the master can no longer keep up, odds are that the slaves are struggling just as much.

Filtering

An easy solution to the problem is filtering. As described in Chapter 7, MySQL provides the ability to filter the replication stream selectively on both the master and the slave. The problem is that you can filter based only on database or table names. Filtering is therefore not an option if you use data-based partitioning. MySQL has no facility to filter based on the queries themselves, only the names of the databases and tables involved.

Filtering may work well in a role-based partitioning setup in which the various slave clusters don't need full copies of the master's data (for instance, where a search cluster needs two particular tables, and the user cluster needs the other four). If you use role-based partitioning, it's probably worthwhile to set up each cluster to replicate only the tables or databases the cluster needs to do its job. The filtering must be on the slaves themselves, as opposed to the master, so the slaves' IO thread will still copy all the master's write queries. However, the SQL thread will read right past queries the slaves aren't interested in (those that are filtered out).

Separate clusters

Aside from Moore's Law, the only real solution to scaling the write side with this model is to use truly separate clusters. By going from a single master with many slaves to several independent masters with their own slaves, you eliminate the bottlenecks associated with a higher volume of write activity, and you can get away with using less expensive hardware.

Figure 8-4 illustrates this logical progression. As before, there are two groups of slaves, one for search and one for user lookups, but this time each group is served by its own master.

High Availability

So far we've concerned ourselves with the slaves. Using a proper heartbeat setup and load balancer, you can achieve a high degree of availability and transparency for MySQL-based applications. In its current state, MySQL doesn't offer a lot in the way of high availability support on the master, but that doesn't mean all hope is lost.

In this section, we'll look at several high-availability solutions (both commercial and free). Each of the options considered has pros and cons, which we've done our best to document.

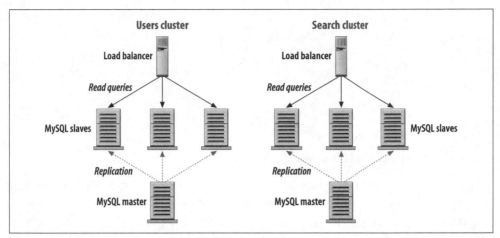

Figure 8-4. Multicluster partitioning

NDB Cluster

As we were putting the finishing touches on this book, MySQL AB was completing the initial integration work on the newest storage engine: NDB. In 2003, MySQL AB acquired Alzato, a company started by Ericsson in 2000. The company developed NDB Cluster, a clustered database system designed for both high availability and scalability.

When the integration is complete, MySQL's NDB storage engine will provide an interface to a backend NDB cluster. For the first time, MySQL will have built-in clustering with automatic failover capabilities. See the MySQL web site and manual for more details on the NDB technology.

Dual-Master Replication

We looked at dual-master replication back in Chapter 7. While it doesn't help in scaling an application (both servers must handle the full write load), you can achieve much improved availability and transparency by putting a load balancer in the mix. Figure 8-5 illustrates this arrangement.

Aside from the downsides mentioned in Chapter 7 (mostly a lack of conflict resolution), there isn't a lot that can go wrong with this setup. The worst problem is the potential for data loss, but that's really no different from master/slave replication. After a query writes a record to *master 1*, MySQL records the query in the binary log, and the other master has a chance to read it. If *master 1* happens to crash between the time that the record is written and when the binary log is updated, however, the other master (and any slaves) will never know about the query. As far as *master 2* is

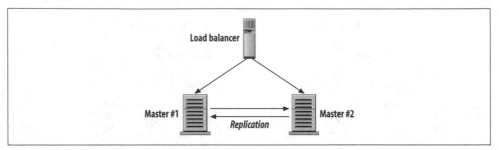

Figure 8-5. Dual-master replication for high availability

concerned, the query never happened. The solution would be for MySQL to provide synchronous replication with two-phase commit, but it doesn't.

On the plus side, this solution is relatively easy to set up and understand. If you already know how to configure replication and have a working load balancer set up with good health checks, dual-master replication isn't much extra work. If you need to perform maintenance on the masters, you can simply take *master 1* offline, do the work, bring it back online, and repeat the process on the other as soon as the first has caught up. Of course, it's best to do this gracefully. Set the health check to fail, and wait until clients are no longer accessing the master before shutting it down. Otherwise you risk interrupting in-progress transactions.

If your load balancer is sophisticated enough, you can virtually eliminate the problem of conflict resolution. Here's how it works: rather than having both masters active, configure the load balancer so that *master 1* is active, and *master 2* is on standby. Only when *master 1* goes down should the load balancer send any traffic to *master 2*. Most load balancers provide a mechanism for doing this.

However, a wrinkle occurs when *master 1* comes back online. What should the load balancer do? If it begins sending connections to *master 1* again, you'll have a situation in which writes could be occurring to both masters at the same time. That's a recipe for conflict. Remember, MySQL connections can be long-running, so the load balancer can't assume that clients will suddenly disconnect from *master 2*. The load balancer needs to be configured so that the notion of the "live master" changes only when the current live master goes down.

Shared Storage with Standby

By increasing the cost and complexity of your infrastructure, you can eliminate the problem of lost updates described previously. Instead of two servers with their own copies of the data using replication to stay in sync, you can configure the active and standby masters to use shared storage.* It's very important to realize that the standby master shouldn't mount the filesystem or start MySQL until the first is offline.

Figure 8-6 shows one implementation of shared storage. It's worth pointing out that a load balancer isn't strictly necessary in this scenario. All you really need is an agent running on each node to monitor the other. If the agent running on *master 2* finds that *master 1* is unavailable, it takes over *master 1*'s IP address and starts up MySQL with an identical configuration (same data directory, log filenames, etc.). If the configuration is truly identical, starting up MySQL on *master 2* is logically no different from fixing *master 1* and bringing MySQL up there. However, in reality there is an important difference: time. *Master 2* is already booted and ready to go. Starting up MySQL takes a matter of seconds. The only delay is imposed by consistency checks on the data. Shared storage means the possibility of share corruption if you're not using InnoDB or BDB tables.

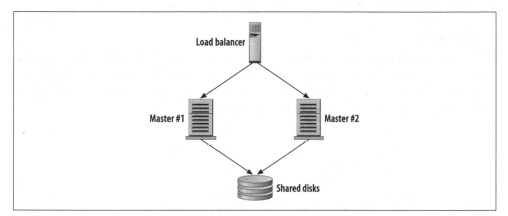

Figure 8-6. A live master and a warm standby master using shared storage

Writing such an agent is a tricky undertaking. We don't recommend you try it unless you have a lot of time available for testing all the possible edge cases you're likely to encounter with flaky network equipment. Instead, spend some time looking at existing tools. There are numerous open source projects that can be adapted to do this for MySQL. The best candidate is *keepalived* (*http://keepalived.sourceforge.net/*), a keep-alive health check facility written to work in conjunction with LVS. There are also two commercial solutions on the market today, described in the next section.

---

* The exact type of shared storage isn't terribly important. You see greater performance from directly attached systems than network attached storage, however, due mainly to the reduced latency.

Commercial Solutions

As of this writing, there are two commercial products worthy of consideration for high availability. Each takes a completely different approach to solving the problem, so different sites may find one or the other suitable, or neither. Keep an eye on this market: we expect to see a lot of new development in this area in the next year or so.

Veritas cluster agent

Veritas has a well established reputation for providing the technology necessary to build many sorts of clusters. Their MySQL offering builds on the shared storage with standby model we just looked at. The cluster agent runs on both the active and standby nodes, monitoring the health of the primary master. When the agent detects a problem on the master, it brings the standby instance online and takes over the primary master's functionality.

EMIC Networks

EMIC Networks provides a full-blown clustering solution for MySQL. By combining a number of relatively inexpensive servers running EMIC's version of MySQL, you can create incredibly robust MySQL clusters without needing to worry about the single point of failure most other architectures have.

## CHAPTER 9

Backup and Recovery

Ask your favorite system administrator what the least favorite part of her job is and there's a good chance she'll mutter, "backups," with a sullen look on her face. Running backups ranks right up there with a visit to the dentist on most people's list of least fun things to do.*

If you already rely on standard backup software to handle your MySQL servers, you probably have a false sense of security about backups. There aren't many popular backup tools that know how to back up MySQL properly, so that there is no corruption, half-committed transactions, or other assorted problems.

In this chapter we'll begin by considering why you need backups in the first place. Then we'll examine the issues that arise when trying to back up a running database server, including a look at why most backup software isn't well suited to MySQL backups. That leads to a discussion of the various backup-related tools for MySQL and how you can put them to use. Finally, we'll consider what's involved in creating a custom backup script.

Most of the how-to material is in the second half of the chapter. Much of the initial discussion revolves around understanding your backup options and how to go about selecting the right one.

Why Backups?

Strangely, some people never stop to consider *why* they need to back up their servers. The data is important, so we just assume that backing it up is equally important. That's good, because backups *are* important and do need to be done. But by understanding the various ways in which backups may be used, we gain some perspective on the utility of various backup strategies.

---

* If Dr. Huntley ever reads this, Jeremy hopes he doesn't take it personally.

Disaster Recovery

Disaster recovery is the most popular motivation for running backups, but in reality it is often not as relevant as some of the other reasons we'll look at.

What is a disaster? For our purposes, a disaster is any event that causes significant portions of the data to be corrupted or unavailable. Some examples of disasters include the following:

- Hardware failure
- Software failure
- Accidental erasure of data*
- Stolen server
- Physically destroyed server

Any of these disasters can occur at any time. The odds of any one of them occurring are pretty low, but none of them are impossible. Having a known good copy of your data on hand will greatly minimize the pain of having to recover. It's a form of insurance—and cheap insurance at that.

Some of these disasters might be the result of a natural disaster (tornado, earthquake, mudslide, etc.). Unlike a simple disk failure, nature's catastrophes have a habit of physically damaging and even destroying entire buildings. To be truly safe, you need to have off-site backups. Something as simple as taking the tapes home with you every other week or sending a set to a remote office may prove to be invaluable if nature strikes.

Auditing

There are times when you'd like to be able to go back in time and see what a database, table, or even a single record looked like. Having older backups available makes this relatively easy to do. Just pull out the correct files, load them onto a test server, and run some queries. Depending on the type of data you store, there may even be legal reasons why you need to keep old copies of your data around.

Why else might you need the ability to go back in time and examine older copies of your data? You might have to:

- Look for data corruption
- Decide how to fix a newly discovered bug retroactively
- Compute the rate of growth for your databases
- Provide evidence for a lawsuit or investigation

---

* The day after writing this section, Jeremy received a late phone call from a coworker who had accidentally mistyped the WHERE clause in a DELETE query. Luckily there was a good backup on hand.

Of course, there are countless other situations in which older data can be invaluable. The trouble is, you may not realize that until it is too late.

Testing

It's usually a good idea to test changes to an application before putting them into production. To do that, you'll probably have a separate database server you can load data onto to run various tests. Over the course of development, you may need to wipe the data clean and reload it several times.

If you have a recent backup of your production server available, setting up a test server can be downright trivial. Just shut down MySQL, restore the data, start MySQL, and begin testing.

Considerations and Tradeoffs

We considered calling this section "Things You Really Need To Think About" because backing up a running database is more complex than it may first appear to be. This isn't because backups are inherently difficult; it's because MySQL is a bit more complex that you might think.

When it comes to actually performing the backups, you can script the process yourself, use one of the prebuilt tools, or both. It all depends on your needs. In this section, we'll examine the major decisions you'll need to make and how they influence the backup techniques you can use. Then in the next section we'll look at the most popular tools.

Dump or Raw Backup?

One of the first decisions to make is the format of the backups you'd like to create. The result of a database *dump* is one or more files that contain the SQL statements (mostly INSERT and CREATE TABLE) necessary to re-create the data. Dumps are produced using *mysqldump*, described in more detail in "Tools and Techniques," later in this chapter. You can perform dumps over the network so that your backups are created on a host other than your database server. It's possible to produce dumps of any MySQL table type.

Having the contents of the tables as SQL files provides a lot of flexibility. If you simply need to look for a few records, you can load the file in your favorite editor or use a tool such as *grep* or *less* to locate the data. The dumped data is quite readable.

Restoring a dump is easy. Because the dump file contains all the necessary information to re-create the table, you simply need to feed that file back into the *mysql* command-line tool. And if you need to restore only some of the records, you can directly edit the file directly or write a script to prefilter out the records you don't need. Raw backups don't provide this flexibility. You can't easily filter out records from a table when using a raw backup; you can operate only on whole tables.

There are some downsides to using dumps. A dump file consumes far more disk space than the table or database it represents. Not only are there a lot of INSERT statements in the file, all numeric data (which MySQL stores quite efficiently) becomes ASCII, using quite a bit more space. Dumps are more CPU-intensive to produce, so they'll take longer than other methods. Dump files compress rather well using tools such as *gzip* or *bzip2*. Also, reloading a dump requires that MySQL spend considerable CPU time to rebuild all the indexes.

Because there's often a fair amount of unused space and overhead in InnoDB's data files, you'll find that InnoDB tables often take far less space that you might expect when backed up.

While dumps have a lot of advantages, the extra space, time, and CPU power they require are often not worth expending—especially as your databases get larger and larger. It's more efficient to use a *raw backup* technique rather than using dumps. A raw backup is a direct copy of MySQL's data files as they exist on disk. Because the records aren't converted from their native format to ASCII, raw backups are much faster and more efficient than dumps. For ISAM and MyISAM tables, this means copying the data, index, and table definition files. For BDB and InnoDB tables, it also involves preserving the transaction logs and the data.

Both *mysqlhotcopy* and *mysqlsnapshot*, which we describe in some detail later, can be used to produce raw backups of ISAM and MyISAM tables. They do so by locking and flushing the tables before copying the underlying files. The tables may not be written to during the backup process. The InnoDB Hot Backup tool, also discussed later in this chapter, provides a raw backup of your InnoDB data without the need for downtime or locking. There is no equivalent tool for BDB tables.

Raw backups are most often used to back up a live server. To get a consistent backup, ISAM and MyISAM tables need to be locked so that no changes can occur until the backup completes. InnoDB tables have no such restriction.

Restoring a raw backup is relatively easy. For ISAM and MyISAM tables, you simply put the data files in MySQL's data directory. Unless you're using InnoDB's multiple-tablespace support in Version 4.1 or newer, InnoDB tables can't be restored individually from a raw backup because they are stored in shared tablespace files rather than individually. Instead, you'll need to shut down MySQL and restore the tablespace files.

If you have the luxury of shutting down MySQL to perform backups, the backup and restore processes can be greatly simplified. In fact, that's the next decision to consider.

Online or Offline?

Being able to shut down MySQL during backups means not having to worry about consistency problems (discussed in the next section), locking out changes from live applications, or degrading server performance. A nonrunning MySQL instance can be backed up using standard backup software. There's no danger of files changing. If MySQL isn't running, the backup process will likely be faster too; it won't be competing with MySQL for I/O and CPU cycles.

If you're planning to shut down MySQL during backups, make sure that your backup software is configured to back up all of the MySQL-related data. Ideally, you'd back up the entire system, but there may be cases when that isn't feasible. Large MySQL installations often span several filesystems. The binaries may be in one place, config files in another, and the data files elsewhere. Having them on different backup schedules could leave you with a difficult problem if you need to restore just after a major upgrade. The config files may not match the data file locations, for example.

Table Types and Consistency

Maintaining consistency is one of the most tricky and often overlooked issues in database backups. You need to ensure that you're getting a consistent snapshot of your data. Doing so requires an understanding of the types of tables you need to back up and how MySQL handles them.

If you're using MyISAM tables, simply making copies of the various data files isn't sufficient. You must guarantee that all changes have been flushed to disk and that MySQL won't be making changes to any of the tables during the backup process. The obvious solution is to obtain a read lock on each table before it is backed up. That will prevent anyone from making changes to the table while still allowing them to read from it.

That technique works well for a single table, but in a relational database, tables are often related to each other. Records inserted into one table depend on those in another. If that's not accounted for, you can end up with an inconsistent backup—records may exist in one table but have no counterparts in another. It all depends on the order in which the tables were copied and the likelihood that changes were made to one while the other was backed up.

So a good backup program needs to lock groups of related tables before they are copied. Rather than deal with that complexity, the popular solutions for MySQL give you the option of either locking all tables and keeping them locked until the backup is done, or locking and backing up tables one at a time.[*] If neither option appeals to you, there's a good chance that you need to script your own solution. See "Rolling Your Own Backup Script," later in this chapter, for details.

Storage Requirements

The amount of space required to store backups must factor into the decision-making process. How much room does your backup media have? Tape, CD, DVD, and hard disks all have capacity limits, costs, and lifetimes.[†]

After you've determined how much space you can afford and manage effectively, you need to consider how frequently you really need to perform backups. Do you need to back up all your data every day? Can you get by with backing up only your most active tables or databases daily and performing a full backup on the weekend? That will save a lot of space if much of your data changes infrequently.

When dealing with backups, it's a good idea to consider compression. If you're backing up to a tape drive with hardware compression, it's handled for you automatically. Otherwise, you can choose any compression scheme you'd like. Most dump files and raw backups compress rather well. However, if a lot of your data is already compressed (either compressed MyISAM tables or tables with BLOB fields that contain compressed data), there will be little benefit in further compression attempts.

If you have more than a few compressed MyISAM tables, not only should you avoid trying to compress them further, but you should also consider backing them up less frequently. Compressed MyISAM tables are read-only; by definition, they don't change often. You'd have to uncompress the table, make changes, and recompress it. That's rare.

The final issue to think about is retention. How long do you need to keep backups around? Rather than simply throwing out backups when you begin to run out of space, it's best to plan ahead. By taking into account the amount of data you must back up, the amount of space you need, and how long you want to keep data around, you won't run into surprises.

If you find yourself running out of space, consider staggering the backups that you do save. Rather than always deleting the oldest backups, you can use an alternative approach such as removing backups that fall on odd-numbered days. That would allow you to double the age of your oldest backup.

---

[*] Ideally, we'd have the option to unlock each table selectively after it is copied, but MySQL doesn't allow that yet.

[†] But hard disks seem to be growing in capacity without bound. It shouldn't be long before you can buy a terabyte hard disk.

Replication

If you're using MySQL's replication features (described in Chapter 7), you can be a lot more flexible in your approach to backups. In fact, you may want to set up a slave just to simplify backups.

By performing backups on a slave, you eliminate the need ever to interrupt systems that may need to make changes on the master. In a $24 \times 7 \times 365$ operation, this is an excellent way to ensure that you always have a copy of your data on another machine (this method is commonly used at Yahoo!). And since you can switch to the slave if the master dies, it significantly reduces the downtime when something does go wrong.

When backing up a slave, it's important always to save the replication files as well. That includes the *master.info* file, relay logs, relay index, and so on. Without them, you can't easily restore a slave that has suffered a failure. The files contain information about where the slave left off in the replication process. See Chapter 7 for more information.

Tools and Techniques

With an understanding of the various backup-related issues you need to consider, let's move on to examining the tools available. If you have a complex configuration or unusual needs, there's a chance that none of these alone will do the job for you. Instead, you'll need to build a custom solution—possibly using one or more of the tools described here.

This section isn't intended to be a comprehensive reference for each tool. Instead, it focuses on presenting the relevant features of each one so that you better understand your choices. Once you've selected a tool, be sure to consult the documentation for it. There's a good chance that the tool has options that didn't exist when this book was written. We will post news about available tools at our web site: *http://highperformancemysql.com* (see the Preface for more information).

mysqldump

For a long time, *mysqldump* was the only backup tool available for MySQL. It is a command-line utility for dumping tables of any type into SQL flat files. It even handles foreign-key constraints properly. *mysqldump* comes with MySQL, so you're guaranteed to have it installed already.

Using *mysqldump* to perform dumps is ideally suited to backing up small databases. The resulting files are large compared to the data being dumped, and it's not a very efficient process.

To back up all the databases on a server, execute the following command:

```
$ mysqldump -u root -pPassword -x --all-databases > dump.sql
```

The -x flag tells *mysqldump* to lock all tables during the backup to ensure consistency.

There are a few drawbacks to that method. Most importantly, the entire dump will go to a single file, which can result in a very large file if you have a lot of data to back up. *mysqldump* doesn't have an option to split the output into separate files based on database or table name.

If you need to back up a subset of all the databases, you can provide a list of database names on the command line:

```
$ mysqldump -u root -pPassword -x --databases db1 db2 db3 > dump.sql
```

This creates a dump file with the information necessary to recreate the db1, db2, and db3 databases.

If you need to back up only a few tables from a single database, you can provide the database and table names:

```
$ mysqldump -u root -pPassword -x db1 table1 table2 table3 > dump.sql
```

mysqldump works well over the network, too. By adding a -h argument, you tell it to connect to a remote MySQL host instead:

```
$ mysqldump -h db.example.com -u root -pPassword -x --all-databases > dump.sql
```

Restoring

No matter which options you use, restoring a dump is always straightforward. Simply feed the dump file back through the *mysql* command-line tool:

```
$ mysql -u root -pPassword < dump.sql
```

If you find yourself restoring dump files frequently (perhaps on a test server), consider using *mysqldump*'s --extended-insert option. It tells *mysqldump* to bundle many insert statements together using MySQL's bulk insert syntax:

```
INSERT INTO mytable (col1, col2, col3)
VALUES (val1, val2, val3) (val1, val2, val3) ...
```

This makes the restore run far faster than the default method, which uses one insert statement per row. It also results in much smaller dump files.

Normally, *mysqldump* requests all the rows for the table it is dumping, buffers them in memory, and writes the data to disk. It does this to minimize the amount of time tables are locked on the server. However, when dumping large tables, you need to use the --quick option; it prevents the buffering, instead telling *mysqldump* to fetch rows from the server one at a time. While it's a bit slower* than the default method,

---

* That's not a typo. The --quick option causes the dump process to take a bit more time.

it's the only option when your tables are too big to fit in memory on the host that's running the dump.

In fact, you might consider using the `--opt` option. It enables several useful options at once, including `--quick` and `--extended-insert`.

Windows users should use the `--result-file` option to specify an output file:

```
$ mysqldump -u root -pPassword --all-databases --result-file=dump.sql
```

Otherwise, Windows converts all newline characters (\n) to a carriage return plus newline (\r\n). The silent conversion will cause endless frustration when you need to restore a table in a hurry.

mysqlhotcopy

Originally created by Tim Bunce (the architect of Perl's DBI), *mysqlhotcopy* is a Perl script included in the standard MySQL distributions. Its purpose is to automate the process of backing up a database consisting of ISAM and MyISAM tables while the server is running. It's the most popular tool available for performing online raw backups and is best suited to backing up single databases on a live server. It operates by getting a read lock on all the tables to be copied, copying them, and then releasing the lock. This means it doesn't scale very well as traffic or size increase.

To back up a live database, such as the test database, run:

```
$ mysqlhotcopy -u root -p Password test /tmp
```

You'll end up with a *test* subdirectory in */tmp* that contains all the tables from the backed up database.

```
$ ls -l /tmp/test
total 108
-rw-rw----  1 mysql  users  8550 May  3 12:02 archive.frm
-rw-rw----  1 mysql  users    25 May  3 12:02 archive.MYD
-rw-rw----  1 mysql  users  2048 May 23 12:58 archive.MYI
-rw-rw----  1 mysql  users  8924 Mar  4 21:52 contacts.frm
-rw-rw----  1 mysql  users  7500 Mar  5 21:11 contacts.MYD
-rw-rw----  1 mysql  users  5120 May 23 12:58 contacts.MYI
-rw-rw----  1 mysql  users  8550 May  3 12:02 dirty.frm
-rw-rw----  1 mysql  users    25 May  3 12:02 dirty.MYD
-rw-rw----  1 mysql  users  2048 May 23 12:58 dirty.MYI
-rwxr-xr-x  1 mysql  users  8558 Feb 26  2001 maybe_bug.frm*
-rwxr-xr-x  1 mysql  users    45 Feb 26  2001 maybe_bug.MYD*
-rwxr-xr-x  1 mysql  users  2048 May 23 12:58 maybe_bug.MYI*
-rwxr-xr-x  1 mysql  users  8715 Jan 15  2001 test_more_info.frm*
-rwxr-xr-x  1 mysql  users   784 Jan 16  2001 test_more_info.MYD*
-rwxr-xr-x  1 mysql  users  2048 May 23 12:58 test_more_info.MYI*
```

As you can see, *mysqlhotcopy* copies the data (*.MYD*), index (*.MYI*), and table definition (*.frm*) files for each table in the test database. To conserve space, you may choose to back up only the *.frm* and *.MYD* files in their entirety. Given the `--noindices` option, *mysqlhotcopy* copies only the first 2,048 bytes of each *.MYI* file. That's all MySQL needs to reconstruct the indexes at a later date.

```
$ mysqlhotcopy -u root -p Password --noindices test /tmp
```

Because it is written in Perl, *mysqlhotcopy* has support for regular expressions too. To back up every database that contains the string test in its name, run:

```
$ mysqlhotcopy -u root -p Password --regexp=test /tmp
```

In practice, few users use that capability, but it is there.

Restoring

To restore one or more tables, simply copy the files into the proper subdirectory of MySQL's data directory. For example, if you need to restore the test_more_info table into the test database, run:

```
$ cp /tmp/test/test_more_info.* datadir/test
```

If you used the --noindices option to truncate the *.MYI* files, you need to repair the tables before you can use them. You can use either the myisamchk -r command:

```
$ cd datadir/test
$ myisamchk -r test_more_info
```

or the REPAIR TABLE test_more_info command from within MySQL:

```
mysql> REPAIR TABLE test_more_info
```

That's all there is to it. You can then freely use the restored table.

mysqlsnapshot

Jeremy originally wrote *mysqlsnapshot* to simplify the process of configuring replication slaves at Yahoo! using MySQL 3.23.xx. As the amount of data grew, he realized one day that a better online backup system was needed. After working with the code for *mysqlsnapshot*, Jeremy realized that if he added one more feature it would do the job quite well. In addition, it would be a much smaller and easier to maintain than *mysqlhotcopy*.

He hasn't yet submitted *mysqlsnapshot* for inclusion in the MySQL distribution. It may be there by the time you read this, but if not, you can find it at *http://jeremy. zawodny.com/mysql/mysqlsnapshot/*.

mysqlsnapshot is best used to back up an entire database server without taking it offline. It has no options for specifying particular databases or tables to include or exclude in the process. It copies everything.

To back up all databases on a server, run:

```
$ mysqlsnapshot -u root -p Password -s /tmp/snap --split -n
checking for binary logging... ok
backing up db database... done
```

```
backing up db jzawodn... done
backing up db mysql... done
backing up db nuke... done
backing up db phplib... done
backing up db prout... done
backing up db test... done
snapshot completed in /tmp/snap/
```

This results in one tar file for each database, written to the */tmp/snap* directory. If you remove the --split option, *mysqlsnapshot* puts all the data in a single tar file. If you supply the -z argument, it compresses the backup using gzip.

Restoring

Restoring a backup created with *mysqlsnapshot* is just a matter of untarring the files in MySQL's data directory. To restore the prout database, you execute:

```
$ cd datadir/test
$ tar -xvf /tmp/prout.tar
```

This illustrates one reason you ought to consider keeping each database in a separate tar file. By doing so, your backups will be more manageable (you can selectively delete them on a per-database basis), and you can be selective about what you restore.

InnoDB Hot Backup

If you're keeping a large amount of data in InnoDB and would like online backups, the InnoDB Hot Backup tool is the best choice. Unlike MySQL, it's not free. Rather, it's a relatively inexpensive commercial tool developed by the makers of InnoDB. See *http://www.innodb.com/hotbackup.html* for details.

To use the Hot Backup Tool (*ibbackup*), you create a configuration file that tells *ibbackup* where to archive the data. Then run it like this:

```
$ ibbackup /etc/my.cnf /etc/ibbackup.cnf
```

The backup tool needs to read the MySQL configuration file as well as its own configuration. Recent versions of *ibbackup* have added the ability to compress the backup (--compress).

It's important to note that *ibbackup* doesn't back up the *.frm* files for your tables. So even if you use InnoDB tables exclusively in MySQL, you still need to back up the *.frm* files separately from using *ibbackup*. This is slated to change in the future, so check the InnoDB manual for the most recent news.

Restoring a backup is a straightforward process. With MySQL offline, simply run:

```
$ ibbackup --restore /etc/ibbackup.cnf
```

Then start MySQL.

Offline Backups

As discussed earlier, there are numerous benefits to shutting down MySQL before performing a backup. To recap:

- There will be no consistency problems.
- You can use existing backup software.
- Backups can be very fast.

If you are using a home-grown backup script of some sort, simply add a call to the *mysqladmin* command like this:

```
# Now, shut down MySQL before the backup begins.
mysqladmin -u root -pPassword shutdown

# And start the backup
...

# Then bring MySQL back up
/usr/local/mysql/bin/mysqld_safe &
```

If you use a prepackaged backup system, you need to ensure that MySQL is down before it starts. If the backup software is run locally on the MySQL server, that's easy. Rather than running the software directly, create a small shell script or batch file that handles the stopping and starting of MySQL around the backup process—much like the previous example.

In larger environments, it is common to run client/server backup software. The backup server contacts a daemon running on a remote server when it is time for the backup process to begin. That daemon (running on your MySQL server) then feeds data to the backup server over the network. It is also common in such environments to let the backup software control the exact starting time of the backup.

In a case like that, you may need to find an alternative approach for backing up MySQL, or you'll need to do some digging in the backup software's manual. There's a good chance that you can find a way to make the backup software start and stop MySQL when it needs to. If not, you may be able to use one of the other backup strategies. If you have sufficient disk space, you can perform the backup directly on the MySQL server and let your normal backup process back up those files.

Restoring

Once again, MySQL makes it easy to restore data.* Unless you're restoring the entire MySQL installation, you need to recover the files that make up the tables and databases you need to restore. Once you have them, copy them back into MySQL's data directory and start MySQL.

---

* Your backup software may not, but there's little we can do about that here.

Filesystem Snapshots

Taking a snapshot of MySQL's data is the fastest and least intrusive method of backing up an online server. While the implementation details vary, a snapshot is an online copy of your data—usually stored on the same filesystem or volume. In fact, most systems use a copy-on-write scheme to minimize the free space required to take a snapshot.

MySQL itself provides no support for taking snapshots, but various free and commercial filesystems and storage solutions do. In the Linux world, LVM (the Linux volume manager) has snapshot capabilities. Veritas sells a filesystem product for most versions of Unix (and Linux) that can take snapshots. FreeBSD 5.x may offer snapshot capabilities too.

In the hardware space, Network Appliance's popular "filers" can be used to take filesystem snapshots. EMC has two ways of doing this: snapshots, which are just like the snapshots described above, and BCVs (business continuance volumes). They are, in effect, additional mirrors of a volume that can be broken off and mounted on other systems. They require double the amount of storage and are therefore expensive.

Snapshots are best used with a more traditional backup solution. By itself, a snapshot doesn't do much to guard against hardware failures. Sure, you can use a snapshot to quickly restore an accidentally dropped table, but all the snapshots in the world won't help if the disk controller catches fire.

Be sure that you have sufficient space reserved on your volume for the number of snapshots you plan to keep online. Most snapshot-capable filesystems require that you reserve a minimum amount of disk space for snapshot data. If your server processes a lot of write queries, you can easily exceed the reserved space. Check your filesystem documentation for complete details.

Just as with the other approach to online backups, you must be careful to flush and obtain a read lock on all ISAM and MyISAM tables before initiating a snapshot. The easiest way to do this is to use MySQL's FLUSH TABLES WITH READ LOCK command. It will hold the lock until you disconnect from MySQL or issue an UNLOCK TABLES command. We'll discuss this in the next section.

Rolling Your Own Backup Script

There are always circumstances in which the standard tools aren't enough to get the job done. Perhaps they're not flexible enough, they're too slow, or they just don't work the way you'd like. The solution, of course, is to build your own tool. In doing so, you may decide to use the existing utilities or to just do your own thing.

Let's look at writing a simple MySQL backup script in Perl. While it isn't the most powerful or flexible script in the world, it can serve as a starting point for building a custom solution.

The script (*mysnap.pl*) solves the following problem. You have a MySQL server that keeps all its data on a volume with snapshot capabilities. Every 12 hours, you'd like to perform the following tasks to make a good snapshot and gather a list of tables and their sizes:

1. Flush and lock all MyISAM tables.
2. Assemble a list of every table and its size.
3. Initiate a snapshot.
4. Unlock the tables.
5. Output the list of table sizes.

The script's output can be captured and automatically mailed to a backup administrator. A *cron* entry like this does the job nicely if you're using Vixie *cron* (common on Linux and FreeBSD):

```
MAILTO=backup-admin@example.com
00 */12 * * * /usr/local/bin/mysnap.pl
```

Otherwise, you can use the more traditional format:

```
00 0,12 * * * /usr/local/bin/mysnap.pl | mail backup-admin@example.com
```

You'll find the complete script listed here.

```perl
#!/usr/bin/perl -w
#
# mysnap.pl - snapshot mysql and mail stats to backup admins

use strict;
use DBIx::DWIW;

$|=1;   # unbuffer output

my $db_user = 'backup_user';
my $db_pass = 'backup_pass';
my $db_name = 'mysql';
my $db_host = 'localhost';
my $command = '/usr/local/bin/snapshot';
my $conn    = DBIx::DWIW->Connect(DB => $db_name, User => $db_user,
                                  Pass => $db_pass, Host => $db_host);

my @table_sizes;

# flush and lock all tables
$conn->Execute("FLUSH TABLES WITH READ LOCK");

# gather stats on the tables
my @db_list = $conn->FlatArray("SHOW DATABASES");

for my $db (@db_list)
{
    $conn->Execute("USE $db") or die "$!";
    my @table_info = $conn->Hashes("SHOW TABLE STATUS");
```

```
    for my $table (@table_info)
    {
        my $name = $table->{Name};
        my $size = $table->{Data_length};
        push @table_sizes, ["$db.$name", $size];
    }
}

# run the snapshot
system($command);

# unlock the tables
$conn->Execute("UNLOCK TABLES");
$conn->Disconnect;

# sort by size and print
for my $info (sort { $b->[1] cmp $a->[1] } @table_sizes)
{
    printf "%-10s  %s\n", $info->[1], $info->[0];
}

exit;

__END__
```

Let's walk through the basic flow. The first thing to notice is that the script requires a module from CPAN. DBIx::DWIW simplifies most Perl work with MySQL.* After using the necessary modules, define the necessary variables for the connection to MySQL. Then you execute a FLUSH TABLES WITH READ LOCK to make sure all changes are on disk and that no further changes will happen.

Once the tables have all been flushed and locked, the script collects a list of all the databases on the server and iterates through them. In each database, the script gets the status of all the tables using SHOW TABLE STATUS, which produces records that look like this:

```
mysql> SHOW TABLE STATUS \G
*************************** 1. row ***************************
           Name: journal
           Type: MyISAM
     Row_format: Dynamic
           Rows: 417
 Avg_row_length: 553
    Data_length: 230848
Max_data_length: 4294967295
   Index_length: 5120
      Data_free: 0
 Auto_increment: NULL
    Create_time: 2001-12-09 23:18:06
```

* The DWIW stands for Do What I Want, a play on Perl's Do What I Mean.

```
     Update_time: 2002-06-16 22:20:13
      Check_time: 2002-05-19 17:03:35
   Create_options:
          Comment:
```

The script grabs the `Name` and `Data_length` fields for each table and stores them in the `@table_sizes` list. Once that data has been gathered, the script calls the `snapshot` command. Finally, it unlocks the tables and prints the list of tables and sizes (sorted by size).

Running *mysnap.pl* produces output like this:

```
$ mysnap.pl
9300388448  Datascope.SymbolHistory
1458868716  Chart.SymbolHistory
773481608   logs.pfs
749644404   IDX.LinkLog
457454228   SEC.SEC_Filings
442951712   IDX.BusinessWireArticles
343099968   Datascope.Symbols
208388096   IDX.Headlines
...
```

As expected, the largest tables are listed first—regardless of which databases they reside in.

There are many ways *mysnap.pl* can be improved or enhanced. It could:

- Perform more error checking.
- Compare the current table sizes with those from the previous run.
- Notice whether a table has grown beyond a preset threshold.
- Ignore Heap tables, since they don't reside on disk.

None of those enhancements are particularly difficult. With even a basic grasp of Perl and a bit of time, you can transform that script to something custom-tailored for your needs.

## CHAPTER 10

Security

Keeping MySQL secure is critical to maintaining the integrity and privacy of your data. Just as you have to protect Unix or Windows login accounts, you need to ensure that MySQL accounts have good passwords and only the privileges they need. Because MySQL is often used on a network, you also need to consider the security of the host that runs MySQL, who has access to it, and what someone could learn by sniffing traffic on your network.

In this chapter we'll look at how MySQL's permissions work and how you can keep control of who has access to the data. We'll also consider some of the basic operating system and network security measures you can employ to keep the bad guys out of your databases. Finally, we'll discuss encryption and running MySQL in a highly restricted environment.

Account Basics

Consider first the example of a typical Unix login. You have a username and a password, along with, possibly, some other information such as the login owner's full name, telephone number, or other information. There is no distinction between the user *dredd* coming from *foo.example.com* and *dredd* coming from *bar.example.com*. To Unix, they are one and the same.

Each account in MySQL is composed of a username, password, and location (usually hostname, IP address, or wildcard). As we'll see, having a location associated with the username adds a bit of complexity to an otherwise simple system. The user *joe* who logs in from *joe.example.com* may or may not be the same as the *joe* who logs in from *sally.example.com*. From MySQL's point of view, they are completely different. They may even have different passwords and privileges.

Database-Specific Passwords

We indicated that users are stored as username/password/location. It's important to note that one qualifier not included is the database. For instance:

```
mysql> GRANT SELECT ON Foo.* to 'nobody'@'localhost' IDENTIFIED BY 'FooPass';
mysql> GRANT SELECT ON Bar.* to 'nobody'@'localhost' IDENTIFIED BY 'BarPass';
```

You might think, to look at that, that user *nobody* connects to Foo using *FooPass* as his password and to Bar using *BarPass* as his password. That's not the case. What actually happens is that *nobody* has his password changed in the users table to *BarPass*, and any connections to the Bar database using *FooPass* will fail to authenticate.

This is especially important because it means that if you want to limit access for an application to one database and not another, your codebase may have the password to "its" database encoded into it. If someone sees that source code, and you use the same MySQL user for some other application that accesses a different database, the person who sees one set of source code will now know how to gain access to the other database.

MySQL uses a series of *grant tables* to keep track of users and the various privileges they can have. The tables are ordinary MyISAM tables[*] that live in the mysql database. Storing the security information itself in MySQL makes a lot of sense. It allows you to use standard SQL queries to make any security changes. There are no additional configuration files for MySQL to process. But, this also means that if the server is improperly configured, any user could make security changes!

Over the lifetime of a typical database connection, MySQL may perform three different types of security checks:

Authentication
> Who are you? For each incoming connection, MySQL checks your username, the password you supplied, and the host from which you are connecting. Once it knows who you are, the information is used to determine your privileges.

Authorization
> What are you allowed to do? Shutting down the server, for example, requires that you have the shutdown privilege.

Access control
> What data are you allowed to see and/or manipulate? When you try to read or modify data, MySQL checks to see that you've been granted permission to see or change the columns you are selecting.

---

[*] And they must remain ordinary MyISAM tables. Don't change their type.

As you'll see, authorization and access control can be a bit difficult to distinguish in MySQL. Just remember that authorization applies to global privileges (discussed shortly), while access control applies to typical queries (SELECT, UPDATE, and so on).

Privileges

Access control is made up of several *privileges* that control how you may use and manipulate the various objects in MySQL: databases, tables, columns, and indexes. For any combination of objects, the privileges are all boolean—either you have them or you don't. These per-object privileges are named after the SQL queries you use to trigger their checks. For example, you need the select privilege on a table to SELECT data from it.

Here's the full list of per-object privileges:

- Select
- Insert
- Update
- Index
- Alter
- Create
- Grant
- References

Not all privileges apply to each type of object in MySQL. The insert privilege is checked for all of them, but the alter privilege applies only to databases and tables. That makes perfect sense, because you insert data into columns all the time, but there's no ALTER COLUMN command in SQL. Table 10-1 lists which privileges apply to each type of object in MySQL.

Table 10-1. Access control privileges

Privilege	Databases	Tables	Columns
Select	✓	✓	✓
Insert	✓	✓	✓
Update	✓	✓	✓
Delete	✓	✓	
Index	✓	✓	
Alter	✓	✓	
Create	✓	✓	
Drop	✓	✓	
Grant	✓	✓	
References	✓	✓	✓

While most of those privileges are rather straightforward, a few deserve some additional explanation:

Select

> The select privilege is required for `SELECT` queries that access data stored in MySQL. No privilege is needed to perform simple math (`SELECT 2*5`), date/time conversions (`SELECT Unix_TIMESTAMP(NOW())`) and formatting, or various utility functions (`SELECT MD5('hello world')`).

Index

> This single privilege allows you to create and drop indexes. Even though index changes are made via `ALTER TABLE` commands, the index privilege is what matters.

Grant

> When using the `GRANT` command (described later), you may specify `WITH GRANT OPTION` to give the user the grant privilege on a table. This privilege allows the user to grant any rights you have granted him to other users. In other words, he can share his privileges with another user.

References

> The references privilege controls whether or not you may reference a column in a given table as part of a foreign key constraint.

Global privileges

In addition to the per-object privileges, there is a group of privileges that are concerned with the functioning of MySQL itself and are applied server-wide. These are the authorization checks mentioned earlier:

Reload

> The reload privilege is the least harmful of the server-wide privileges. It allows you to execute the various `FLUSH` commands, such as `FLUSH TABLES`, `FLUSH STATUS`, and so on.

Shutdown

> This privilege allows you to shut down MySQL.

Process

> The process privilege allows you to execute the `SHOW PROCESSLIST` and `KILL` commands. By watching the processlist in MySQL, you can capture raw SQL queries as they are being executed—including the queries that set passwords.

File

> This privilege controls whether you can execute a `LOAD DATA INFILE...` command. The danger in allowing this is that a user can use the command to read an arbitrary file into a table, as long as it is readable by the `mysqld` process.

Super

> This privilege allows you to `KILL` any query on the server. Without it, you're limited to only those queries that belong to you.

Each server-wide privilege has far-reaching security implications, so be very cautious when granting any of them!

The Grant Tables

MySQL's grant tables are the heart of its security system. The information in these tables determines the privileges of every user and host that connects to MySQL. By correctly manipulating the records, you can give users exactly the permissions they need (and no more). Incorrectly manipulating them can open up your server to the possibility of abuse and damage.

Let's take a brief look at the five grant tables before really digging in. We've included them here in the order that MySQL consults them. You'll see why that becomes important in a minute.

user
> The user table contains the global privileges and encrypted passwords. It is responsible for determining which hosts and users may connect to the server.

host
> The host table assigns privileges on a per-host basis, regardless of the user. When deciding to accept or reject a connection, MySQL consults the user table as noted earlier. Though we list it as a grant table, the host is never modified through use of the GRANT or REVOKE commands. You can add and remove entries manually, however.

db The db table sets database-level privileges.

tables_priv
> The tables_priv table controls table-specific privileges.

columns_priv
> Records in the columns_priv table specify a user's privileges for a single column of a single table in a particular database.

Privilege Checks

For each query issued, MySQL checks to make sure the user has the required privileges to perform the query. In doing so, it consults each of the tables in a specific order. Privileges set in one table may be overridden by a table checked later.

In other words, the privilege system works through inheritance. Privileges granted in the user table are passed down through all the other checks. If there are no matching records in any of the other tables, the original privileges set forth in the user table apply.

MySQL uses different criteria when checking each grant table. Records in the host table, for example, are matched based on the host from which the user has connected and the name of the database that the query will read from or write to. Records in the db table, on the other hand, match based on the host, database, and username. Table 10-2 summarizes the fields used for matching records in each of the grant tables.

Table 10-2. Fields used for matching grant table records

Table	Password	User	Host	Db	Table	Column
user	✓	✓	✓			
host			✓	✓		
db		✓	✓	✓		
tables_priv		✓	✓	✓	✓	
columns_priv		✓	✓	✓	✓	✓

Let's look at the schema for each table as well as the privileges each affects.

The user Table

MySQL's user table contains authentication information about users as well as their global privileges. It contains fields for the username, hostname, and password. The remainder of the fields represent each of the privileges, which are all off by default. As you'll see, many of the other tables also contain the Host and User fields as well as a subset of the privilege fields that are present in the user table, but only the user table contains passwords. In a way, it is the */etc/passwd* of MySQL.

Even if a user has no global privileges at all, there must be a record in the user table for her, if she is to issue a command successfully. See the section "Grant Mechanics," later in this chapter, for an example.

In the meantime, let's have a look at the fields in the user table:

```
mysql> DESCRIBE user;
+-----------------+---------------------+------+-----+---------+-------+
| Field           | Type                | Null | Key | Default | Extra |
+-----------------+---------------------+------+-----+---------+-------+
| Host            | varchar(60)         |      | PRI |         |       |
| User            | varchar(16)         |      | PRI |         |       |
| Password        | varchar(45)         |      |     |         |       |
| Select_priv     | enum('N','Y')       |      |     | N       |       |
| Insert_priv     | enum('N','Y')       |      |     | N       |       |
| Update_priv     | enum('N','Y')       |      |     | N       |       |
| Delete_priv     | enum('N','Y')       |      |     | N       |       |
| Create_priv     | enum('N','Y')       |      |     | N       |       |
| Drop_priv       | enum('N','Y')       |      |     | N       |       |
| Reload_priv     | enum('N','Y')       |      |     | N       |       |
| Shutdown_priv   | enum('N','Y')       |      |     | N       |       |
| Process_priv    | enum('N','Y')       |      |     | N       |       |
| File_priv       | enum('N','Y')       |      |     | N       |       |
```

```
| Grant_priv            | enum('N','Y')                    |   |   | N |   |   |
| References_priv       | enum('N','Y')                    |   |   | N |   |   |
| Index_priv            | enum('N','Y')                    |   |   | N |   |   |
| Alter_priv            | enum('N','Y')                    |   |   | N |   |   |
| Show_db_priv          | enum('N','Y')                    |   |   | N |   |   |
| Super_priv            | enum('N','Y')                    |   |   | N |   |   |
| Create_tmp_table_priv | enum('N','Y')                    |   |   | N |   |   |
| Lock_tables_priv      | enum('N','Y')                    |   |   | N |   |   |
| Execute_priv          | enum('N','Y')                    |   |   | N |   |   |
| Repl_slave_priv       | enum('N','Y')                    |   |   | N |   |   |
| Repl_client_priv      | enum('N','Y')                    |   |   | N |   |   |
| ssl_type              | enum('','ANY','X509','SPECIFIED')|   |   |   |   |   |
| ssl_cipher            | blob                             |   |   |   |   |   |
| x509_issuer           | blob                             |   |   |   |   |   |
| x509_subject          | blob                             |   |   |   |   |   |
| max_questions         | int(11) unsigned                 |   |   | 0 |   |   |
| max_updates           | int(11) unsigned                 |   |   | 0 |   |   |
| max_connections       | int(11) unsigned                 |   |   | 0 |   |   |
+-----------------------+----------------------------------+---+---+---+---+---+
```

When a user first connects to MySQL, it checks the user table to decide if the user is allowed to connect and is who she says she is (the password check). But how exactly does MySQL make those decisions?

Matching a username is a simple test of equality. If the username exists in the table, it's a match. The same is true of the password. Because all MySQL passwords are hashed using the built-in PASSWORD( ) function, expect MySQL to do something like this:

```
SELECT *
  FROM user
 WHERE User = 'username'
   AND Password = PASSWORD('password')
```

However, this query could return multiple records. The user table's primary key is composed of the fields User and Host, not just User, which means a single user can have multiple entries in the table—especially if she is allowed to connect from several specifically named hosts. MySQL must check all those records to see which one matches.

Things get more interesting when you realize that the Host field may contain any of the standard SQL wildcard characters: _ (matches a single character) and % (matches any number of characters). What does MySQL do if the user *jane* attempts to connect from the host *jane.example.com*, and the user table contains records for *jane@jane.example.com* as well as *jane@%.example.com*?

Host matching

The first rule you need to know about MySQL's privilege system is this: the most specific match always wins. MySQL will always prefer an exact match over one that uses a wildcard of any sort.

MySQL accomplishes this by internally sorting the records in the user table based on the Host and User fields—in that order. Hostnames and IP addresses without wildcards come before those that contain them.

Given a list of host entries such as this:

- %
- *localhost*
- *jane.example.com*
- *%.example.com*
- *192.168.1.50*
- *joe.example.com*
- *192.168.2.0/255.255.255.0*

MySQL sorts them in this order:

- *localhost*
- *192.168.1.50*
- *jane.example.com*
- *joe.example.com*
- *192.168.2.0/255.255.255.0*
- *%.example.com*
- *%*

To clarify what "most specific" means to MySQL, let's consider how MySQL will match several username and hostname combinations. Assuming that the user *jane* and the "any user" (represented here as the absence of a username) can connect from some of the various hosts listed earlier, MySQL sorts the entries like this:

- *jane@jane.example.com*
- *jane@joe.example.com*
- *@localhost*
- *@192.168.1.50*
- *@jane.example.com*
- *@joe.example.com*
- *@%.example.com*
- *jane@%.example.com*
- *jane@%*

When *jane* connects from *jane.example.com*, she may have a different set of privileges from when she connects from *joe.example.com*. Other users connecting from *web.example.com* will match the *%@%.example.com* record and receive whatever privileges have been granted in that row. When *jane* connects from *web.example.com*, she'll receive the privileges granted to *jane@%.example.com*.

The host Table

The host table assigns database-level privileges for users connecting from specific hosts (or groups of hosts). Let's look at the table:

```
mysql> DESCRIBE host;
+--------------------+--------------+------+-----+---------+-------+
| Field              | Type         | Null | Key | Default | Extra |
+--------------------+--------------+------+-----+---------+-------+
| Host               | char(60)     |      | PRI |         |       |
| Db                 | char(64)     |      | PRI |         |       |
| Select_priv        | enum('N','Y')|      |     | N       |       |
| Insert_priv        | enum('N','Y')|      |     | N       |       |
```

```
| Update_priv           | enum('N','Y') |   | N |   |   |
| Delete_priv           | enum('N','Y') |   | N |   |   |
| Create_priv           | enum('N','Y') |   | N |   |   |
| Drop_priv             | enum('N','Y') |   | N |   |   |
| Grant_priv            | enum('N','Y') |   | N |   |   |
| References_priv       | enum('N','Y') |   | N |   |   |
| Index_priv            | enum('N','Y') |   | N |   |   |
| Alter_priv            | enum('N','Y') |   | N |   |   |
| Create_tmp_table_priv | enum('N','Y') |   | N |   |   |
| Lock_tables_priv      | enum('N','Y') |   | N |   |   |
+-----------------------+---------------+------+-----+---------+-------+
```

With the exception of the Db field, this table is a subset of the user table. It is missing all the global privileges (such as the shutdown privilege), but all the privileges that can be applied to a database objects are there. As expected, they all default to No.

Records might appear in this table to enforce a rule that all connections from hosts in the *public.example.com* domain are forbidden from changing any data. You can also allow anyone connecting from *secure.example.com* to have full privileges on tables in the security database.

The db Table

The db table specifies database-level privileges for a particular user and database:

```
mysql> DESCRIBE db;
+-----------------------+---------------+------+-----+---------+-------+
| Field                 | Type          | Null | Key | Default | Extra |
+-----------------------+---------------+------+-----+---------+-------+
| Host                  | char(60)      |      | PRI |         |       |
| Db                    | char(64)      |      | PRI |         |       |
| User                  | char(16)      |      | PRI |         |       |
| Select_priv           | enum('N','Y') |      |     | N       |       |
| Insert_priv           | enum('N','Y') |      |     | N       |       |
| Update_priv           | enum('N','Y') |      |     | N       |       |
| Delete_priv           | enum('N','Y') |      |     | N       |       |
| Create_priv           | enum('N','Y') |      |     | N       |       |
| Drop_priv             | enum('N','Y') |      |     | N       |       |
| Grant_priv            | enum('N','Y') |      |     | N       |       |
| References_priv       | enum('N','Y') |      |     | N       |       |
| Index_priv            | enum('N','Y') |      |     | N       |       |
| Alter_priv            | enum('N','Y') |      |     | N       |       |
| Create_tmp_table_priv | enum('N','Y') |      |     | N       |       |
| Lock_tables_priv      | enum('N','Y') |      |     | N       |       |
+-----------------------+---------------+------+-----+---------+-------+
```

This table is virtually identical to the host table. The only difference is the addition of the User field, which is needed in order to create per-user privileges.

By making the appropriate entries in this table, you could ensure that *joe* has full privileges on the sales database when connecting from either *accounting.example.com* or *cfo.example.com*.

The tables_priv Table

Going a level deeper, the tables_priv table controls table-level privileges (those applied to all columns in a table) for a particular user:

```
mysql> DESCRIBE tables_priv;
+-------------+---------------------+------+-----+---------+-------+
| Field       | Type                | Null | Key | Default | Extra |
+-------------+---------------------+------+-----+---------+-------+
| Host        | char(60) binary     |      | PRI |         |       |
| Db          | char(64) binary     |      | PRI |         |       |
| User        | char(16) binary     |      | PRI |         |       |
| Table_name  | char(60) binary     |      | PRI |         |       |
| Grantor     | char(77)            |      | MUL |         |       |
| Timestamp   | timestamp(14)       | YES  |     | NULL    |       |
| Table_priv  | set(...)            |      |     |         |       |
| Column_priv | set(...)            |      |     |         |       |
+-------------+---------------------+------+-----+---------+-------+
```

This table probably looks a bit odd. The creators of MySQL decided to use a SET( ) function to represent privileges in both the tables_priv and columns_priv tables. In doing so, they made it difficult for authors to present a nice clean listing of all the grant tables in their books (we're sure that wasn't their intent).

The ... in the Table_priv field should actually read:

```
'Select','Insert','Update','Delete','Create','Drop','Grant'
```

and the ... in the Column_priv field really contains:

```
'Select','Insert','Update','References'
```

Both are new fields not seen in previous tables. As their names imply, they control table and column privileges. There's another new field in the table: Grantor. This 77-character field records the identity of the user who granted these privileges. It is 77 characters in size because it is intended to hold a username (up to 16 characters), an @ symbol, and a hostname (up to 60 characters).

The Timestamp field also makes its first appearance in this table. As you'd expect, it simply records the time when the record was created or modified.

Using table-level privileges isn't very common in MySQL, so don't be surprised if your server has no records in its tables_priv table. If you've installed the popular *phpMyAdmin* utility (discussed in Appendix C), however, you might see something like this:

```
mysql> SELECT * FROM tables_priv \G
*************************** 1. row ***************************
       Host: localhost
         Db: mysql
       User: phpmyadmin
 Table_name: user
    Grantor: root@localhost
```

```
      Timestamp: 20020308185823
     Table_priv:
    Column_priv: Select
```

This entry grants the phpmyadmin user access to the database, with the Select privileges he needs to obtain information from MySQL. This table doesn't grant privileges on any particular data; that has to be done in another table, as you'll see in the next section.

The columns_priv Table

The final table, columns_priv, is similar to the tables_priv table. It specifies individual column privileges in a particular table:

```
mysql> DESCRIBE columns_priv;
+-------------+---------------------+------+-----+---------+-------+
| Field       | Type                | Null | Key | Default | Extra |
+-------------+---------------------+------+-----+---------+-------+
| Host        | char(60) binary     |      | PRI |         |       |
| Db          | char(64) binary     |      | PRI |         |       |
| User        | char(16) binary     |      | PRI |         |       |
| Table_name  | char(64) binary     |      | PRI |         |       |
| Column_name | char(64) binary     |      | PRI |         |       |
| Timestamp   | timestamp(14)       | YES  |     | NULL    |       |
| Column_priv | set(...)            |      |     |         |       |
+-------------+---------------------+------+-----+---------+-------+
```

Just as in the previous table, the ... in the Column_priv field really contains:

```
'Select','Insert','Update','References'
```

Column-level privileges also aren't very common in MySQL. But there are cases when you're likely to encounter them. Again, *phpMyAdmin* is a great example:

```
mysql> SELECT * FROM columns_priv LIMIT 1 \G
*************************** 1. row ***************************
        Host: localhost
          Db: mysql
        User: phpmyadmin
  Table_name: tables_priv
 Column_name: Column_priv
   Timestamp: 20020308185830
 Column_priv: Select
```

This record allows the phpmyadmin user to select data from the Column_priv column of the tables_priv table in the mysql database.

Confused yet? Can't blame you. The grant tables can be quite confusing at first. Until you spend some time working with them, you won't really appreciate the flexibility this design provides.

We wouldn't recommend spending that time unless absolutely necessary. Instead, read the next section. It reviews the GRANT and REVOKE commands and then looks at how they interact with the grant tables so that you don't have to. It's only worth delving deeply into the grant tables if you find a situation that can't be set up (or is too complex) using the GRANT command.

Grant and Revoke

The recommended way to change privileges in MySQL is to use the GRANT and REVOKE commands. They provide a simple syntax for making most changes without needing to understand the underlying grant tables and their various matching rules.

There's nothing to prevent you from using normal INSERT, UPDATE, and DELETE queries to manipulate the grant tables directly. In fact, many long-time MySQL users still find it easier to do so. But as MySQL continues to evolve, it is likely that the grant tables will change. Columns may be added, renamed, or removed (it has happened before). There may even be additional tables involved in the process at some point. By sticking to the GRANT and REVOKE commands, you can insulate yourself from those changes. It is also very easy to make very bad mistakes when modifying the table directly. The GRANT and REVOKE commands will continue to be the recommended way of managing privileges.

If you do decide to manipulate the grant tables by hand rather than using the GRANT and REVOKE commands, you must tell MySQL that you've done so by issuing a FLUSH PRIVILEGES command. MySQL caches the information contained in the grant tables so that it doesn't have to go through the expensive process of reading and interpreting them each time it needs to check a privilege. As a result, any changes you make with an INSERT or other generic command will go unnoticed until the server is restarted or a FLUSH PRIVILEGES is executed.

Grant Mechanics

With an understanding of the layout of the grant tables, let's walk through some examples to see exactly how the tables are affected. We'll create a fictional organization, *widgets.example.com*, and see what kind of access various individuals within that organization might require. Each example is intended to demonstrate how you might use various GRANT commands to set up real-world permissions.

System administrator account

In most large organizations, you have two important administrators. The *system administrator* manages the "physical" server including the operating system, Unix login accounts, etc., and the *database administrator* concentrates on the database server.

You may want to restrict the access of the root account to the database, for various reasons. You can accomplish this by issuing the following command:

```
mysql> REVOKE ALL PRIVILEGES ON *.* FROM 'root'@'localhost';
```

Database administrator account

When more than one DBA has access to MySQL, it's a good idea to give each one a separate account rather than having them share the root account. This setup provides greater accountability, and you don't have to give out the root password if you'd rather not. *widgets.example.com* has two database administrators; let's call them Raymond and Diana.

To give the user *raymond* full privileges on the server when connecting from any host, a GRANT command like this does the trick:

```
mysql> GRANT ALL PRIVILEGES ON *.* TO 'raymond'@'%' IDENTIFIED BY '27skuw!'
    -> WITH GRANT OPTION;
```

Behind the scenes, that command adds a record to the user table:

```
mysql> SELECT * FROM user WHERE User = 'raymond' \G
*************************** 1. row ***************************
            Host: %
            User: raymond
        Password: 11417e201753de4b
     Select_priv: Y
     Insert_priv: Y
     Update_priv: Y
     Delete_priv: Y
     Create_priv: Y
       Drop_priv: Y
     Reload_priv: Y
   Shutdown_priv: Y
    Process_priv: Y
       File_priv: Y
      Grant_priv: Y
 References_priv: Y
      Index_priv: Y
      Alter_priv: Y
```

You might decide that while Raymond travels around the world and needs to be able to get access from anywhere,[*] Diana needs access from only the office, in which case you would execute a command like this one:

```
mysql> GRANT ALL PRIVILEGES ON *.* TO 'diana'@'%.widgets.example.dom' IDENTIFIED BY
    -> 'yu-gi-oh' WITH GRANT OPTION;
```

This would limit Diana's access such that she connects only if she is coming from a machine within the *widgets.example.com* domain, which hopefully corresponds to a trusted machine. For even higher security, it might make sense to change the %.widgets. example.com clause to use an IP address or IP network, specifying the office Diana works in, perhaps, or possibly only her workstation.

---

[*] Obviously, opening up MySQL from anywhere in the world is a really bad idea, and Raymond should come up with a better way to connect to the server.

Of course, Diana has the ability to alter her own privileges, but there's not a lot you can do about that.

Average employee account

The average *widgets.example.com* employee is a customer service representative, entering orders taken over the phone, updating existing orders, etc. Tera, a customer service representative, logs into a custom application that passes her username and password through to the MySQL server for any activity. The command to create Tera's account might look like this:

```
mysql> GRANT INSERT,UPDATE PRIVILEGES ON widgets.orders
    -> TO 'tera'@'%.widgets.example.com'
    -> IDENTIFIED BY 'rachel!94';
```

Tera can provide her username and password to the application, and she can add new orders or update existing orders, but she can't go back and delete entries, etc. In this configuration, every employee of *widgets.example.com* that needs to enter an order into the system has her own individual database access. Instead of a shared "application account," each employee's transactions are logged under her own username, and each employee has only the privileges she needs to enter or work with orders.

Notice the lack of a WITH GRANT OPTION clause. There's no need to give Tera the ability to assign privileges to anyone else.

Logging, write-only access

It is common to use MySQL as the backend for logging various types of data. Whether you have Apache recording every request in MySQL or you're keeping track of when your doorbell rings, logging is a write-only application that probably needs to write to only a single database or table.

To set up write-only access for logging, you might use a command like this:

```
mysql> GRANT INSERT ON logs.* TO 'logger'@'%.widgets.example.com'
    -> IDENTIFIED BY 'blah0halb';
```

This command adds a record to the user table, of course:

```
mysql> SELECT * FROM user WHERE User = 'logger' \G
*************************** 1. row ***************************
        Host: %.widgets.example.com
        User: logger
    Password: 2d502d346553f4f3
 Select_priv: N
 Insert_priv: N
 Update_priv: N
 Delete_priv: N
 Create_priv: N
   Drop_priv: N
 Reload_priv: N
```

```
       Shutdown_priv: N
        Process_priv: N
           File_priv: N
          Grant_priv: N
     References_priv: N
          Index_priv: N
          Alter_priv: N
```

However, this command grants no privileges. The only purpose of the record here is to allow the user to connect from any host and to provide a password.

Because we specified a privilege that applies to a specific database, the interesting bits were added to the db table:

```
mysql> SELECT * FROM db WHERE User = 'logger' \G
*************************** 1. row ***************************
           Host: %.widgets.example.com
             Db: logs
           User: logger
    Select_priv: N
    Insert_priv: Y
    Update_priv: N
    Delete_priv: N
    Create_priv: N
      Drop_priv: N
     Grant_priv: N
References_priv: N
     Index_priv: N
     Alter_priv: N
```

As expected, the only privilege granted by this record is the insert privilege—just what we wanted.

Operations and monitoring

There are times when you want to give someone (a network operations center) or some thing (monitoring software) access to your MySQL server to check its health, kill long-running queries, or even shut down the server. Let's say that the *widgets. example.com* network operations center has a staff that works 24/7 monitoring various processes and services, including the health of the MySQL server.

The Network Operation Center's (NOC) user account needs to be able to connect, issue the KILL and SHOW commands, and shut down the server. Further, because this ability is very powerful, it has to be limited to a single host, so that even if the password is somehow compromised, the unauthorized user would have to be in the NOC do anything.

This statement accomplishes that:

```
mysql> GRANT PROCESS, SHUTDOWN on *.*
    -> TO 'noc'@'monitorserver.noc.widgets.example.com'
    -> IDENTIFIED BY 'q!w@e#r$t%';
```

The result is in a new user row:

```
mysql> SELECT * FROM user WHERE User = 'noc' \G
*************************** 1. row ***************************
            Host: monitorserver.noc.widgets.example.com
            User: noc
        Password: 7abf52ce38207ca0
     Select_priv: N
     Insert_priv: N
     Update_priv: N
     Delete_priv: N
     Create_priv: N
       Drop_priv: N
     Reload_priv: N
   Shutdown_priv: Y
    Process_priv: Y
       File_priv: N
      Grant_priv: N
 References_priv: N
      Index_priv: N
      Alter_priv: N
```

Common Problems and Limitations

MySQL doesn't always act the way you expect it to. Often this is because the flexibility of its privilege system leads you to expect it to act in a more sophisticated way than it is designed to act. Let's take a look at a couple of common ways MySQL can demonstrate unexpected behavior.

Can't revoke specific privileges

One day you decide that *raymond* shouldn't have read access to the payroll database. He currently has all privileges. So you try to take away his select privilege for that database:

```
mysql> REVOKE SELECT ON payroll.* FROM raymond;
ERROR 1141: There is no such grant defined for user 'raymond' on host '%'
```

What? Raymond is a DBA and has all privileges, doesn't he? Let's check:

```
mysql> SHOW GRANTS FOR raymond \G
*************************** 1. row ***************************
Grants for raymond@%: GRANT ALL PRIVILEGES ON *.* TO 'raymond'@'%'
IDENTIFIED BY PASSWORD '11417e201753de4b' WITH GRANT OPTION
```

Sure enough, he has every privilege. What's the problem?

MySQL isn't as smart is it appears to be. It provides a way to grant privileges, through the user and host and other tables shown earlier, but it doesn't have a parallel system to deny privileges. It doesn't have a system for granting all access except for certain specific items (like the *hosts.allow* and *hosts.deny* files familiar to Unix system administrators). Essentially, you can't deny a more specific privilege than you have granted to a given user.

The solution to this problem is rather ugly. You have to remove all the user's privileges, then specifically grant those you want to keep. This gets messy because you need a GRANT command for every database except payroll.

```
mysql> GRANT ALL PRIVILEGES ON db1.* TO raymond WITH GRANT OPTION;
mysql> GRANT ALL PRIVILEGES ON db2.* TO raymond WITH GRANT OPTION;
mysql> GRANT ALL PRIVILEGES ON db3.* TO raymond WITH GRANT OPTION;
```

And so on. This example illustrates the class of problems that we'll look at next.

Host and database matching can't exclude matches

The previous example would have been a lot easier if you could write something like this:

```
mysql> GRANT ALL PRIVILEGES ON *.* EXCEPT payroll.* TO raymond;
```

But MySQL can't do that. Similarly, if you want to restrict access from just one host (*insecure.example.com*), there's no way to do it. You can't do this:

```
mysql> GRANT ALL PRIVILEGES ON *.* TO raymond@"%"
    -> EXCEPT raymond@insecure.example.com;
```

Neither of these work because MySQL was designed to make it easy to grant privileges but not to deny privileges. From MySQL's point of view, you deny a privilege by never granting it in the first place. The result is a system that makes it easy to build *inclusive* rules but makes it impossible to build *exclusive* rules.

If you want to allow *raymond* to connect from any host except *insecure.example.com,* you have to either block that host at the network level or add a record with a bogus password to the user table for *raymond@insecure.example.com.* In the latter case, Raymond can connect but authentication will always fail.

Privileges don't vanish when objects do

It should be noted that there is one serious design flaw in the way MySQL handles privileges. That problem is that there is no GRANT clean-up when database objects are removed.

For example, let's say you've done the following:

```
mysql> GRANT ALL PRIVILEGES ON my_db.* TO raymond;
```

You later run the following command:

```
$ mysqladmin drop my_db
```

In a well-designed privileges system, that GRANT would find itself destroyed as part of the dropping of the databases it referenced.* With MySQL, however, the privileges remain in the db table.

At first glance, you may think to yourself, "Why do I care? Since my_db is dropped, there's nothing there to see." But what if a couple months or years later, you create a new database called my_db? Do you still want Raymond to have access to the new table? Do you even remember that he has access to it?

The solution—let's call it a workaround, because that's what it is—is for the admin, when dropping a database or table, to scour and directly access the appropriate privileges tables. In the my_db example, if you drop the my_db table, you might want to do something like this:

```
mysql> DELETE FROM db where Db='my_db';
mysql> DELETE FROM tables_priv where Db='my_db';
mysql> DELETE FROM columns_priv where Db='my_db';
mysql> FLUSH PRIVILEGES;
```

In some cases, it might be possible to do this using the REVOKE command multiple times for each user that may have been granted privileges, but it's probably much faster and more secure to access the privileges tables as just shown, and be sure to make a clean sweep across them. Likewise, if you dropped only a particular table in my_db, say, my_db.my_table, you might do this:

```
mysql> DELETE FROM tables_priv where Db='my_db' AND Table_name='my_table';
mysql> DELETE FROM columns_priv where Db='my_db' AND Table_name='my_table';
mysql> FLUSH PRIVILEGES;
```

Obviously, no DELETE is needed against the db table because it isn't a database-wide privilege that needs to be revoked.

In some cases, you might find this useful. For example, if you're dropping a table just to reload it again from backup, it's much more convenient not to have to worry about revoking and regranting privileges.†

In an ideal world, this would be an option to commands like ALTER TABLE or DROP DATABASE, to allow the system to hunt down and destroy granted privileges automatically. Alternatively, MySQL could default to a theoretically "secure" methodology of destroying stale privileges but offer the option to leave the privileges intact.

---

* At the very least, there would be a configuration option to permit the destruction to happen.

† An argument can be made that if you're restoring from a backup and leaving the existing privileges in place, you're not necessarily restoring to the backed-up state and might be leaving any security holes that were created afterwards still in place.

Operating System Security

Even the most well thought out and secure grant tables will do you little good if any random cracker can get root access to your server. With unlimited access, someone could simply copy all your data files to another machine running MySQL.* Doing so would effectively give the cracker an identical copy of your database.

Data theft isn't the only threat to guard against. A creative cracker may decide that it's more fun to make subtle changes to your data over the course of weeks or even months. Depending on how long you keep backups around and when the data corruption is noticed, such an attack could be quite devastating.

Guidelines

The general guidelines discussed here aren't a comprehensive guide to system security. If you are serious about security—and you should be—we recommend a copy of O'Reilly's *Practical Unix and Internet Security* by Simson Garfinkel, Gene Spafford, and Alan Schwartz. That said, here are some ideas for maintaining good security on your database servers:

Don't run MySQL from a privileged account
> The root user on Unix and the system (Administrator) user on Windows possess ultimate control over the system. If a security bug is discovered in MySQL, and you're running it as a privileged user, a hacker can gain extensive access to your server. The installation instructions are quite clear about this, but it bears repeating. Create a separate account, usually *mysql*, for the purpose of running MySQL.

Keep your operating system up to date
> All operating system vendors (Microsoft, Sun, RedHat, SUSE, etc.) provide notifications when a security-related update is available. Find your vendor's mailing list and subscribe to it. Pay special attention to the security list for MySQL itself, obviously, as well as anything that may interact directly with the database, such as PHP or Perl.

Restrict logins on the database host
> Does every developer building a MySQL-based application need an account on the server? Certainly not; only system and database administrators need accounts on the machine. All the developers need to be able to do is issue queries against the database remotely using TCP/IP.

Have your server audited
> Many larger organizations have internal auditors who can assess the security of a server and make recommendations for improving it. If you aren't lucky enough

---

* Remember: MyISAM data files are portable across operating systems and CPU architectures.

to have access to auditors, you can hire a security consultant to perform the audit.

Backups are important here as well. If your server is broken into, you'll need to reinstall the operating system from an untainted source. Once that's done, you'll be faced with the task of having to restore all the data. If you have the luxury of time, you might compare the hacked server to a known good backup in an effort to determine how the hacker was able to get in. Chapter 9 is devoted to backup and recovery issues.

Network Security

We'd love to say simply, "Don't ever put a MySQL server on the Internet." Period. End of story. But the fact is that you may need to have a MySQL server that is accessible on the Internet. To help keep your server secure, we'll look at several techniques you can use to limit its exposure.

Even if your server is used only on an internal network at your organization, there are steps you should take to keep data away from prying eyes. After all, some of the most serious security threats in a company come from the inside, not Joe Random Hacker.

Keep in mind that this information is only a starting point in the process of ensuring your MySQL servers are well protected. There are numerous good network security books available, including *Building Internet Firewalls* by Elizabeth D. Zwicky, Simon Cooper, D. Brent Chapman, and *TCP/IP Network Administration* by Craig Hunt, both from O'Reilly. If you're serious about network security, do yourself a favor and pick up a book on the topic (after you finish this one!).

As with operating-system security, having a third-party audit of your network can be quite helpful in spotting weaknesses before they are exploited.

Localhost-Only Connections

If your MySQL server is used in an application that resides on the same host (common with small and mid-sized web sites), there's a good chance you won't need to allow any access to MySQL over the network. By eliminating the need to accept external connections, you dramatically reduce the number of ways in which a hacker can get data from your MySQL server.

Disabling network access limits your ability to make administrative changes remotely (add users, rotate logs, etc.). So you'll need to either log in to the MySQL server using SSH or install a web-based application that allows you to make those changes. The remote login requirement can be difficult on some Windows systems, but there are other remote-access alternatives on the market. One solution to the problem might be to install *phpMyAdmin* (discussed in Appendix C).

The skip-networking option tells MySQL not to listen on any TCP socket. It will, however, listen for connections on a Unix socket. Starting MySQL without networking support can be accomplished using the following very simple command:

```
$ mysqld_safe --skip-networking
```

You can instead put the skip-networking option in the [mysqld] section of your *my.cnf* file:

```
[mysqld]
skip-networking
```

No matter which option you use, the result is the same. MySQL won't accept any TCP connections.*

---

localhost's Special Meaning in MySQL

Sometimes even the best tools just don't do what you'd expect, and MySQL is no exception. The hostname *localhost* has special meaning to the MySQL client library. And because most other languages' APIs (Perl, Python, PHP, etc.) build on that library, they're all affected by this "feature."

To the client library, a hostname of *localhost* means "connect using the local socket (not TCP) because we know the server is on the local machine." (Note that because it doesn't have Unix Sockets available to it, the Windows version of MySQL treats *localhost* no differently from any other host and connects to 127.0.0.1 via TCP sockets.)

The practical effects of this occur in two circumstances:

1. When dealing with GRANT commands, if a user is connecting from *localhost*, the GRANT command must specify *localhost* as the hostname. MySQL won't match *localhost* when given a % wildcard. In other words, by specifying permissions for *user@%* and *user@localhost*, you're not being redundant.

2. When setting up tunneling using SSH, if you attempt to connect to the forwarded TCP port on *localhost*, you'll be surprised that it doesn't work. You must use the IP address 127.0.0.1 instead.

---

* You can end up with an interesting configuration if you have a MySQL slave server configured with skip-networking. Because it initiates its connection to the master, the slave still gets all its data updates, but because no remote connections are permitted, you can have a more secured "backup replica" that can't be remotely tainted. It should be noted, though, that obviously you can't use such a replica in a failover configuration: no other client could connect to it.

It's also important to note that the JDBC doesn't support Unix Domain sockets, so using this configuration means that JDBC clients can't connect.

Firewalling

As with any other network-based service, it is important that you allow connections only from authorized hosts. As we showed earlier, you can use MySQL's GRANT command to restrict the hosts from which users can connect, but it's a good idea to have a dual protection. By filtering connections at the network level using a firewall, you gain additional security.*

Having multiple ways to filter connections means that a single mistake, such as a typo in a GRANT command, won't allow connections from unauthorized hosts. In many organizations, network security is administered by a group of people that is separate from those developing applications. This further helps reduce the possibility that a single person's change can expose a server.

The most secure approach to use when firewalling a machine is to deny all connections by default. Then you can add rules that allow access to the few services that other hosts may need access to. For a system limited to providing a MySQL server, you should allow connections only to TCP port 3306 (MySQL's default) and possibly a remote login service such as SSH (typically on TCP port 22).

No default route

Consider not having a default route configured on your firewalled MySQL servers. That way, even if the firewall configuration is compromised, and someone tries to contact your MySQL server from the outside, the packets will never get back to them. They'll never leave your local network.

Let's say your MySQL server is 192.168.0.10, and the local network has a 255.255.255.0 netmask. In this configuration, any packet from 192.168.0.0/24 is considered "local" because it can be reached directly via the attached network interface (probably *eth0* or the host operating system's equivalent). Traffic from any other address would have to be directed to a gateway to reach its final destination, and since there is no default route, there is no way for those packets to find their gateway and get to their destination.

If you must allow a select few outside hosts to access your otherwise firewalled server, add static routes for those hosts. Doing so ensures that the server responds to as few outside hosts as possible.

MySQL in a DMZ

Simply firewalling MySQL servers often isn't secure enough for some installations. If one of your web or application servers is compromised, an attacker could use the server to attack a MySQL server directly. Once the attacker has access to a single

---

* For our purposes, a firewall is simply a device that network traffic passes through for the purposes of filtering and possibly routing. Whether it's a "real" firewall, a router, or an old 486 PC doesn't matter.

computer on the firewalled network, she has relatively unrestricted access to all the other servers on that network.*

By moving the MySQL servers to their own separate network segment that isn't accessible from the outside, you can greatly improve security. For instance, imagine a LAN containing the web or other application servers and a firewall. Behind the firewall, on a different physical network segment and a different logical subnet, is one or more MySQL servers. The application servers have restricted access to the MySQL servers: all of their traffic must first pass through the firewall, which can be configured in a very restrictive way.

Taking things a step further, you can argue that the application servers should be either in the DMZ or in their own separate DMZ. Is that going too far? Maybe. As is always the case in security matters, you may need to trade security for convenience and should be aware of the risks you're taking in doing so.

Connection Encryption and Tunneling

Any time you need to communicate with a MySQL server across a network that is public (such as the Internet) or otherwise open to traffic sniffing (many wireless networks), consider using some form of encryption. By doing so, you can make it far more difficult for anyone who might try to intercept the connection and either sniff or spoof the data.

As an added benefit, many encryption algorithms result in a compressed data stream. So not only is your data more secure, but you're also better using the available network bandwidth.

While this discussion is focused on a client accessing a MySQL server, the client could be another MySQL server. This is common when using MySQL's built-in replication. Each slave server connects to the master using the exact same protocol that normal MySQL clients use.

Virtual private networks

A company with two or more offices in distant locations may set up a virtual private network (VPN) between them using a variety of technologies. A common solution is for the external routers at each office to encrypt all traffic destined for another office. In such a situation, there's little to worry about. All the traffic is already being encrypted as it is sent out over whichever public or private network happens to connect the offices.

---

* That's not entirely true. Many modern network switches allow you to configure multiple Virtual LANs (VLANs) on a single physical network. Machines that aren't on the same VLAN may not be able to talk to each other.

Does the existence of the VPN mean that there is no benefit to applying a MySQL-specific solution? Not necessarily. In the event that the VPN must be disabled for some reason, it would be nice if MySQL's network traffic remained secret. Also, there may be a benefit to restricting access to the data to prevent it from being viewed by the prying eyes of the network administrator, who can easily watch it flow across the network, if he so desired.

SSL in MySQL

As of Version 4.1, MySQL has native support for Secure Sockets Layer (SSL)—the same technology that keeps your credit card number safe when you're buying books on Amazon or airline tickets on your favorite travel site. Specifically, MySQL uses the freely available OpenSSL library.

Unfortunately, the binary versions of MySQL that ship with most Linux distributions (and those available for download from the MySQL.com web site) don't have SSL enabled by default.* To check your server, simply inspect the value of the have_openssl variable:

```
mysql> SHOW VARIABLES LIKE 'have_openssl';
+----------------+-------+
| Variable_name  | Value |
+----------------+-------+
| have_openssl   | NO    |
+----------------+-------+
1 row in set (0.00 sec)
```

If it says NO, you'll need to compile your own MySQL server.

If it says YES, whole new levels of security in database access are opened to the administrator, depending on the security needs of your particular application.

At its most basic, you may wish to allow only encrypted sessions, relying on the SSL protocol to protect the user's password. You can require a user to connect via SSL using optional arguments to the GRANT command:

```
mysql> GRANT ALL PRIVILEGES ON ssl_only_db.* to 'raymond'@'%'
    -> IDENTIFIED BY "FooBar!" REQUIRE SSL;
```

That GRANT, however, doesn't place any restrictions on the SSL certificate being used by the connecting client. As long as the client and the MySQL server can negotiate an SSL session, the validity of the client certificate won't be checked.

---

* SSL can be compiled into the Windows version of MySQL after you download OpenSSL for Windows. If you aren't in a situation in which you can recompile MySQL using the OpenSSL libraries, another solution might be to use STunnel, located at *http://www.stunnel.org*. It won't be nearly as fully featured as actually using the OpenSSL hooks directly, but at least you can encrypt your client connections.

Minimal checking of the client certificate can be performed by using the `REQUIRE x509` option:

```
mysql> GRANT ALL PRIVILEGES ON ssl_only_db.* to raymond@%
    -> IDENTIFIED BY "FooBar!" REQUIRE x509;
```

This requires that the client certificate be at least verifiable against the CA certificates the MySQL server has been set up to recognize.

One step up might be to permit only a specific client certificate to access the database. You can do that using the `REQUIRE SUBJECT` syntax:

```
mysql> GRANT ALL PRIVILEGES ON ssl_only_db.* to 'raymond'@'%'
    -> IDENTIFIED BY "FooBar!"
    -> REQUIRE SUBJECT "/C=US/ST=New York/L=Albany/O=Widgets Inc./CN=client-ray.
example.com/emailAddress=raymond@example.com";
```

Maybe you don't care specifically what client license is used, but only that it be one issued using your organization's CA certificate. In this case, you might use the `REQUIRE ISSUER` syntax to do something like the following:

```
mysql> GRANT ALL PRIVILEGES ON ssl_only_db.* to 'raymond'@'%'
    -> IDENTIFIED BY "FooBar!"
    -> REQUIRE ISSUER "/C=US/ST=New+20York/L=Albany/O=Widgets Inc./CN=cacert.example.
com/emailAddress=admin@example.com";
```

For the ultimate in authentication, you can require both the issuer and subject to be predefined values, requiring Raymond to use the specific certificate issued using your organization's CA certificate, for example, by combining the two syntaxes:

```
mysql> GRANT ALL PRIVILEGES ON ssl_only_db.* to 'raymond'@'%'
    -> IDENTIFIED BY "FooBar!"
    -> REQUIRE SUBJECT "/C=US/ST=New York/L=Albany/O=Widgets Inc./CN=client-ray.
example.com/emailAddress=raymond@example.com"
    -> AND ISSUER "/C=US/ST=New+20York/L=Albany/O=Widgets Inc./CN=cacert.example.com/
emailAddress=admin@example.com";
```

One other minor SSL-related option is the `CIPHER` requirement option, which allows the administrator to permit only "trusted" (strong) encryption ciphers to be used. SSL is cipher-independent, and the potentially strong SSL encryption can be invalidated if a really weak cipher is used to protect the data being transferred. You can restrict the choice of protocols to a set you consider to be secure by issuing a command like the following:

```
mysql> GRANT ALL PRIVILEGES ON ssl_only_db.* to 'raymond'@'%'
    -> IDENTIFIED BY "FooBar!"
    -> REQUIRE CIPHER "EDH-RSA-DES-CBC3-SHA";
```

It should be noted that managing individual client certificates may seem like excellent security, but it can be an administrative nightmare. When you create a client certificate, you have to assign it an expiration date, preferably something not too long in duration. You want it to be long enough in life so that you're not constantly having to regenerate a new certificate, but short enough in life that if the certificate holder leaves the company, or the certificate falls into the hands of a hostile entity, it doesn't give them access to your data forever.

In a small environment of a couple of employees, it may be very easy to keep track of individual certificate ownership. When your organization scales upward to hundreds or thousands of employees with certificates, keeping track of which certificates expire when and making sure that client certificates don't expire before they've been replaced can become quite cumbersome.

For some organizations this problem is solved using a combination of REQUIRE ISSUER and a series of monthly client certificates that are distributed via a trusted distribution path, such as a company intranet. Clients can download and connect to the MySQL server using certificates that are good for a month or two. This way, if an employee loses access to the company intranet, or a partner is no longer given access to the monthly key, then even if the administrator isn't told to remove their access, their ability to connect naturally expires in a predetermined schedule.

SSH tunneling

If you're using an older version of MySQL or simply don't want to hassle with setting up SSL support, consider using SSH instead. If you use Linux or Unix, there's a good chance you're already using SSH to log in to remote machines.[*] What a lot of people don't know is that SSH can be used to establish an encrypted tunnel between two hosts.

SSH tunneling is best illustrated with an example. Let's suppose that we want an encrypted connection from a Linux workstation to the MySQL server running on *db. example.com*. On the workstation, you execute the following command:[†]

```
$ ssh -N -f -L 4406:db.example.com:3306
```

This establishes a tunnel between TCP port 4406 on the workstation and port 3306 on *db.example.com*. You could connect to MySQL through the tunnel from the workstation by doing this:

```
$ mysql -h 127.0.0.1 -P 4406
```

SSH is a very powerful tool that can do far more than this simple example illustrates. We suggest reading O'Reilly's *SSH, The Secure Shell: The Definitive Guide* by Daniel J. Barrett and Richard E. Silverman if you'd like to learn more about SSH.

---

[*] A variant of OpenSSH is also available for Windows clients. There is a full tutorial on how to set up SSH tunnels to connect to MySQL machines at *http://www.vbmysql.com/articles/security/sshtunnel.html*.

[†] Assuming SSH Version 2 is installed. SSH Version 1 has no -N option. See your SSH documentation for details.

TCP Wrappers

MySQL can be compiled with support for TCP wrappers on Unix systems. If a full-blown firewall isn't an option, TCP wrappers provide a basic level of defense. You'll gain additional control over which hosts MySQL will or will not talk to without having to change your grant tables.

To use TCP wrappers, you need to build MySQL from source and pass the `--with-libwrap` option to `configure` so that it will know where to find the proper header files on your operating system:

```
$ ./configure --with-libwrap=/usr/local/tcp_wrappers
```

Assuming you have an entry in your */etc/hosts.deny* file that denies all connections by default:

```
# deny all connections
ALL: ALL
```

you can explicitly add MySQL to your */etc/hosts.allow* file:

```
# allow mysql connections from hosts on the local network
mysqld: 192.168.1.0/255.255.0.0 : allow
```

The only other catch is that you need an appropriate entry in */etc/services* for MySQL. If you don't already have one, add a line such as the following:

```
mysql    3306/tcp  # MySQL Server
```

Of course, if you are running MySQL on a nonstandard port, use that number instead of 3306.

Automatic Host Blocking

MySQL provides some help in preventing network-based attacks. If MySQL notices too many bad connections (those that don't result in a valid MySQL session) from a particular host, it starts blocking connections from that host. The server variable `max_connection_errors` determines how many bad connections MySQL will allow before it begins blocking.

When a host is blocked, MySQL records in the error log a message that looks like this:

```
Host 'host.badguy.com' blocked because of many connection errors.
Unblock with 'mysqladmin flush-hosts'
```

As that message indicates, you can use the `mysqladmin flush-hosts` command to unblock the host, presumably after you have figured out why that host was having problems connecting and have addressed whatever issue is relevant. The `mysqladmin` *flush_hosts* command simply executes a FLUSH HOSTS SQL command, which empties MySQL's host cache tables. The result is that *all* blocked hosts are unblocked; there's no way to unblock a single host.

If you find that this becomes a common problem for some reason, you can set the max_connection_errors variable to a relatively high number to avoid the problem.

```
$ mysqld_safe -O max_connection_errors=999999999
```

It's currently not possible to set max_connection_errors to zero and disable the check entirely. The only way to do that is to remove the check from the source code.

Data Encryption

In applications that store sensitive data, such as banking records, you may want the data to be stored in an encrypted format. Doing so makes it very difficult for someone to use the data even if they walk up to your server and take it home. A full discussion of the relative merits of encryption algorithms and techniques is beyond the scope of this book.

Hashing Passwords

In less sensitive applications, you may need to protect just a few pieces of information, such as a password database for another application. Passwords really shouldn't be stored in the clear, so they are commonly encrypted in applications. But rather than use encryption, it may be wise to follow the lead of most Unix systems and even MySQL itself: use a hashing algorithm on the password and store the result in your table.

Unlike traditional encryption, which can be reversed, hashing is a one-way process that can't be reversed. The only way to determine the password that generated a particular hash value is to use a very computationally expensive brute-force attack (trying all possible combinations of input).

MySQL provides four functions for hashing passwords: PASSWORD( ), ENCRYPT( ), SHA1( ), and MD5( ).* The best way to see the results of each function is to try each one on the same source text. Let's see how the string pa55word hashes in each:

```
mysql> SELECT MD5('pa55word');
+----------------------------------+
| MD5('pa55word')                  |
+----------------------------------+
| a17a41337551d6542fd005e18b43afd4 |
+----------------------------------+
1 row in set (0.13 sec)
```

---

* MySQL's ENCRYPT( ) simply calls the C library's crypt( ) function. On some Unix variants, crypt( ) is an MD5 implementation, making it no different from using MD5( ). On others, it is the traditional DES encryption algorithm.

```
mysql> SELECT PASSWORD('pa55word');
+----------------------+
| PASSWORD('pa55word') |
+----------------------+
| 1d35c6556b8cab45     |
+----------------------+
1 row in set (0.00 sec)

mysql> SELECT ENCRYPT('pa55word');
+---------------------+
| ENCRYPT('pa55word') |
+---------------------+
| up2EcbOHdj25A       |
+---------------------+
1 row in set (0.17 sec)
```

Each function returns a fixed-length alphanumeric string that can be stored in a CHAR column. To cope with the possibility of mixed-case characters in the result of ENCRYPT( ), it's best to declare the column CHAR BINARY.

Storing hashed data is as easy as:*

```
INSERT INTO user_table (user, pass) VALUE ('jzawodn', MD5('pa55word') )
```

To verify user's password, take the username and password supplied and run a SELECT query to see if they match. Using a language such as Perl or PHP, the query might look like this:

```
SELECT *
  FROM user_table
 WHERE user = '$username'
   AND pass = MD5('$password')
```

Password hashing is an easy-to-use and relatively secure way to store passwords in a database without them being easily recoverable.

Encrypted Filesystems

Because MySQL's various table handlers all store their data as regular files on whatever filesystem you may be using, it's possible to use an encrypted filesystem. Most popular operating systems have at least one encrypted filesystem available, either free or commercial.

The main advantage of this approach is that you don't have to do anything special for MySQL to take advantage of it. Because all the encryption and decryption takes place outside MySQL, it just performs reads and writes without any knowledge of what's happening under the hood. All you need to do is make sure your data and

---

* While you can do it the way we describe here, there are a number of reasons why it is much better to do the MD5 calculations on the client machine if possible, because the clear-text password might appear in the process list or in a query log.

logs are stored on the proper filesystem. From your application's point of view, there's nothing special about this arrangement either.

There are a few downsides to using an encrypted filesystem with MySQL. First of all, because all the data, indexes, and logs are being encrypted, there will be a fair amount of CPU overhead involved in encrypting and decrypting the data. If you're thinking about using an encrypted filesystem, be sure to perform good benchmarks so that you understand how it behaves under heavy load.

A more subtle problem with this setup occurs when you consider making backups of your data. To copy the data to another location (disk, tape, CD-ROM, server, etc.), the data must be decrypted. To keep the data safe, you need to find backup software that can encrypt your backups. The only real workaround is to take a complete dump of the disk partition. You can safely store a copy elsewhere because the data remains encrypted. However, there's no way to selectively restore pieces of the data; you'd need to restore the entire partition.

Application-Level Encryption

A more common approach to encryption is to build it into the application (or middleware). When the application needs to store sensitive data, it first encrypts the data and stores the result in MySQL. Similarly, when the application retrieves information from MySQL, it must decrypt it.

This approach provides a lot of flexibility. It doesn't tie you to a particular filesystem, operating system, or even database (if your code is written in a generic fashion). It gives the application designer the freedom to choose an encryption algorithm that's most appropriate (balancing speed and strength) for the data being stored.

Because the data is stored encrypted, backups are very easy. No matter where you copy the data, it is encrypted. However, it also means that access to the data must go through software that understands how to decrypt it. You can't just fire up the mysql command-line tool and begin issuing queries.

Application-level encryption does have some drawbacks, though. It is a lot harder for MySQL to effectively index the data, for example. You may find yourself suffering from significant performance issues.

Design issues

This freedom and flexibility have interesting implications for database design. You need to ensure that the field types you are using are appropriate for the type of encryption you're using. Some algorithms produce blocks of data with fixed minimum sizes. That means you may need a column that can hold 256 bytes just to hold a piece of data that is significantly smaller before encryption. Many popular encryption libraries produce binary data, so you'll need to create columns that can store binary data. As an alternative, you can convert the binary data to a hex or base-64 representation, but that would require more space and time.

Deciding exactly what data should and shouldn't be encrypted isn't easy either. You need to balance security against making the information in your tables difficult to query. For example, you might have an account table that represents bank accounts and contains the following fields:

- id
- type
- status
- balance
- overdraft_protection
- date_established

Which fields make sense to encrypt? If you encrypt the balance, which seems reasonable, it would be difficult to answer common reporting questions. For example, you might try to write the following query to find the minimum, maximum, and average balance of accounts of each account type:

```
SELECT MIN(balance), MAX(balance), AVG(balance)
    FROM account
GROUP BY type
```

But the results would be meaningless. MySQL has no clue what the balance field means, so it would just try to perform those functions on the encrypted data in the balance field.

The obvious but painful solution is for your application to read all the records from the account table and do the math for the report you need. That may not be terribly difficult, but it's annoying. Not only are you reimplementing functionality MySQL already provides, you're also slowing down the process considerably.

What all this boils down to is a tradeoff between security and the advantages of using a relational database in the first place. Any field that contains encrypted data is basically useless to MySQL's built-in functions because they need to operate on the unencrypted data. Similar problems arise in query optimization. In an unencrypted setup, you can easily find all the accounts with a balance greater than $100,000 by doing this:

```
SELECT *
    FROM account
WHERE balance > 100000
```

If there is an index on the balance field, MySQL will probably locate the records in a split second. But if the data is encrypted, you have to get all the records in your application and filter them after they're decrypted. There's just no way for MySQL to help you out.

Source Code Modification

If you're looking for a more flexible approach than either encrypted filesystems or application-based encryption, you can always build a custom solution. The source code for MySQL is freely available under the GNU General Public License.

This sort of work requires that you either know C++ or hire someone who does. Beyond that, you'll be looking to create your own table handler with native encryption support, or you might find it easier to extend an existing table handler (the MyISAM and BDB handlers are easiest to understand) with encryption.

You'll find the relevant files in the *sql* directory of the MySQL source code. Each table handler is composed of at least two C++ files. The MyISAM handler code, for example, is in *ha_myisam.h* and *ha_myisam.cc*.

MySQL in a chrooted Environment

Running a server in a chrooted environment greatly enhances overall system security on a Unix system. It does this by setting up an isolated environment in which files outside of a given directory are no longer accessible. That way, even if a security flaw is found in the server and exploited, the potential for damage is limited to the files in that directory, which should only be the files for that particular application.

The first thing to do is compile your MySQL from source. Many administrators already do this, but this is an absolute must in a chrooted application, because many prepackaged MySQL installations will put some files in */usr/bin*, some in */var/lib/mysql*, etc., and all the files in the chrooted installation need to reside under the same directory structure.

What we tend to do is to have a */chroot* path where all chrooted applications live. Configure your MySQL installation using something like this:

```
$ ./configure --prefix=/chroot/mysql
```

Compile MySQL as you normally would, and let the installation procedure install the MySQL files in the */chroot/mysql* tree.

The next thing to do is a little magic, to make everything happier. chroot actually stands for Change ROOT. If you enter:

```
chroot /chroot/mysql
```

the / directory is now actually */chroot/mysql*. Because the MySQL files are used both by server (running chrooted) and client (which won't be), it's important to set up the filesystem so that both the server and the clients can find the files they need to. An easy solution to this problem is to do the following:

```
$ cd /chroot/mysql
$ mkdir chroot
```

```
$ cd chroot
$ ln -s /chroot/mysql mysql
```

This creates a symbolic directory path */chroot/mysql/chroot/mysql*, which actually points to */chroot/mysql*. Now, even if the application is chrooted and trying to get to */chroot/ mysql*, it will reach the proper directory. Meanwhile, if the client application is running outside the chroot environment, it can find the files it needs.

The last step is to send the proper commands to `mysqld_safe`, so that the MySQL server can start itself up and *chroot* to the proper directory. To do this, you might enter something like this:

```
$ mysqld_safe --chroot=/chroot/mysql --user=1001
```

You'll notice we used the Unix UID of the MySQL user, instead of `--user=mysql`. This is because in the chrooted environment, the MySQL server may no longer be able to query your authentication backend to do username-to-UID lookups.[*]

There are some caveats when using a chrooted MySQL server. `LOAD DATA INFILE` and other commands that directly access filenames may behave significantly differently than you expect because the server no longer considers / to be the filesystem root. So, if you tell it to load data from */tmp/filename*, you should be sure that the file is actually */chroot/mysql/tmp/filename,* or MySQL won't be able to find it.

---

[*] From our experience in testing this, it might be as simple as copying `libnss*` to your MySQL library directory in the chrooted environment, but from a practical standpoint, it's probably best not to worry about such things, and just enter the UID directly in your startup script.

The SHOW STATUS and SHOW INNODB STATUS Commands

SHOW STATUS

The SHOW STATUS command allows you to view a snapshot of the many (over 120) internal status counters that MySQL maintains. These counters track particular events in MySQL. For example, every time you issue a SELECT query, MySQL increments the Com_select counter.

This command is valuable because early signs of performance problems often appear first in the SHOW STATUS output—but you have to be looking for them. By learning which counters are most important to server performance and how to interpret them, you'll be well prepared to head off problems before they become an issue for your users.

This appendix is designed to do just that. Here you'll find a brief summary of the more important counters MySQL provides, as well as some discussion of what to watch out for and how you might correct some of the problems highlighted here. We've attempted to group related items together rather than simply using an alphabetical list. And we've omitted the counters that have little relevance to MySQL performance. See the *MySQL Reference Manual* for a full list of the counters available in your version of MySQL.

Running the SHOW STATUS command repeatedly and examining the results is a very tedious process. To make life a bit easier, *mytop* automates much of the process. See Appendix B for more about *mytop*.

Note that these counters are stored as unsigned integers. On a 32-bit platform such as Intel x86, that means the counters will wrap just over the 4.2 billion mark. This can lead to very confusing numbers and wildly incorrect conclusions. So be sure to check how long your server has been online (Uptime) before jumping to conclusions. The odds of a counter wrapping increase as time goes on.

As you read the descriptions in this appendix, consider how you might add some of these counters to your monitoring infrastructure. Third-party MySQL modules already exist for most of the freely available *rrdtool*-based systems (Cricket, Cacti, etc.). If none are available for your system, consider using one of the free plug-ins as a starting point for building your own. They're not very complicated.

Thread and Connection Statistics

Just because connections to MySQL are very lightweight doesn't excuse applications that poorly use their connections. A rapid-fire connect/disconnect cycle will slow down a MySQL server. It may not be noticeable under most circumstances, but when things get busy you don't want it getting in the way.

Using information in the following counters, you can get a high-level picture of what's going on with MySQL's connections and the threads that service them.

Aborted_clients
> This is the number of connections to the server that were aborted because the client disconnected without properly closing the session. This might happen if the client program dies abruptly from a runtime error or is killed.

Aborted_connects
> This counter contains the number of connection attempts that failed. These failures may be because of user privilege issues, such as an incorrect password, or communications issues such as malformed connection packets or connect_timeout being exceeded—often as the result of a network or firewall problem.

Bytes_received
> Number of bytes received from all clients, including other MySQL servers involved in replication.

Bytes_sent
> Number of bytes sent to all clients, including other MySQL servers.

Connections
> Total number of connection attempts, both successful and failed, to the MySQL server.

Max_used_connections
> The peak number of simultaneous connections.

Slow_launch_threads

Number of threads that have taken longer than `slow_launch_time` to be created. A nonzero value here is a often a sign of excessive CPU load on the server.

Threads_cached

Number of threads in the thread cache. See Chapter 6 for more about MySQL's thread cache.

Threads_connected

Number of currently open connections.

Threads_created

Total number of threads that have been created to handle connections.

Threads_running

Number of threads that are doing work (not sleeping).

Uptime

How long (in seconds) the MySQL server has been up and running.

Command Counters

A large percentage of MySQL's counters are devoted to counting the various commands or queries that you issue to a MySQL server. Everything from a SELECT to a RESET MASTER is counted.

Com_*

The number of times each * command has been executed. Most names map directly to SQL queries or related commands. Some are derived from function names in the MySQL C API. For example, `Com_select` counts SELECT queries, while `Com_change_db` is incremented any time you issue a USE command to switch databases. `Com_change_db` can also count the number of times you change databases programmatically using the `mysql_change_db( )` function from the C API or a language such as PHP.

Questions

The total of number of queries and commands sent to the server. It should be the same as summing all the `Com_*` values.

Temporary Files and Tables

During normal operations, MySQL may need to create temporary tables and files from time to time. It's completely normal. If this happens excessively, however, performance may degrade as a result of the additional disk I/O required.

Created_tmp_disk_tables

The number of temporary tables created while executing statements that were stored on disk. The decision to put a temporary table on disk rather than in memory is controlled by the `tmp_table_size` variable. Tables larger than the value of this variable will be created on disk, while those smaller will be created in memory. But temporary tables created explicitly with `CREATE TEMPORARY TABLE` aren't governed by this. They always reside on disk.

Created_tmp_tables
Similar to `Created_tmp_disk_tables` except that it counts the number of implicit temporary tables created in memory and on disk.

Created_tmp_files
How many temporary files `mysqld` has created.

Comparing `Created_tmp_tables` to `Created_tmp_disk_tables` will tell you the percentage of your temporary tables that are being constructed on the much slower disk as opposed to being created in much faster memory. Obviously, you will never be able to completely eliminate the use of on-disk temporary tables, but if too many of your tables are being created on disk, you may want to increase your `tmp_table_size`.

Data Access Patterns

The handler counters track the various ways that rows are read from tables at the lower level. MySQL communicates with each storage engine through a common API. Because storage engines used to be known as table handlers, the counters still refer to handler operations.

Studying these values will tell you how often MySQL can fetch the exact records it needs as opposed to fetching lots of records and checking field values to see if it really wanted the records. Generally, the counters help to highlight when MySQL is or isn't effectively using your indexes. For example, if the `Handler_read_first` is too high, the server is doing a lot of full index scans, which is probably not what you want it to do.

On the other hand, if the `Handler_read_key` value is high, MySQL is using the indexes to optimum effect and going right after the row it needs quite often without having to dig around and look for it, and your queries and tables are using indexes to optimum effect.

Handler_commit
Number of internal `COMMIT` commands.

Handler_delete
Number of times MySQL has deleted a row from a table.

Handler_read_first
Number of times the first entry was read from an index.

Handler_read_key
Number of times a row was requested based on a key. The higher this value is, the better. It means that MySQL is effectively using your indexes.

Handler_read_next

Number of requests to read next row using the key order. This is incremented if you are querying an index column with a range constraint or doing an index scan.

Handler_read_prev

Number of requests to read previous row in key order. This is mainly used when you have a query using `ORDER BY ... DESC`.

Handler_read_rnd

Number of requests to read a row based on a fixed position. If you do a lot of queries that require sorting of the result, this figure will likely be quite high.

Handler_read_rnd_next

How many times MySQL has read the next row in a datafile. This figure will be high if you are doing a lot of table scans. If that is the case, it's likely that either your tables need to be indexed, or the queries you are submitting need to be changed to take better advantage of the indexes that do exist.

Handler_rollback

Number of internal `ROLLBACK` commands.

Handler_update

Number of requests to update a table row.

Handler_write

Number of table rows that have been inserted.

MyISAM Key Buffer

As described in Chapter 4, the key buffer is where MySQL caches index blocks for MyISAM tables. Generally speaking, a large key buffer means hitting a disk less frequently, so queries will run more efficiently. Increasing the size of the key buffer is often the single biggest "bang for your buck" adjustment you can make on a server that uses mostly MyISAM tables.

Key_blocks_used

The number of 1024-byte blocks contained in the key cache.

Key_read_requests

The number of times a block is requested to be read. It might be found in cache, or it might be read from disk (in which case `Key_reads` are also incremented).

Key_reads

The number of physical reads during which a key block was read from disk.

Key_write_requests

The number of requests for a key block to be written.

Key_writes

The number of physical writes during which key blocks were written to the disk.

These last four counters tell you how often MySQL needed to read/write a key block. Each time a "request" occurs, there may or may not be an actual read or write to match it. If there's not, that's good, because it means the data was already in memory, and the request never hit the disk.

As a general rule of thumb, you want the request numbers to be roughly 50–100 times higher than the corresponding read or write numbers. Higher is better! If they're smaller than that, increasing the size of the key buffer is likely in order.

File Descriptors

On a MySQL server that handles hundreds or thousands of simultaneous queries, you need to keep an eye on the number of open file descriptors MySQL is using. The table_cache setting has the largest impact on MySQL's file descriptor usage if you're mainly using MyISAM tables. For MyISAM tables, the numbers work out like this: each *.frm* file is opened once when the table is first accessed. The contents are cached, and it is immediately closed. The index file (*.MYI*) is opened once and is shared among all clients accessing it. The data file (*.MYD*) is opened by each client using the table. The table cache may reduce the number of times that the *.frm* file is reopened on a system with many active tables.

The following counters help keep track of MySQL's file descriptor usage:

Open_tables
    The total number of tables that are currently open.

Open_files
    The total number of open files.

Open_streams
    Number of streams that are open. (These are mostly used for logging.)

Opened_tables
    Number of tables that have been opened since the server started. If Opened_tables is significantly higher than Open_tables, you should increase the size of table_cache.

Query Cache

As described in Chapter 5, the query cache can provide an impressive performance boost to applications that issue identical queries in a repetitive manner. The following counters will help you understand how effective the query cache is and whether you can safely increase or decrease its size.

Qcache_queries_in_cache
    How many query results are in the query cache.

Qcache_inserts
    How many times MySQL has inserted the results of a query into the cache.

Qcache_hits

> The number of times MySQL has found a query in the cache instead of having to actually execute the query.

Qcache_lowmem_prunes

> Each time MySQL needs to prune the query cache (remove some entries) because it has run out of memory, it increments this counter. Ideally this counter should be 0. If the number increases with any regularity, consider increasing the query_cache_size.

Qcache_not_cached

> This is the number of queries that aren't cachable, either because the query explicitly opted out of the cache, or the result was larger than query_cache_limit.

Qcache_free_memory

> Free space (in bytes) remaining in the cache.

Qcache_free_blocks

> How many free (unused) blocks exist in the cache.

Qcache_total_blocks

> This is the total number of blocks in the cache. By subtracting Qcache_free_blocks from this value, you can derive the number of nonempty blocks. Because the query cache blocks are allocated on an as-needed basis, this information isn't terribly useful for anything other than impressing your coworkers.

SELECTs

This group of counters tracks SELECT queries that may be problematic. Typically they're queries that might have been run more efficiently if MySQL had been able to find an appropriate index to use. If any of these are nonzero and growing at even a moderate rate, go back to Chapter 4 to refresh your memory on how MySQL's indexes work—you probably need to add at least one.

Select_full_join

> Number of joins without keys. If this figure isn't 0, you should check your indexes carefully.

Select_full_range_join

> Number of joins that used a range search on reference table.

Select_range

> Number of joins that used ranges on the first table. It's normally not critical even if this number is big.

Select_scan

> Number of joins that did a full scan of the first table.

Select_range_check
> Number of joins that check for key usage after each row. If this isn't 0, you should check your indexes.

Slow_queries
> Number of queries that have taken more than `long_query_time`.

Unfortunately, there is no easy way to find out which query triggered a particular counter increase. By enabling the slow query log, however, you can at least capture all queries that take more than a predefined number of seconds to complete. Sometimes you'll find that those slow queries are also suffering from one of the problems listed above. See Chapter 5 for more about MySQL's query cache.

Sorts

Queries with `ORDER BY` clauses are commonplace, but sorting a nontrivial number of rows can become a burden if done frequently. The section "Multicolumn indexes" in Chapter 4 discusses some of the index-based sorting optimizations present in MySQL 4.0 and beyond. If MySQL can't use an index for sorting, however, it must resort to old-fashioned sorting techniques.

Sort_merge_passes
> Number of merge-passes the sort algorithms have performed. If this value gets too high, you may wish to increase `sort_buffer`.

Sort_range
> Number of sorts done on ranges. This is better than sorting an entire table.

Sort_rows
> The total number of rows that have been sorted.

Sort_scan
> Number of sorts that were done using a table scan. Ideally, this shouldn't happen often. If it does, you probably need to add an index somewhere.

Table Locking

Any time MySQL waits for a table lock, it is a bad thing. How much of a bad thing is often a function of the application and usage patterns, but there's no way around the fact that a MySQL thread waiting for a lock is getting absolutely no work done. To help track locks and lock contention on tables, MySQL provides the following two counters.

Table_locks_immediate
> Number of times the server acquired a table lock immediately.

Table_locks_waited
> Number of times the server had to wait on a table lock.

The goal is to have Table_locks_immediate as high as possible and Table_locks_waited as close to zero as possible. Realistically, there has to be a middle ground, but those are the ideals we would hope for in a perfect world. For lower-volume or single user applications, table locks are often a nonissue. However, on large multiuser systems or high-volume web sites, table locks can be a very serious problem.

A high percentage of Table_locks_waited is a sign either that you need to make queries more efficient (so that they hold locks for a short period of time) or that you may need to consider an alternative table type. Moving from MyISAM to InnoDB tables will often greatly reduce lock contention—but not always. See Chapter 2 for more details about table locking.

SHOW INNODB STATUS

As noted in Chapter 1, the SHOW INNODB STATUS command produces detailed statistics about what's going on inside the InnoDB storage engine (far more detailed than anything in MyISAM). A detailed understanding of all the statistics InnoDB provides is beyond the scope of what most database administrators will ever need. Much of the information InnoDB presents is useful only in rare and very specific diagnostic activities, so we'll keep the discussion fairly basic here and focus on the more commonly used values.

Sample output from SHOW INNODB STATUS command is included at the end of this section. The output is broken up into several labeled groups. For most day to day use, the most informative sections are Transactions, Buffer Pool and Memory, and Row Operations.

Semaphores
This section details the various locks used inside InnoDB. Higher values here generally indicate a busy server with frequent contention inside InnoDB. They are cumulative statistics, however, so the longer your server has been up, the higher you can expect them to be.

Transactions
Each of the active or pending transactions is listed in this section. For each, InnoDB lists the MySQL thread ID as well as the IP address and MySQL username responsible for initiating the transaction. You may see indications of transactions waiting on locks here. If so, there's a good chance your application is encountering deadlocks.

File I/O
Here InnoDB lists the state of each file I/O thread and provides counts of other I/O-related activity.

Insert Buffer and Adaptive Hash Index

When records are added to InnoDB, they are first put into the insert buffer. From there InnoDB merges records into the tablespace. This section provides a few metrics generated during those operations.

Log

The transaction log statistics are presented here, including the current sequence number and the highest sequence numbers from the most recent log flush and checkpoint operations. InnoDB also provides average values for the number of log-related I/O operations per second.

Buffer Pool and Memory

This section tells you how well InnoDB is using the memory you've given it via the innodb_buffer_pool setting. The "buffer pool size" and "free buffers" values give you an idea of how much of that memory is in use. InnoDB also provides read/create/write-per-second statistics that indicate how quickly the database pages are changing.

Row Operations

Here you'll find some very useful high-level numbers that track the frequency of INSERTs, UPDATEs, DELETEs, and SELECTs as well as counting the number of rows affected by each.

Here's some sample output from a SHOW INNODB STATUS command:

```
mysql> SHOW INNODB STATUS \G
*************************** 1. row ***************************
Status:
=====================================
031218  8:29:53 INNODB MONITOR OUTPUT
=====================================
Per second averages calculated from the last 3 seconds
----------
SEMAPHORES
----------
OS WAIT ARRAY INFO: reservation count 5, signal count 5
Mutex spin waits 0, rounds 0, OS waits 0
RW-shared spins 6, OS waits 3; RW-excl spins 2, OS waits 2
------------
TRANSACTIONS
------------
Trx id counter 0 1039616
Purge done for trx's n:o < 0 454662 undo n:o < 0 0
Total number of lock structs in row lock hash table 0
LIST OF TRANSACTIONS FOR EACH SESSION:
---TRANSACTION 0 0, not started, OS thread id 49162
MySQL thread id 16, query id 112 216.145.52.107 jzawodn
show innodb status
--------
FILE I/O
--------
```

```
I/O thread 0 state: waiting for i/o request (insert buffer thread)
I/O thread 1 state: waiting for i/o request (log thread)
I/O thread 2 state: waiting for i/o request (read thread)
I/O thread 3 state: waiting for i/o request (write thread)
Pending normal aio reads: 0, aio writes: 0,
  ibuf aio reads: 0, log i/o's: 0, sync i/o's: 0
Pending flushes (fsync) log: 0; buffer pool: 0
155 OS file reads, 4 OS file writes, 4 OS fsyncs
0.00 reads/s, 0 avg bytes/read, 0.00 writes/s, 0.00 fsyncs/s
-------------------------------------
INSERT BUFFER AND ADAPTIVE HASH INDEX
-------------------------------------
Ibuf for space 0: size 1, free list len 314, seg size 316,
0 inserts, 0 merged recs, 0 merges
Hash table size 138401, used cells 0, node heap has 0 buffer(s)
0.00 hash searches/s, 0.00 non-hash searches/s
---
LOG
---
Log sequence number 0 900654168
Log flushed up to   0 900654168
Last checkpoint at  0 900654168
0 pending log writes, 0 pending chkp writes
9 log i/o's done, 0.00 log i/o's/second
----------------------
BUFFER POOL AND MEMORY
----------------------
Total memory allocated 54384729; in additional pool allocated 1167488
Buffer pool size   2048
Free buffers       1983
Database pages     65
Modified db pages  0
Pending reads 0
Pending writes: LRU 0, flush list 0, single page 0
Pages read 65, created 0, written 0
0.00 reads/s, 0.00 creates/s, 0.00 writes/s
No buffer pool page gets since the last printout
--------------
ROW OPERATIONS
--------------
0 queries inside InnoDB, 0 queries in queue
Main thread id 14344, state: waiting for server activity
Number of rows inserted 0, updated 0, deleted 0, read 0
0.00 inserts/s, 0.00 updates/s, 0.00 deletes/s, 0.00 reads/s
----------------------------
END OF INNODB MONITOR OUTPUT
============================

1 row in set (0.09 sec)
```

APPENDIX B

mytop

This appendix is a basic reference for Version 1.5 of *mytop*, a tool you can use to monitor various aspects of MySQL. *mytop* began as a simple Perl script that Jeremy wrote back in 2000 after getting sick of repeatedly running SHOW FULL PROCESSLIST and SHOW STATUS in an attempt to get a handle on what a MySQL was doing. After a bit of hacking on it, he realized that it would be useful it the tool felt a bit like the Unix *top* utility. Since then it has evolved to become quite a bit more popular and powerful. It is especially useful when tracking down problematic queries or trying to figure out what's keeping your server so busy.

mytop is an evolving piece of software. Be sure to check the *mytop* web site (*http://jeremy.zawodny.com/mysql/mytop/*) for *mytop* news, downloads, and information about the mailing list. It's likely that new features have been added since Version 1.5.

Note that when discussing "queries" in this chapter (and many other places in the book), we're doing so in a general sense: SELECT, INSERT, UPDATE, and DELETE.

Overview

mytop does much of the hard work involved in summarizing MySQL performance data. There are three primary display modes in *mytop*. The default, *thread view* (or *top view*), closely resembles the Unix *top* command, as seen in Figure B-1. It produces a multiline summary at the top of the screen followed by a listing of threads in MySQL. The *command view* aggregates the data from MySQL's Com_* command counters (see Appendix A), as seen in Figure B-2. Finally, Figure B-3 illustrates *status view*, which tracks all the other values in the output of SHOW STATUS. Like *top*, *mytop* refreshes the display periodically. The default *refresh interval* is five seconds, but that's easily adjusted.

Let's take a closer look at *mytop*'s display modes.

Thread View

In *mytop*'s default display (Figure B-1), the first several lines of the screen are consumed by the *mytop* header. The first line identifies the hostname of the MySQL server as well as its version number. On the right side it displays the server's uptime in Days ┤HH:MM:SS form followed by the current time.

```
MySQL on db.example.com (4.0.15)                          up 2+22:52:17 [16:04:48]
Queries: 93.0M  qps:  382 Slow:    2.1k      Se/In/Up/De(%):    62/29/02/05
                qps now:   12 Slow qps: 0.0  Threads:    26 (  10/  51) 36/15/20/25
Cache Hits: 135.0 Hits/s:  0.0 Hits now:    0.0  Ratio:  0.0% Ratio now:  0.0%
Key Efficiency: 99.5%  Bps in/out: 15.4k/13.8k  Now in/out: 10.0k/574.6k

      Id      User      Host/IP        DB    Time   Cmd Query or State
      --      ----      -------        --    ----   --- ----------
  317134    client       www02    catalog      0  Query SELECT COUNT(DISTINCT OR
  317108    client       www03      mysql      0  Query show full processlist
  276987    client       www01    catalog      2  Sleep
  276969    client       www02       test      3  Sleep
  317129    client       www01    catalog      3  Sleep
  317131    client       www01      mysql      3  Sleep
  317133   jzawodn       www01    catalog      4  Sleep
  317132    client       www01    catalog      5  Sleep
  317130      root       www01    catalog      5  Sleep
  314252  readonly       www02    catalog      6  Sleep
  234961  readonly       www01    catalog      6  Sleep
  276910    client       www02    catalog      9  Sleep
  317062      root   localhost       test     10  Sleep
  317048    client       www02    catalog     10  Sleep
  273970      root       www02    catalog     10  Sleep
  317127      root       www01    catalog     16  Sleep
  315979      repl         db1               878  Binlog Slave: waiting for binlo
  299354    client       www03    catalog   12075  Sleep
  265235      repl        db14             33981  Binlog Slave: waiting for binlo
  259924      repl        db25             37581  Binlog Slave: waiting for binlo
  237800      repl        db22             54927  Binlog Slave: waiting for binlo
  237799      repl        db24             54927  Binlog Slave: waiting for binlo
  237796      repl        db21             54930  Binlog Slave: waiting for binlo
  142404      repl        db13            124119  Binlog Slave: waiting for binlo
   40678      repl        db12            215526  Binlog Slave: waiting for binlo
      18      repl        db11            255122  Binlog Slave: waiting for binlo
-- paused. press any key to resume --
```

Figure B-1. mytop thread view

The next two lines display statistics about queries and threads. The first provides a cumulative count of the number of queries executed, followed by the average number of queries executed per second, then the total number of slow queries. Finally, the Se/In/Up/De(%): section displays the relative percentage of SELECT, INSERT, UPDATE, and DELETE queries that the server has executed.

The third line also displays queries per second (qps) and slow queries, but they reflect only queries executed during the last refresh interval. This line provides a count of the connected, running, and cached threads followed by Se/In/Up/De(%):. Again, those numbers reflect only the most recent queries.

The rest of the screen is used to display connected threads. Each thread listing shows the thread ID, username, database, hostname or IP address, time, and information about what state the thread is in. Generally, threads are either idle (Sleep) or executing a query or command (Query). When a thread is executing a query, you see the beginning of the query in the rightmost column of the display. The time represents how long a thread has been in the same state. So if you see a thread with a time of 10 running a SELECT query, that means the query has been running for 10 seconds. The display is also color-coded by default. Idle threads are the default color, while yellow indicates a thread running a query, and green indicates a thread that is in the process of handing a new connection.

From here you can use *mytop*'s runtime keystrokes (see Table B-1 later in this chapter) to control its behavior and appearance. For example, by pressing **f** and entering the ID number of a thread, you can make *mytop* display the full query.

Command View

This view provides some insight into the relative number of times the server is asked to execute various queries or commands: SELECT, INSERT, UPDATE, and so on. Figure B-2 shows an example of *mytop*'s command view.

The first column lists the command being counted. Sometimes the commands map directly to queries (SELECT, INSERT, etc.), while others represent a calls of commands. For example, set option covers all SET commands, such as SET AUTOCOMMIT=1, SET GLOBAL.wait_timeout, etc. Still others represent components of the MySQL C API. The best examples of this are admin commands, which represents the ping command (and a few others), and change db, which represents mysql_select_db( ) calls, including those generated by the USE command.

The remaining columns measure the number of times each command has been executed, both in absolute and relative terms. The Total and Pct columns represent the total number of command executions and the relative percentages of each. The second set of numbers, Last and Pct, do the same thing but consider only commands executed in the last refresh cycle

Status View

The newest view in *mytop* complements command view. Status view summarizes the noncommand-related counters in SHOW STATUS output. Even without the command counters listed, there are quite a number of values (over 60 as of MySQL 4.0). To see them all, you'll need a tall window. Figure B-3 shows an example on a moderately busy server.

The Total column displays the current value of each counter, while the Change column contains the delta from the last refresh interval. On a color display, positive changes are reported in yellow and negative in red. Unchanging values are shown in

```
          Command      Total  Pct  I  Last  Pct
          -------      -----  ---  I  ----  ---
           select   60030319  61%  I  1342  78%
           insert   17013017  17%  I    10   0%
          replace   11600046  11%  I    55   3%
           delete    5158335   5%  I    31   1%
           update    2143269   2%  I   279  16%
       set option     469303   0%  I     0   0%
           commit     469302   0%  I     0   0%
     delete multi      49079   0%  I     0   0%
   admin commands      21241   0%  I     0   0%
      show status      16443   0%  I     1   0%
      lock tables      15276   0%  I     0   0%
 show processlist      10583   0%  I     0   0%
show slave status       6916   0%  I     0   0%
show master status      6196   0%  I     0   0%
    unlock tables       5128   0%  I     0   0%
        change db       4694   0%  I     0   0%
      show tables       4397   0%  I     0   0%
            check       1029   0%  I     0   0%
   show variables        745   0%  I     0   0%
       drop table        512   0%  I     0   0%
     create table        474   0%  I     0   0%
      show fields        305   0%  I     0   0%
     rename table        118   0%  I     0   0%
   show databases         95   0%  I     0   0%
     create index         72   0%  I     0   0%
           repair         42   0%  I     0   0%
 show slave hosts         20   0%  I     0   0%
show innodb status        12   0%  I     0   0%
    insert select          8   0%  I     0   0%
      alter table          3   0%  I     0   0%
      show binlogs          3   0%  I     0   0%
            purge          3   0%  I     0   0%
      show create          2   0%  I     0   0%
-- paused. press any key to resume --
```

Figure B-2. mytop command view

the default color. The **i** keystroke can be used in this view to filter out unchanging values from the display. This can be quite useful on small displays because many of the values aren't changing frequently.

Getting mytop

Getting *mytop* installed and running is fairly painless. If you've ever installed Perl modules from CPAN before, you'll feel right at home with *mytop*. It is also written in Perl and packaged much like a typical Perl module.

As of this writing, *mytop* has been packaged for several Linux and Unix distributions. FreeBSD users will find *mytop* available in the FreeBSD Ports system and can install it using pkg_add -r mytop. Debian GNU/Linux users can simply execute sudo apt-get install mytop, and SUSE Linux users will find an RPM package on the *mytop* web site.

```
              Counter      Total   Change
              -------      -----   ------
       Aborted_clients:     33307        0
      Aborted_connects:         7        0
       Bytes_received: 1690019594   156708
          Bytes_sent: 1013917210    23539
          Connections:     23193        0
 Created_tmp_disk_tables:    3890        0
     Created_tmp_tables:     3894        0
      Created_tmp_files:        0        0
  Delayed_insert_threads:       0        0
        Delayed_writes:         0        0
        Delayed_errors:         0        0
         Flush_commands:        1        0
        Handler_commit:     72886       19
        Handler_delete:   1613306        0
     Handler_read_first:       38        0
       Handler_read_key:  3581942      110
      Handler_read_next: 83880457       88
      Handler_read_prev:        0        0
       Handler_read_rnd:  2745412       57
   Handler_read_rnd_next: 36566543        0
      Handler_rollback:      5787        0
        Handler_update:  2154433       57
         Handler_write:  5975014      267
        Key_blocks_used:   375052        0
     Key_read_requests: 50594275      444
             Key_reads:   412307        0
    Key_write_requests: 12568078       88
            Key_writes:   7517370       40
    Max_used_connections:     108        0
   Not_flushed_key_blocks:       0        0
 Not_flushed_delayed_rows:       0        0
           Open_tables:       512        0
            Open_files:       964        0
          Open_streams:         0        0
```

Figure B-3. mytop status view

Requirements

To install and use *mytop*, you'll also need the following Perl modules:

- DBI
- DBD::mysql
- Term::ReadKey

Additionally, if you've installed any of the following optional modules, *mytop* will detect that and take advantage of them:

- Time::HiRes
- Term::ANSIColor

Of course, you'll also need Perl. Any version as of 5.005 and beyond should work.

Installation

Once you have the required software installed, download and extract the latest version of *mytop* from *http://jeremy.zawodny.com/mysql/mytop/*:

```
$ wget http://jeremy.zawodny.com/mysql/mytop/mytop-1.5.tar.gz
$ tar zxvf mytop-1.5.tar.gz
```

Then run the Perl *Makefile* and install *mytop*:

```
$ cd mytop-1.5
mytop-1.5$ perl Makefile.PL
Checking if your kit is complete...
Looks good
Writing Makefile for mytop
mytop-1.5$ make install
Installing /usr/local/man/man1/mytop.1p
Installing /usr/bin/mytop
Writing /usr/local/lib/perl/5.8.0/auto/mytop/.packlist
Appending installation info to /usr/local/lib/perl/5.8.0/perllocal.pod
```

Finally, try executing *mytop* to make sure it's installed properly along with all the prerequisites.

Configuration and Usage

mytop's behavior is controlled by a combination of command-line arguments, configuration file options, and runtime keystrokes. Most command-line arguments appear in single letter (-p) and longer GNU-style (--password) forms. Table B-1 lists the keystrokes, command-line arguments, configuration file directives, and the actions they perform.

Upon startup, *mytop* looks for a ~/.mytop. If it finds one, it reads in the settings and uses them as defaults, which are then overridden by any command-line arguments. The configuration file format is composed of key/value pairs, one per line. A sample file might look like this:

```
user=jzawodn
pass=blah!db
host=localhost
```

Most of the command-line arguments have a counterpart option in the configuration file. Future versions of *mytop* are expected to read MySQL's */etc/my.cnf* and *~/.my.cnf* as well, possibly deprecating *~/.mytop* at some point.

Table B-1. mytop configuration and control

Key	Argument(s)	Config file	Action
?			Display help screen
	--batch or --batchmode	batchmode=1	Run in batch (noninteractive) mode. Useful when called from *cron* or another script.

Key	Argument(s)	Config file	Action
c	-m=cmd or --mode=cmd	mode=cmd	Command summary view.
C	--color or --nocolor	color=[0|1]	Use colors in the display. (Requires the Term::ANSIColor module.) The key toggles color on/off.
d		filter_db=*dbname*	Show threads using one specific database.
	-d or --database	db=*dbname*	Connect to this database.
e			Explain the query a thread is running.
f			Show the full query a thread is executing.
F			Unfilter the display; return to defaults.
	-h or --host	host=*hostname*	Specify the host on which MySQL is running; default is localhost.
h			Show only connections from a particular host.
H	--header or --noheader		Display the header *mytop*'s display (key toggles the header display).
i	-i or --idle	idle=[0|1]	Filter idle (sleeping) threads from the display. Key toggles this.
I	-m= or --mode=innodb	mode=innodb	Show InnoDB status.
k			Kill a thread.
m	-m= or --mode=[qps|top|cmd|innodb]	mode=[qps|top|cmd|innodb]	Mode switch. Cycle between thread view, queries per second, and command summary.
o	--sort=[0|1]	sort=[0|1]	Reverse the sort order. Default is ascending based on time.
p			Pause the display. Any key resumes.
	-p or --password	pass=*password*	Connect using this password.
	--prompt	prompt=[0|1]	Prompt for password interactively.
q			Quit *mytop*.
r			Reset status counters (via FLUSH STATUS).
R	-r or --resolve	resolve=[0|1]	Resolve IP addresses into hostnames. This is useful when MySQL is configured with skip-name-resolve.
s	-s or --delay	delay=*number*	Adjust the refresh interval.
S	-m= --mode=status	mode=status	Switch to SHOW STATUS mode.
	-S or --socket	socket=*/path/to/socket*	Specify the socket to use when connecting to localhost.
t	-m= or --mode=top	mode=top	Switch to thread view (the default).
u		filter_user=*username*	Show only a particular user's threads.
	-u or --user	user=*username*	Connect as this user.

Table B-1. mytop configuration and control (continued)

Key	Argument(s)	Config file	Action
V			Switch to SHOW VARIABLES mode.
:			Enter a complex command.

Common Tasks

With the basic operation of *mytop* covered, let's look at the steps you take to perform common tasks using *mytop*. This it intended to give you a hands-on feel for using *mytop*.

Find, analyze, and kill long-running queries

When *mytop* starts, it sorts threads by the Time column—that is, how long the thread has been in that state. Those that have most recently changed appear at the top of the screen. To locate long-running queries, first remove all idle threads from the display by pressing **i**, then reverse the sort order by pressing **o**. The resulting display will show the longest running queries at the top of the screen.

Once you've located a long-running query, you can obtain the full query by pressing **f** and entering the thread ID when prompted. When looking at the full query, you can ask MySQL to explain the query by pressing **e**. Or you may kill the query by pressing **k** and supplying the thread ID.[*]

Determine what type of queries MySQL has been running

It's often useful to know whether MySQL is running more SELECT or more INSERT queries. Maybe you suspect an application is misbehaving, or perhaps you'd simply like to compute your server's typical read to write ratio. In *mytop*'s thread view (Figure B-1), it displays the percentage of SELECT, INSERT, UPDATE, and DELETE queries. On the right side of the header, you'll see something like this:

```
Se/In/Up/De(%): 61/30/02/05
       ...    63/07/12/10
```

The first line means that, overall, 61% of the server's queries are SELECTs, 30% are INSERTs, 2% are UPDATEs, and 5% are DELETEs. The second line displays values that apply to the last refresh interval (5 seconds by default) only. The two together can give a quick feel for what your server has been doing recently and how that compares to the longer term average.

If you want more detail, press **c** to switch *mytop* into command view. There you'll find detailed counts and percentages for each type of command or query executed. The first column of numbers summarizes overall counts (since the

---

[*] In MySQL 3.23 and 4.0, killing a query also terminates the client's connection to the server. In other words, it kills the connection, and the query dies as a byproduct of that.

server was started or counters reset), while the second set of numbers reflects the last refresh interval only.

Kill a group of queries

Use *mytop*'s "super-kill" feature by pressing **K**. You'll be prompted for a username, and *mytop* will then kill all of that user's threads. In the future this may be extended to evaluate more complex expressions, such as killing all nonidle threads from a given hostname or IP address.

Limit the display to a particular user or host

You can ask *mytop* to filter out all threads except those from a given host or those owned by a given user. If you press **u**, *mytop* prompts for a username to filter on. Similarly, pressing **h** allows you to provide a hostname or IP address which is used to filter the display. If you supply both, *mytop* restricts the display based on both criteria.

To clear the filtering, you can press **F** to remove all filters at once. Otherwise, you can use the **u** or **h** keys to remove either of the filters manually.

phpMyAdmin

There are a number of third-party user interfaces to MySQL that make it easier to access and alter the data stored in your MySQL databases. The most popular of these, by far, is *phpMyAdmin*, a web-based application written in PHP.

To install *phpMyAdmin*, you need first make sure you have a web server running PHP 4.x or later that either includes or has been configured to include MySQL database support. You will also need network connectivity to a MySQL server, even if that MySQL server happens to be on the same host as the web server running *phpMyAdmin*. The *phpMyAdmin* package can be downloaded from *http://www.phpmyadmin.net/*, or your Unix/Linux distribution might make a binary package available through its native package management system. Debian Linux users, for example, can simply run apt-get install phpmyadmin.

The Basics

To use *phpMyAdmin* to access your database, you need a username and password that are valid for connections from your web server. Your web server might be on the same machine as your MySQL server, in which case, obviously, the user only needs to be able to access the server from *localhost*.

Once you have logged in using a valid user account, you will see something that looks like Figure C-1.

As you can see in Figure C-2, there are some links to basic server information. Via the Status link, *phpMyAdmin* provides a way to see the status of your server without logging into it and issuing commands via a command-line interface.

To drill into a specific database, the first step is to select the database name from the pull-down menu on the left menu bar. *phpMyAdmin* then displays all the tables within that database, as shown in Figure C-3. This page is extremely useful at a quick glance for checking the relative sizes of your tables, which storage engine is used for each table, and the number of records contained in each.

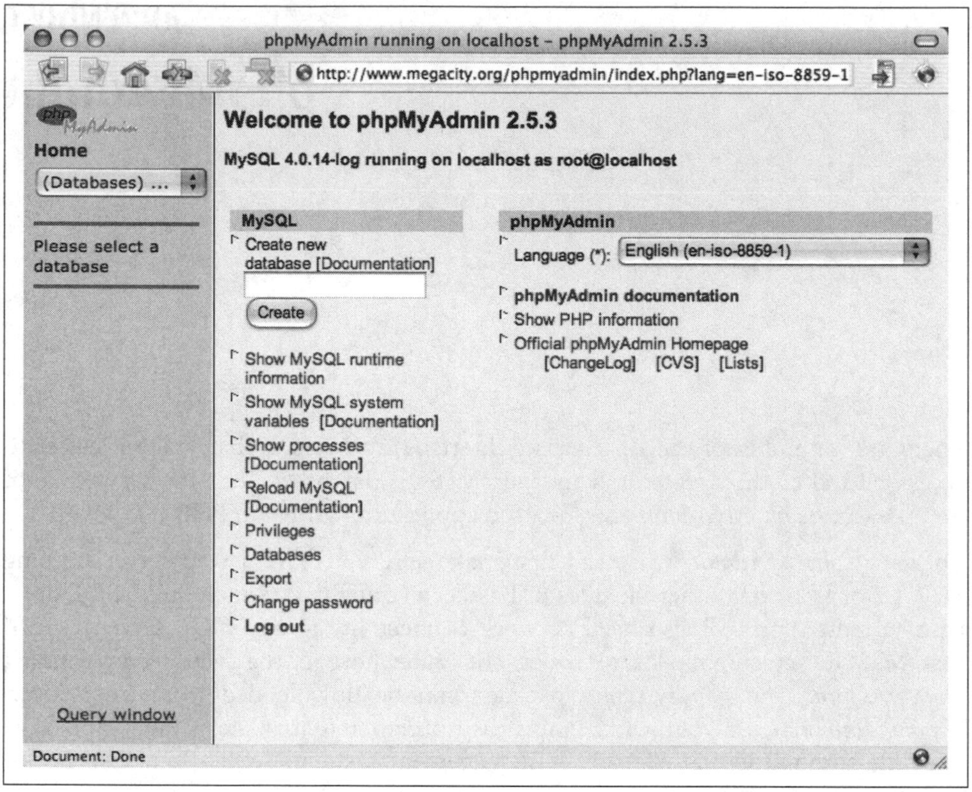

Figure C-1. phpMyAdmin start page

A step-by-step tutorial in how to use *phpMyAdmin* is outside the scope of this book, but we'd like to show you some common examples of where you might find it useful to have *phpMyAdmin* installed because it can make your job as the database administrator significantly easier, or at least faster. It can also allow you to grant people access to issue raw SQL commands and perform maintenance without actually giving them a login on the machine or requiring them to use the MySQL command-line interface.

Practical Examples

In the rest of this appendix we'll describe how to use *phpMyAdmin* to accomplish some common tasks.

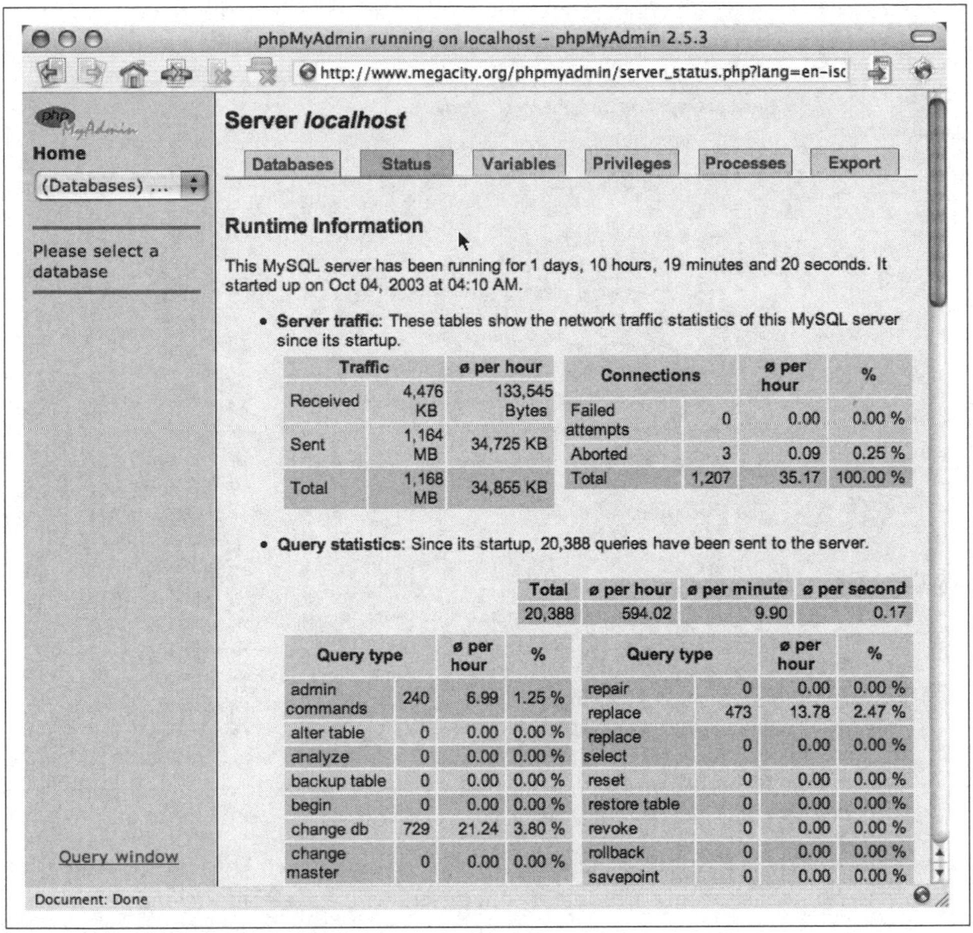

Figure C-2. phpMyAdmin Runtime Information screen

User Maintenance

User maintenance in *phpMyAdmin* functions much as it does in command-line MySQL operation. The administrator can deal with global as well as database and table-level privileges.

To administer global privileges, select Privileges from the start page, which then displays something similar to Figure C-4. Once you have chosen a user to add or remove privileges from, click the "edit" link, which will present you with a user editing interface, as shown in Figure C-5.

From here, most of the functions are self-explanatory; they allow administrators to add or remove global privileges, edit any table-specific privileges the user may have, or change the user's password. You can also clone the user, creating one with the

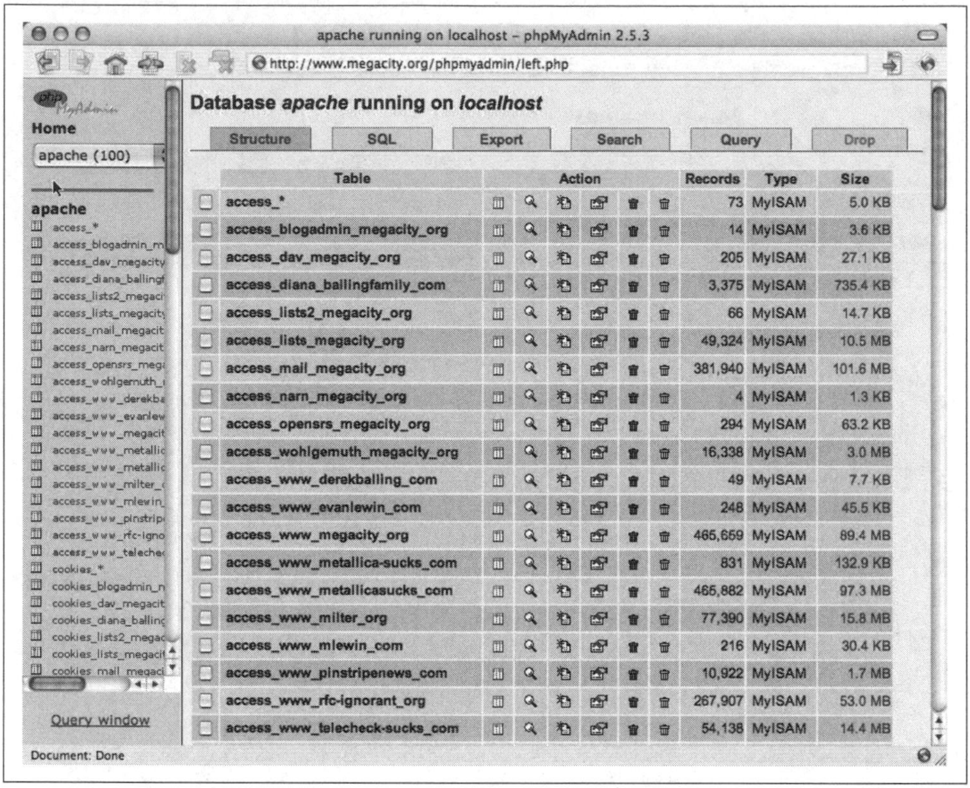

Table	Action	Records	Type	Size
access_*		73	MyISAM	5.0 KB
access_blogadmin_megacity_org		14	MyISAM	3.6 KB
access_dav_megacity_org		205	MyISAM	27.1 KB
access_diana_ballingfamily_com		3,375	MyISAM	735.4 KB
access_lists2_megacity_org		66	MyISAM	14.7 KB
access_lists_megacity_org		49,324	MyISAM	10.5 MB
access_mail_megacity_org		381,940	MyISAM	101.6 MB
access_narn_megacity_org		4	MyISAM	1.3 KB
access_opensrs_megacity_org		294	MyISAM	63.2 KB
access_wohlgemuth_megacity_org		16,338	MyISAM	3.0 MB
access_www_derekballing_com		49	MyISAM	7.7 KB
access_www_evanlewin_com		248	MyISAM	45.5 KB
access_www_megacity_org		465,659	MyISAM	89.4 MB
access_www_metallica-sucks_com		831	MyISAM	132.9 KB
access_www_metallicasucks_com		465,882	MyISAM	97.3 MB
access_www_milter_org		77,390	MyISAM	15.8 MB
access_www_mlewin_com		216	MyISAM	30.4 KB
access_www_pinstripenews_com		10,922	MyISAM	1.7 MB
access_www_rfc-ignorant_org		267,907	MyISAM	53.0 MB
access_www_telecheck-sucks_com		54,138	MyISAM	14.4 MB

Figure C-3. phpMyAdmin after selecting a database

same privileges as the original user, but a different username. This can be handy for adding new database administrators or other users who have complicated privileges.

Perhaps you wish to see which users have access to a particular database. From the databases list, select Check Privileges next to the database you want to check for access on. A list of all users and the privileges granted to them will be displayed (along with links for editing those privileges), as shown in Figure C-6.

Simple SQL Commands

Often, as an administrator, you will want to give users the ability to issue simple SQL commands against the database, but you don't necessarily want to open up the server to login accounts in general or to give a "non-sysadmin" user the ability to get a login shell. In these types of situations, allowing the user in question to use the *phpMyAdmin* interface may be the ideal solution.

There are two basic interfaces available to the user for issuing SQL commands. One of these is a very simple, raw text area that allows the users to type in the SQL

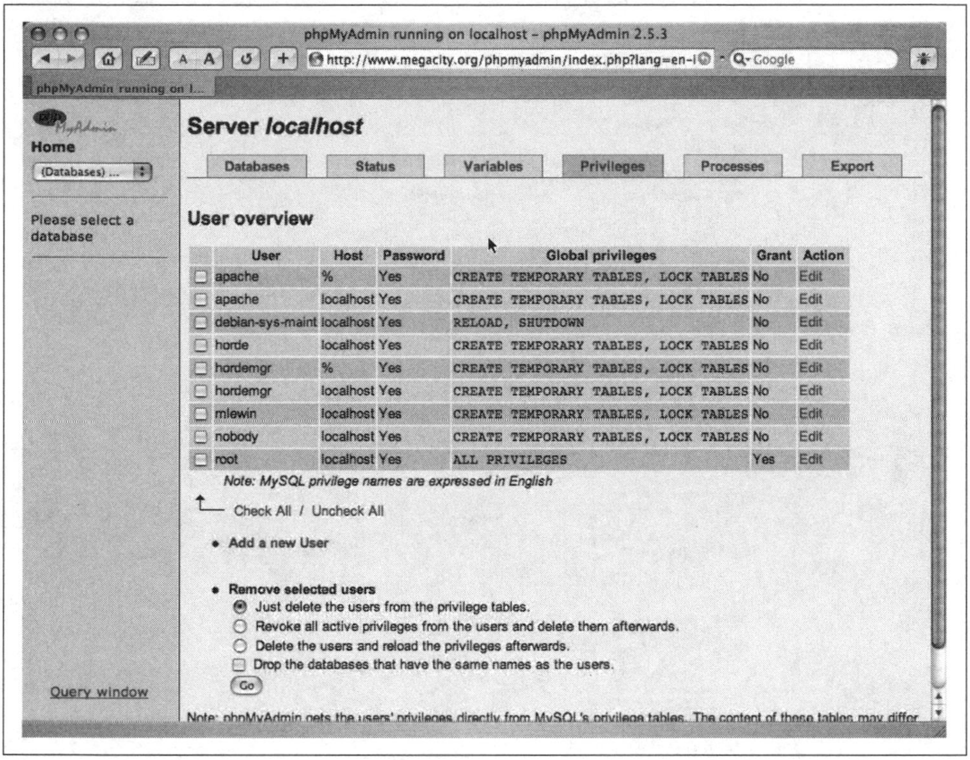

Figure C-4. phpMyAdmin global privileges interface

command they wish to execute. Simply click on the SQL tab after selecting a table to work with.

There is some helpful JavaScript magic on this page that allows the user to select column names from a select element to the right of the free-form text area, so that the user can minimize his typing, as shown in Figure C-7.

Once executed, the resulting records is displayed as returned by the user's query. It is possible to edit, or delete an entry by clicking the note-pad button or the trash-can button, respectively, next to the record you wish to edit or delete.

The other basic record selection method is the Select tab. This is designed for simple queries and allows you to impose simple restrictions on the query being performed, as shown in Figure C-8. The results of that query are displayed in the same format as the results of the SQL query, and likewise allow the user to edit or delete specific entries returned by the query.

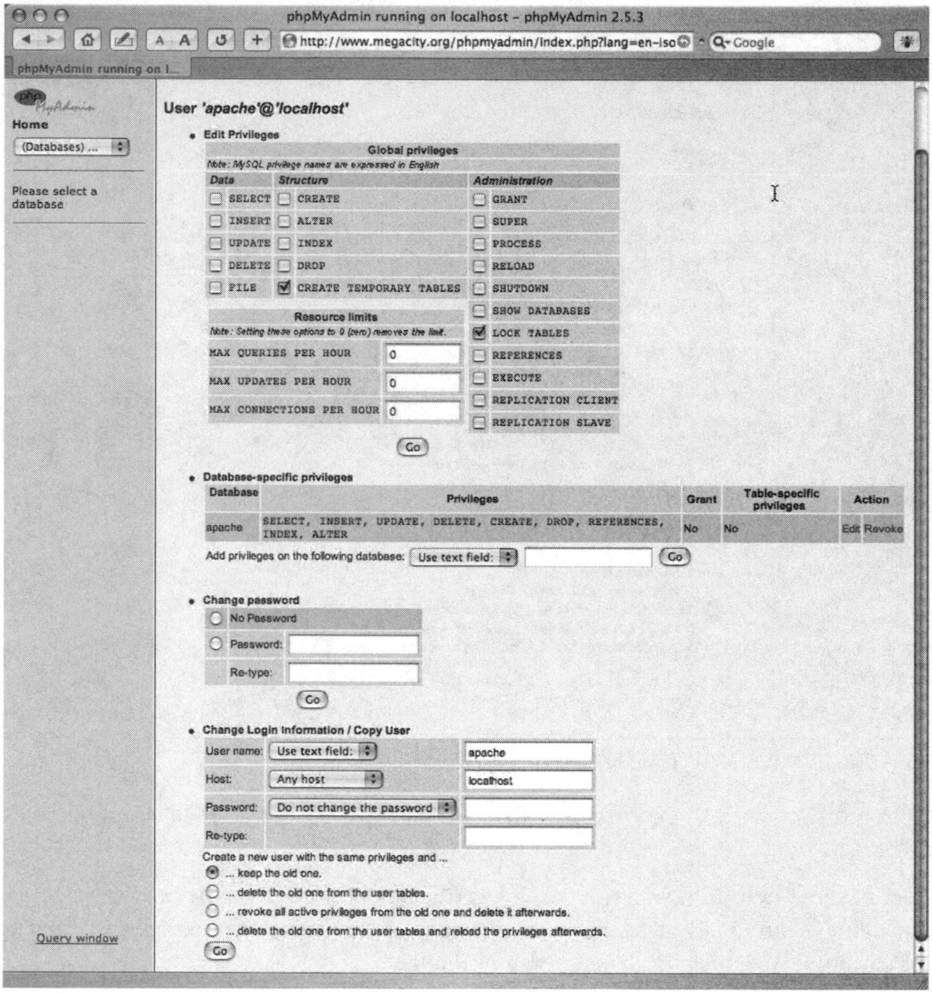

Figure C-5. phpMyAdmin user edit interface

Exporting and Downloading Data

The *phpMyAdmin* interface makes retrieving remote dumps of the database as easy as clicking some buttons on a web form. There are two different Export tabs, one if you are viewing the database as a whole, the other if you are looking at a selected table. They are virtually identical except that the database-wide version also includes a select item for which tables in the database you wish to export. The table-wide interface can be seen in Figure C-9.

As you can see, there are several export options available to the user. If you are looking for a *mysqldump*-style export for possible import into another MySQL

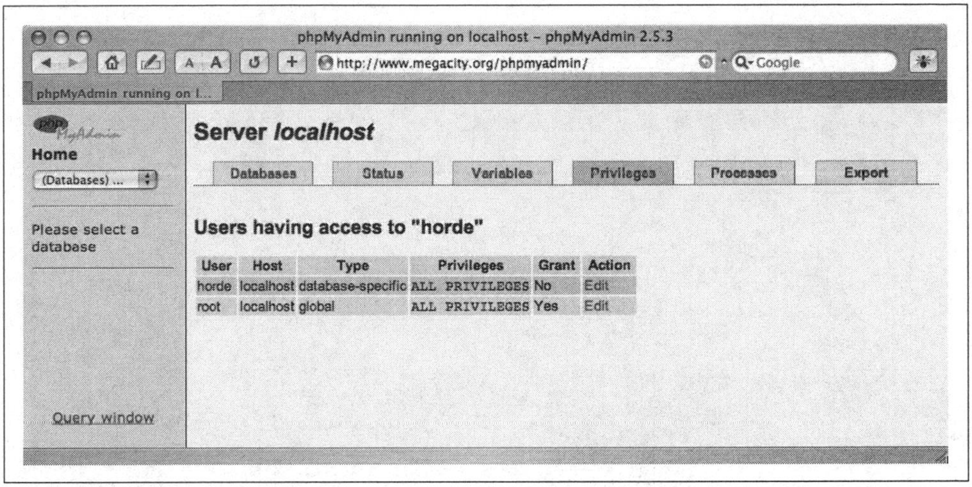

Figure C-6. phpMyAdmin database level privileges interface

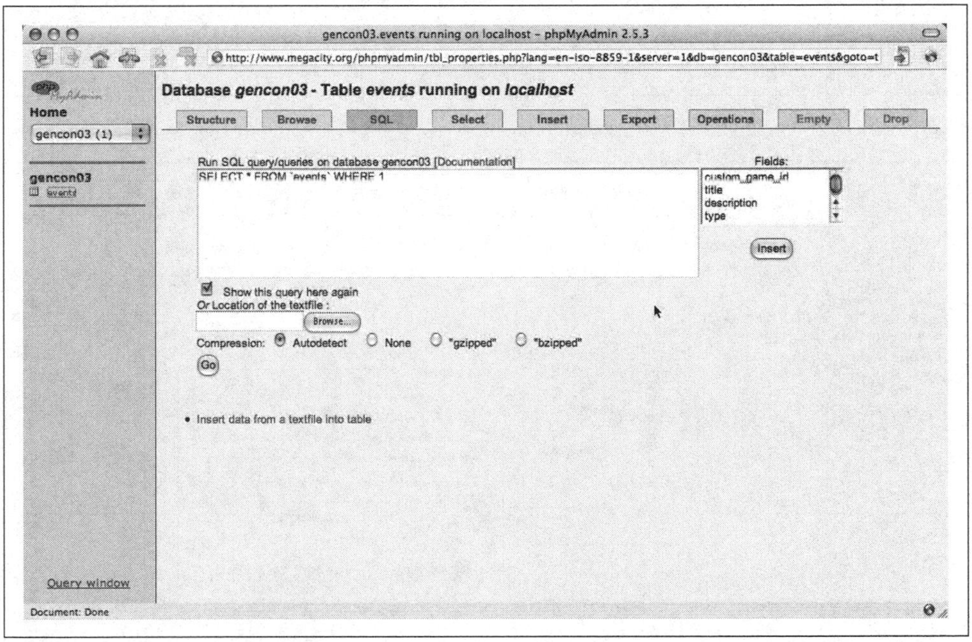

Figure C-7. phpMyAdmin SQL interface

installation, you can select that option. There are CSV options for "normal" use as well as customized CSV output to make Microsoft Excel happy.

The different export options each enable different options in the panel just to the right, specific to the export style in question. Once you select Go, the data will be formatted per your selection and output to your browser via the Web, where you can

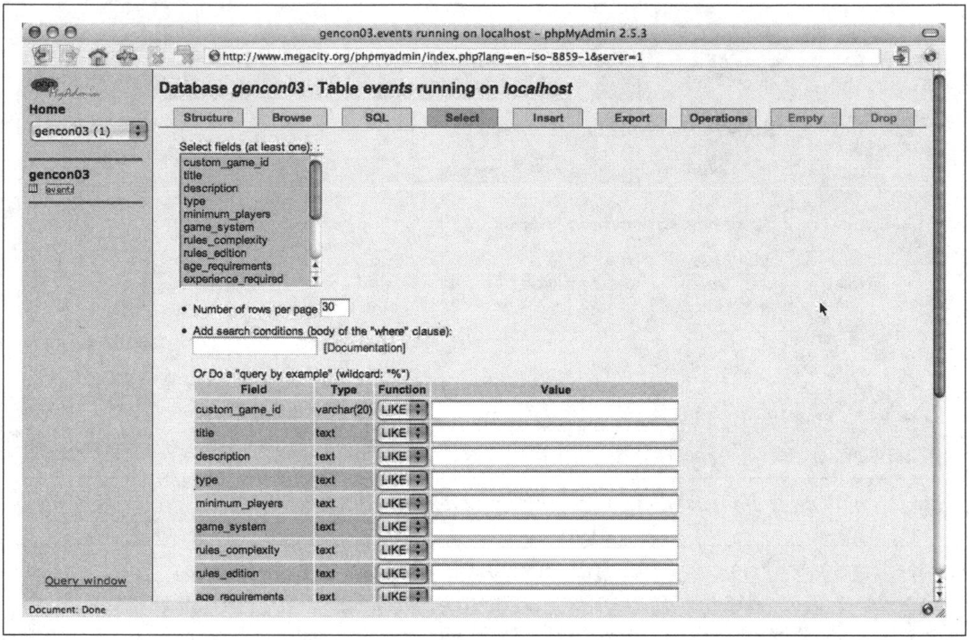

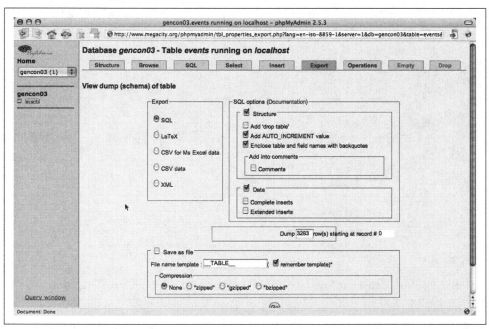

Figure C-8. phpMyAdmin select interface

Figure C-9. phpMyAdmin export interface

copy and paste it or save it to your local disk. Alternatively, you may check the "Save as file" checkbox and simply save the downloaded file to disk. Note that you might see slightly odd behavior, though, if you use this feature to export as XML. Your browser of choice may decide to try to "handle" the XML by displaying it, instead of allowing you to simply save it to disk.

Index

About the Authors

Jeremy D. Zawodny and his two cats moved from northwest Ohio to Silicon Valley in late 1999 so he could work for Yahoo!. He's been at Yahoo! ever since, helping to put MySQL and other open source technologies to use in fun, interesting, and often very big ways. Starting with the popular and high-traffic Yahoo! Finance site, he worked to make MySQL part of the site's core infrastructure in large batch operations as well as real-time feed processing and serving content directly on the site. He then helped to spread "the MySQL religion" to numerous other groups within Yahoo!, including News, Personals, Sports, and Shopping. Nowadays he acts as Yahoo!'s MySQL guru, working with Yahoo!'s many engineering groups to get the most out of their MySQL deployments.

In 2000, he began writing for *Linux Magazine* and continues to do so today as a columnist and contributing editor. Since 2001, Jeremy has been speaking about MySQL at various conferences (O'Reilly's Open Source Conference, PHPCon, The MySQL User Conference, etc.) and user groups in locations as far away as Bangalore, India. His favorite topics are performance tuning, replication, clustering, and backup/recovery. In more recent times, he's rediscovered his love of aviation, earning a Private Pilot Glider license in early 2003. Jeremy rambles almost daily about technology and life in general on his weblog, *http://www.jeremy.zawodny.com/blog/*.

Derek J. Balling has been a Perl programmer and Unix/Linux system administrator since 1996, having helped build two different ISPs from the ground up in the midwestern United States. He spent several years of his career at Yahoo!, working in their Infrastructure Group, where he worked on tools to help improve system uptime. He presently works at a health-care supply company in the New York metropolitan area, helping infiltrate the Open Source virus into their infrastructure. He has also written articles for *The Perl Journal* and a number of online magazines.

When not working on computer-related issues, Derek relaxes with his two cats in his lakeside residence, and has recently taken up the sport of fencing. He also makes his opinion known on current events or whatever is annoying him lately on his blog at *http://www.megacity.org/blog/*.

Colophon

Our look is the result of reader comments, our own experimentation, and feedback from distribution channels. Distinctive covers complement our distinctive approach to technical topics, breathing personality and life into potentially dry subjects.

The animal on the cover of *High Performance MySQL: Optimization, Backups, Replication, and Load Balancing,* is a sparrow hawk (*Accipiter nisus*), a small woodland member of the falcon family found in Eurasia and North Africa. Sparrow hawks have a long tail and short wings; males are bluish-grey with a light brown breast, and females are more brown-grey and have an almost fully white breast. Males are normally somewhat smaller (11 inches) than females (15 inches).

Sparrow hawks live in coniferous woods and feed on small mammals, insects, and birds. They nest in trees and sometimes on cliff ledges. At the beginning of the summer, the female lays 4 to 6 white eggs, blotched red and brown, in a nest made in the boughs of the tallest tree available. The male feeds the female and their young.

Like all hawks, the sparrow hawk is capable of bursts of high speed in flight. Whether soaring or gliding, the sparrow hawk has a characteristic flap-flap-glide action; its large tail enables the hawk to twist and turn effortlessly in and out of cover.

Mary Anne Weeks Mayo was the production editor and proofreader, and Leanne Soylemez was the copyeditor for *High Performance MySQL: Optimization, Backups, Replication, and Load Balancing*. Emily Quill and Claire Cloutier provided quality control. Jamie Peppard and Mary Agner provided production assistance. John Bickelhaupt wrote the index.

Ellie Volckhausen designed the cover of this book, based on a series design by Edie Freedman. The cover image is a 19th-century engraving from the Dover Pictorial Archive. Emma Colby produced the cover layout with QuarkXPress 4.1 using Adobe's ITC Garamond font.

David Futato designed the interior layout. This book was converted by Joe Wizda to FrameMaker 5.5.6 with a format conversion tool created by Erik Ray, Jason McIntosh, Neil Walls, and Mike Sierra that uses Perl and XML technologies. The text font is Linotype Birka; the heading font is Adobe Myriad Condensed; and the code font is LucasFont's TheSans Mono Condensed. The illustrations that appear in the book were produced by Robert Romano and Jessamyn Read using Macromedia FreeHand 9 and Adobe Photoshop 6. The tip and warning icons were drawn by Christopher Bing. This colophon was compiled by Mary Anne Weeks Mayo.

Related Titles Available from O'Reilly

Open Source Database

Managing & Using MySQL, *2nd Edition*

MySQL Cookbook

MySQL Pocket Reference

MySQL Reference Manual

Practical PostgreSQL

Web Database Apps with PHP and MySQL, *2nd Edition*

Keep in touch with O'Reilly

1. Download examples from our books

To find example files for a book, go to:

www.oreilly.com/catalog

select the book, and follow the "Examples" link.

2. Register your O'Reilly books

Register your book at *register.oreilly.com*

Why register your books?
Once you've registered your O'Reilly books you can:

- Win O'Reilly books, T-shirts or discount coupons in our monthly drawing.
- Get special offers available only to registered O'Reilly customers.
- Get catalogs announcing new books (US and UK only).
- Get email notification of new editions of the O'Reilly books you own.

3. Join our email lists

Sign up to get topic-specific email announcements of new books and conferences, special offers, and O'Reilly Network technology newsletters at:

elists.oreilly.com

It's easy to customize your free elists subscription so you'll get exactly the O'Reilly news you want.

4. Get the latest news, tips, and tools

www.oreilly.com

- "Top 100 Sites on the Web"—PC Magazine
- CIO Magazine's Web Business 50 Awards

Our web site contains a library of comprehensive product information (including book excerpts and tables of contents), downloadable software, background articles, interviews with technology leaders, links to relevant sites, book cover art, and more.

5. Work for O'Reilly

Check out our web site for current employment opportunities:

jobs.oreilly.com

6. Contact us

O'Reilly & Associates
1005 Gravenstein Hwy North
Sebastopol, CA 95472 USA

TEL: 707-827-7000 or 800-998-9938
        (6am to 5pm PST)

FAX: 707-829-0104

order@oreilly.com
For answers to problems regarding your order or our products. To place a book order online, visit:

www.oreilly.com/order_new

catalog@oreilly.com
To request a copy of our latest catalog.

booktech@oreilly.com
For book content technical questions or corrections.

corporate@oreilly.com
For educational, library, government, and corporate sales.

proposals@oreilly.com
To submit new book proposals to our editors and product managers.

international@oreilly.com
For information about our international distributors or translation queries. For a list of our distributors outside of North America check out:

international.oreilly.com/distributors.html

adoption@oreilly.com
For information about academic use of O'Reilly books, visit:

academic.oreilly.com

O'REILLY®

Our books are available at most retail and online bookstores.
To order direct: 1-800-998-9938 • order@oreilly.com • www.oreilly.com
Online editions of most O'Reilly titles are available by subscription at safari.oreilly.com